How To
Make Your Car Last Forever

By Tom Torbjornsen

motorbooks

First published in 2010 by Motorbooks, an imprint of MBI Publishing Company, 400 First Avenue North, Suite 300, Minneapolis, MN 55401 USA

The information in this book is true and complete to the best of our knowledge. All recommendations are made without any guarantee on the part of the author or Publisher, who also disclaim any liability incurred in connection with the use of this data or specific details.

We recognize, further, that some words, model names, and designations mentioned herein are the property of the trademark holder. We use them for identification purposes only. This is not an official publication.

Motorbooks titles are also available at discounts in bulk quantity for industrial or sales-promotional use. For details write to Special Sales Manager at MBI Publishing Company, 400 First Avenue North, Suite 300, Minneapolis, MN 55401 USA.

To find out more about our books, join us online at www.motorbooks.com.

ISBN-13: 978-0-7603-3796-7

Editor: Chris Endres
Creative Director: Michele Lanci-Altomare
Design Manager: Jon Simpson
Designer: Danielle Smith

Printed in China

Contents

Acknowledgments

Throughout the writing of this book, many people came to mind, people who have encouraged and supported me throughout my life. They taught me not only the ins and outs of everything automotive, but also how to persist and work toward fulfilling my dreams even when times get rough. There isn't room to name them all, but I want to express my deep gratitude to key individuals who were responsible for teaching me the ways of automotive zen, broadcast, and media.

Don Moquin gave me my start in automotive repair. He gave an aspiring, young, impressionable youth with a dream of being an auto mechanic a chance when I wandered into his gas station in 1972. Thanks, Don.

Bob Loringer saw something in me that I didn't see in myself. Bob entrusted me with the keys to his business, his tools and service bays, and most important, his customers' cars. I learned a lot at Bob Loringer's Sunoco.

Sheldon Siegel taught me the importance of meticulous and vigorous maintenance practices. Sheldon taught me that any car could go 100,000 miles or more if you maintain it properly.

John Mitidieri was my first real mentor in automotive repair. He taught me everything he knew, put up with my idiosyncrasies, trusted me with his toolbox, taught me how to swing a hammer like Thor, and brought me into his home. He was a great friend as well as a teacher, and I sorely miss him.

Mr. Jensen, my auto mechanics teacher at Burlington County Vocational and Technical High School, put up with a difficult kid like me and persevered until "I got it." I also thank the faculty at the high school for their contribution to my education. They equipped me well.

Merrill Rosen believed in me when I came to him with the cockamamie idea of starting an automotive radio talk show 20 years ago. Merrill taught me the ropes of broadcast and media.

Bob Carey saw in me America's premier automotive radio talk show host. Bob took *America's Car Show* from local to national status and taught me about national radio.

This work would have never been published without Kathleen Augustine, my editor. She has the uncanny ability to make sense out of my chicken scratch and bring flavor and personality to the words I put down. Thanks, Kath.

Photo credit: Shutterstock

Introduction

I was born in Brooklyn, New York, in 1956. As a child I ran to my bedroom window every time a loud car passed by on the streets below. One unusually hot summer evening I stared out the window, mesmerized by the image of a 1966 Pontiac GTO as it sat at the light waiting to turn left. The car whined and roared as the driver revved the engine.

In retrospect, the sound of that revving engine was like a large piece of juicy bait, and I was a famished large-mouthed bass in a raging stream. I was hooked. I would pursue cars in every way I could, starting with ¼th scale slot car racing. I purchased cars, worked on cars, and raced cars well into my early twenties. To support this habit I had to work to earn money. Somebody told me once to choose my vocation based on what I love to do. The decision was easy. I would work on cars for a living.

In 1970, I got my first job working on cars at a gas station in the small town of Willingboro, New Jersey. I stayed in and around the auto repair industry either as a technician, a service manager, or an auto service center manager until 1989, when I started my own business as a tool and equipment dealer. I sold tools in a territory in New Jersey for about a year, and then decided to move to western New York to the small city of Jamestown.

One day in late 1990, I walked into a repair shop and saw the owner wringing his hands, upset because he had to make a call to a customer. He had given the customer a quote to replace a timing belt in her car. The car, a 1984 Ford Escort with a four-cylinder engine, was equipped with an interference engine. When the timing belt breaks with this type of engine, the valves collide with the pistons and cause major engine damage. This is

exactly what had happened to her car. The technician was terribly distressed because he quoted the customer $225 to replace the belt when, in fact, the repair would cost the customer more than $2,000 because the engine had to be replaced.

As I watched this fellow pace the floor, wrenched with anxiety over a phone call, I had what I like to call an "a-ha!" moment—a realization that there was a need for a better relationship between the public and the auto repair industry. I decided right then that a radio show, designed to educate motorists on auto repair and maintenance, would meet that need. Such a radio show would be a great public service to those who listened to it. So in January 1991 *America's Car Show with Tom Torbjornsen* was born. The mission statement of the show was this:

To educate consumers and bridge the gap between the auto repair industry and motorists in an effort to build understanding between the two and soften relationships across the service counters.

Nineteen years later, the show is nationally broadcast on Sirius-XM Satellite Radio and the SSI Radio Network. I am an automotive journalist registered with the International Motor Press Association (IMPA), and I write for AOL Autos, Edmunds.Com, CNN, and many other entities on the web.

During the course of my career, the single most-asked question floated to me over the years has been, "Tom, how do I get the most out of my car?" So when I was asked to write a book, I decided to write *How to Make Your Car Last Forever*.

This book is the culmination of all of my answers to this most frequently asked question.

Chapter 1
Maintenance—The Key to the Automotive Fountain of Youth

EXPERIENCE MADE ME A BELIEVER

Back in the old days when I was a young aspiring auto technician out to conquer the world of automotive repair, I was hard pressed to find a car engine that would go over 50,000 miles without needing some major engine work. These engines found their way into our shop, requiring major repairs like replacing a head gasket, doing a valve job, or replacing rod and main bearings or piston rings. I attributed this to what I thought was poor design and inferior lubricants, and I held this philosophy until I met Sheldon Siegel.

Sheldon, an advertising executive in New York City, lived in my little town in southern New Jersey. He commuted 90 miles one way to the city every day. Sheldon drove a 1965 Comet Caliente convertible with a small 289-cid V-8 engine backed by an automatic transmission. He also owned a 1972 Buick Gran Sport. The Buick was his "nice car" for home and "da wife," as he would say.

When I met Sheldon, the Comet had slightly more than 120,000 miles on it, and the Buick registered 75,000 miles. No major engine work had been done on either of these cars. I was amazed and confounded but as I got to know Sheldon, I realized why he was able to get such high mileage out of his cars. Every 3,000 miles Sheldon would bring the Comet in for oil changes. Traveling as much as he did, this translated into every three to four weeks. I became his personal service technician and, month after month, serviced Sheldon's cars. He had the tires rotated and balanced every 5,000 to 6,000 miles, the transmission serviced every 30,000 miles, the cooling system flushed and filled every 24,000 miles, and on it went like clockwork. Sheldon diligently followed the factory-specified maintenance intervals.

Time passed, and the miles racked up on the Comet reached 200,000 without a hitch. Then one day Sheldon decided to retire the Comet because of the external body rust. He gave me the car so I could tear it down and inspect it, hoping to discover the source of its longevity. I assured him that the autopsy of the Comet would serve humanity if I could unlock the mysteries that afforded it such a long life.

Once inside the engine I was amazed that it exhibited little wear, and it was so clean. Apparently, by changing the oil every 3,000 miles, dirt, sludge, and thus engine wear had been averted. Wow! The manufacturers knew what they were talking about after all.

So in the year 1976 I was convinced that the secret to engine longevity lies in systematic and regular maintenance as per the car manufacturers. From that day I vowed to trumpet it from the highest mountains, the lowest valleys, and everywhere in-between. The location of the automotive fountain of youth is in your owner's manual, in the service schedule.

AN INTRODUCTION TO GENERAL MAINTENANCE PRACTICES

So how often should you change your oil and filter and perform any other maintenance services? Again, the answer lies in your owner's manual in the maintenance schedule. Carmakers outline two service intervals, one for severe service and one for normal service applications. Let's take a look at these two applications in depth.

Severe vs. Normal Service Applications

When you are trying to determine what service schedule applies to your driving experience, consult the owner's manual for severe and normal service maintenance intervals. To illustrate the difference between severe and normal intervals, let's look at the definition of each service description as outlined by GM.

Below is the severe service description for a 2000 Chevy Cavalier with a 2.2-liter four-cylinder engine:

Follow the SEVERE schedule if any one of the following are true:

- Most trips are less than 5 to 10 miles (8 to 16km). This is particularly important when outside temperatures are below freezing.
- Most trips include extensive idling (such as frequent driving in stop and go traffic).
- The vehicle is operated in dusty areas frequently.
- Trailer towing or using a carrier on top of the vehicle frequently.
- The vehicle is used for delivery service, police, taxi, or other commercial applications.
- Many GM vehicles have an "Engine Oil Life Monitor" lamp, which can illuminate anytime between intervals depending on driving conditions. The oil should then be replaced at that time, regardless of mileage, and the "Engine Oil Life Monitor" reset.

Next let's look at the recommended service schedule as recommended by GM for this car.

NORMAL SERVICE SCHEDULE

Maintenance Items	7,500	15,000	22,500	30,000	37,500
Air Filter Element				Replace	
Brake Caliper		Inspect		Inspect	
Brake and Traction Control	Inspect	Inspect	Inspect	Inspect	Inspect
Coolant					
Cooling System					
Drive Belt					
Engine Oil	Replace	Replace	Replace	Replace	Replace
Fluid – A/T					
Fluid Filter – A/T					
Ignition Cable					
Oil Filter, Engine	Replace	Replace	Replace	Replace	Replace
Parking Brake Cable	Lubricate	Lubricate	Lubricate	Lubricate	Lubricate
Shift Linkage, A/T	Lubricate	Lubricate	Lubricate	Lubricate	Lubricate
Shift Linkage, M/T	Lubricate	Lubricate	Lubricate	Lubricate	Lubricate
Spark Plug					
Steering	Lubricate	Lubricate	Lubricate	Lubricate	Lubricate
Suspension	Lubricate	Lubricate	Lubricate	Lubricate	Lubricate
Tires	Rotate	Rotate	Rotate	Rotate	Rotate

SEVERE SERVICE SCHEDULE

Maintenance Items	3,000	6,000	9,000	12,000	15,000
Air Filter Element					Inspect
Brake Caliper			Inspect		
Coolant					
Cooling System					
Drive Belt					
Engine Oil	Replace	Replace	Replace	Replace	Replace
Fluid – A/T					
Fluid Filter – A/T					
Ignition Cable					
Oil Filter, Engine	Replace	Replace	Replace	Replace	Replace
Parking Brake Cable		Lubricate		Lubricate	
Shift Linkage, A/T		Lubricate		Lubricate	
Shift Linkage, M/T		Lubricate		Lubricate	
Spark Plug					
Steering		Lubricate		Lubricate	
Suspension		Lubricate		Lubricate	
Tires		Rotate		Rotate	

Now that you've looked over the service description definitions and maintenance tables, I want you to note something. Read again where it says, Follow the *severe* schedule if any one of the following is true:

- Most trips are less than 5 to 10 miles (8 to 16 kilometers). This is particularly important when outside temperatures are below freezing.
- Most trips include extensive idling (such as frequent driving in stop-and-go traffic).
- The vehicle is operated in dusty areas frequently.
- The vehicle tows trailers or uses a carrier on top of the vehicle frequently.
- The vehicle is used for delivery service, police, taxi or other commercial applications.

Correct me if I'm wrong, but don't most of us operate our motor vehicles under one or more of these conditions at least once a week? Does driving in construction areas during roadway construction season count as the dusty area qualifier? For those people who write to me and say that they drive 3,000 miles per year, doesn't that fall under "most trips are less than 5 to 10 miles?" What about all the SUVs and crossovers I see out on the roadways towing a trailer or with a car top carrier affixed to the roof during summer vacation? And on it goes.

Therefore, I submit to you that *we should all maintain our cars according to severe service schedules (the more aggressive approach to maintenance)* if we want to *get the most mileage out of them.*

At this point, some of you are asking, "Why all this maintenance?" Answer: To keep a reliable and safe vehicle on the road for a long time (and save you money). Let's look briefly at a few facts to support this approach.

DRIVERS ASK, TOM ANSWERS: MAINTENANCE PROBLEMS SOLVED

Q Dear Tom,
Does a car get better gas mileage with 89 octane? And why do some cars require it according to the manuals? I own a 2008 Acura TL and the manual recommends 89. With gas prices the way they are, I want to know if it is necessary to buy the recommended octane. Thank you.
　　Sam—Minnesota

A Sam,
Octane has nothing to do with fuel mileage and everything to do with volatility or stability within the combustion chambers of the engine. Low-octane fuel is less stable inside an engine than high-octane fuel. High-performance engines like yours operate at higher combustion chamber temperatures due to higher compression ratios. When low-octane fuel is introduced into a high-compression engine, it pre-ignites, causing a phenomenon called "engine knock." The fuel ignites before it has properly compressed and the electrical spark introduced at the precise time for maximum efficiency. This pre-ignition causes hammering on the tops of the pistons, cylinder head, and valve faces. Over time, this results in premature engine failure. Use the recommended octane fuel in your engine; it's cheaper in the long run than replacing the engine.
　　Tom

Q Tom,
I was reading about your article regarding oil changes in automotive engines at CNN.com and I have a question in regard to detergent and non-detergent oil. I know that today's automobile engines use nondetergent oil. I have just recently rebuilt a 1955 Chris Craft boat with a flathead six-cylinder carburetor engine, and I was advised that I should use nondetergent motor oil in this engine. My question is: Why should I use a nondetergent instead of a detergent oil, which I understand will keep the engine cleaner?
　　Thanks,
　　Texas

A Texas,
On the contrary, today's engines *use* high-detergent oil. That is how they stay clean of sludge deposits, despite their high operating temperatures (assuming the oil is changed regularly according to manufacturer's specs). I see no reason why you can't use today's detergent motor oil in your boat engine. The only concern I have is if the engine has not been run in a long time and it has original seals and wear. Assuming that the seals have been replaced and OEM tolerances restored, I advise you to use the viscosity oil recommended by the engine builders in a high-detergent synthetic motor oil (OEM recommendations being based on the rebuilt engine). AMSOIL makes a great marine application that would work well in that boat of yours.
　　Tom

Q Tom,
Is fuel system cleaning really necessary? If so, at what mileage? Or is it a "fluffy" extra that the dealership wants to talk me into, like rust proofing.
　　Joe—Montana

A Joe,
Fuel system cleaning is a part of your maintenance schedule every 30,000 miles or so (mileage intervals from vary carmaker to carmaker). This is a necessary service to clean out the varnish and dirt buildup that takes place in the fuel delivery system. Fuel injectors are sprayers that have tiny orifices. When these small openings get clogged from dirt and varnish buildup, they dribble fuel instead of delivering a steady properly mixed dose of air and fuel, necessary for efficient combustion. Clogged injectors result in higher tailpipe emissions, poorer fuel economy, and poor engine performance overall.

Intake plenums, cylinder heads, valves, and pistons also get dirty over time from unburned fuel settling on them. This hardened, unburned fuel saps the fuel out of the air-fuel mixture, resulting in a lean condition. The car's computer "sees" this lean condition and richens fuel mixture, resulting in decreased fuel mileage. Fuel system cleaning should be performed every 35,000 to 45,000 miles. As for rust protection, depending on where you live and if salt is used during the winter, a good rust protection will protect your investment, so don't under value it.
　　Tom

Q Greetings Tom,
When paying an aftermarket retailer to order a catalytic converter for me, can I be assured that the converter will fit my existing exhaust system and coupling hardware from the old converter? Or will the new converter have its own hardware?
　　James—Smyrna, Tennessee

A James,
Aftermarket retailers install "one-size-fits-all" converters. How do they do this? The catalytic body is made small so that it fits into the underside of most vehicles; then the inlet and outlets are plumbed with various adapters. In this way, aftermarket retailers can keep a relatively small inventory of converters on hand and adapt them to a large vehicle population. The new cat will be installed using plumbing adapters for your exhaust system, along with clamping and hanging adapters. It will be far from OEM configuration.

A real concern I have is that sometimes aftermarket catalytic converters do not have the unburned gas-processing capability of the OEM cat. So be careful, and ask questions about the processing capability of the replacement cat before installing it.
　　Tom

Photo credit: Shutterstock

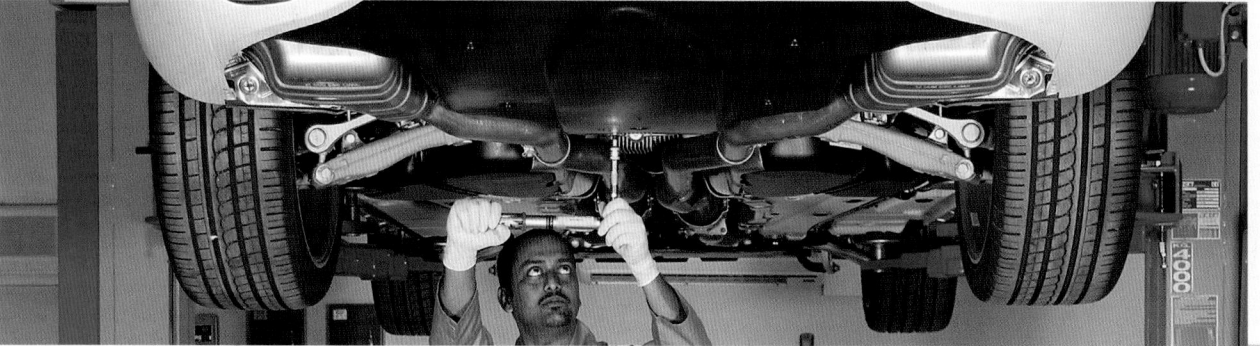

Q Tom,
I've searched for an answer to this question, and absolutely no one seems to be able to answer it. I drive my vehicle quite infrequently. Since November 2005 (the last oil change), I have driven my 1992 Dodge Grand Caravan SE only 1,000 miles. The vehicle has about 94,000 miles on it. I've checked the oil; it's full and appears to be clean. How often should I change the oil since I drive so little? Nearly all of my driving is in town, stop and go, at 25 to 45 miles per hour. Trips vary from 1 to 5 miles one way, about once a week. So I average about 8 miles per week.

Many people tell me to change the oil every 6 months. That would mean I would be changing the oil after driving only 200 miles and that seems ridiculous! I value your opinion. Thanks in advance for your reply.

Ardis—Boston, Massachusetts

A Ardis,
Believe it or not, the use of your vehicle as you described is considered a severe service description. Why? Because the engine never really has a chance to warm up properly and there is a lot of stop-and-go driving. Under such conditions, the engine runs in rich-fuel mode, which results in the spilling of gas down into the crankcase. This dilutes the oil and diminishes its lubricating and rust-inhibiting properties.

I recommend changing the oil and filter once every six months.
Tom

Q Dear Tom,
When would be the proper time for a tune-up on a 2005 Chevy Equinox? I bought it brand new off the lot; it now has 67,000 miles on it. I've changed the oil as recommended by the oil life monitor.

Bruno from The Bronx

A Bruno from The Bronx,
There is no specific tune-up schedule for your vehicle. As a matter of fact, you will find no reference to "tune-up" in the maintenance schedule. If you check the maintenance schedule, it suggests changing the spark plugs at 100,000 miles, a practice I do not subscribe to. I would remove the plugs every 25,000 miles, inspect, clean, and re-gap them. Then apply never-seize compound to the threads and reinstall them, properly torquing them according to manufacturer's specs. Make sure to change the air filters and breather elements according to manufacturer's specs as well and continue to follow the dictates of your OLM in changing the oil. This regimen will keep your chariot in tip-top running condition for many miles to come.
Tom

Q Tom,
Is it true that the Toyota Prius requires car maintenance every 30,000 miles at the cost of $3,000? What do you think of the Prius? I drive 35 miles one way to work and would like a good mpg car.

David—Long Island, New York

A David,
Initially this sounded out of line to me so I checked the Toyota maintenance schedule to confirm my suspicions, and yes, this is indeed an urban legend. Toyota's maintenance schedule for this car indicates no such cost associated with the 30,000-mile maintenance. It is just a regular scheduled maintenance, including an oil and filter change, air filter change, tire rotation, and brake inspection. It will probably cost about $150 for this service, a far cry from three-grand. I like the Prius, as do the majority of the country's motor press core, so buy away.
Tom

TOP TEN FUEL-SAVING TIPS

W ith gas and diesel prices up and continuing to climb, it's worth paying attention to what you drive, when you drive, where you drive, and how you drive.

Here are ten tips for saving fuel:

1. **Drive less.** The best way to save fuel is not to burn it. Consolidate trips, car pool when possible, and drive during off-peak hours to avoid congestion.

2. **Drive slower, perhaps the speed limit for a change.** At freeway speeds, aerodynamics play a measurable role in fuel economy. Driving in the 60- to 65-mile-per-hour range instead of 75-plus-mile-per-hour range will likely increase your fuel mileage by 2 or more miles per gallon.

3. **Keep the engine in tune.** What does that mean with today's electronically fuel-injected engines? Not much, other than making sure the engine is running as it should. Spark plugs, air filters, and oxygen sensors are the primary components that influence fuel economy. Install a new air filter once per year—or more frequently if you live near or drive on dirt or dusty roads—and have the engine scoped on an engine analyzer every 30,000 to 50,000 miles to make sure it's running properly.

4. **Properly inflate your tires.** Pressures at or above 30 to 35 psi are a good choice for most passenger cars. At higher inflation pressures, the tire's rolling resistance decreases. It takes less power to roll the tires down the road. That saves you fuel.

5. **Keep tires and wheels properly aligned.** Not only will this help tires last longer, but properly aligned tires offer less rolling resistance, thus, slightly better fuel mileage.

6. **Keep the front of vehicle clean and free of debris, especially in the grille opening.** Keeping the air conditioning condenser and radiator free of bugs, leaves, and debris allows the engine to cool more efficiently and the air conditioning to work less to keep occupants cool—both of which will save fuel.

7. **Accelerate modestly.** It takes fuel to make power, so the harder you accelerate, the more fuel the engine burns. At freeway speed, accelerate gently to avoid transmission downshifts if possible. Again, lower engine rpm generally means less fuel consumption.

8. **Coast as much and as often as you can.** Anticipate stop signs, traffic lights, and slowdowns. Why keep accelerating toward a stop? Lifting off the throttle and coasting toward the stop or slowdown obviously saves fuel.

9. **Brake gently and as little as possible—within reason, of course.** You still need to stop before the intersection. Applying your brakes converts energy from fuel you've already burned when accelerating the vehicle back into heat. Don't waste what you've already spent; coast as much as possible and brake as little as possible.

10. **Eyes up!** Look as far ahead as possible to maintain good situational awareness. The farther ahead you look, the more time and distance you have to adjust the speed and direction of your vehicle. Good situational awareness is the key to safe driving, and it also saves fuel by helping you anticipate the need to slow or stop early, allowing you to do so gently and progressively.

OIL AND LUBRICANTS

Engine Oil

Engine oil and lubricants such as transmission and power steering fluid lose their ability to flow and lubricate. This is called viscosity breakdown. When viscosity breakdown occurs in engine oil, the oil loses its ability to lubricate, it can't transfer heat away from hot internal engine parts, and it can't keep dirt in suspension. The result is premature engine wear and ultimately, over time, engine failure.

Transmission Fluid

Transmission fluid lubricates, cools, and acts as the medium through which hydraulic pressure is produced within the unit. When transmission fluid is neglected and left inside the transmission for long periods, it gets burnt and loses its viscosity. The result is premature transmission wear and failure.

Power Steering Fluid

Power steering fluid is nothing more than hydraulic fluid (like transmission fluid). It is the medium through which hydraulic power steering assist is achieved. Regular checks of the level and condition will ensure that the power steering pump and rack or steering box (if so equipped) stay in good shape. If a fluid leak ensues, then the levels get low, heat and friction build up, and the pump, rack, or steering box start to grind themselves to pieces.

Drivetrain components such as differentials, transfer cases, and power takeoffs typically use transmission fluid, motor oil, a special limited slip semi-synthetic lubricant, or gear oil. Each manufacturer uses different fluids as per their application. The lubricants in these components should be checked for level, color, and consistency. A milky color means that water or moisture is in the component and, if left in this condition, will damage the unit. Fluid change should be done immediately and the cause for moisture contamination found and repaired.

Engine Coolant (Antifreeze)

Engine coolant is designed to do four things:

1. Absorb heat from the engine and carry that heat to the radiator where it is cooled.
2. Lubricate the water pump.
3. Inhibit rust and scale buildup.
4. Protect against the engine coolant freezing when temperatures dip below freezing.

Over time engine coolant (also referred to as antifreeze) chemically breaks down and can't perform these vital functions. The industry-accepted recommended change interval is every two years or 24,000 miles. Some manufacturers use coolant that is supposed to last 100,000 miles. However, when a leak ensues and oxygen gets into the sealed system, oxidation occurs and produces rust. There's also a buildup of acid and scale, a decrease of lubrication, and ultimately a loss of protection. For this reason, systems that use the high mileage antifreeze should undergo periodic inspection for leaks, rust, and scale buildup to avoid problems caused by leaks.

Brake Fluid

Brake fluid (a hydraulic fluid) is the medium through which the brakes function. More specifically, when the brake pedal is depressed, the fluid courses through the system under intense hydraulic pressure and mechanically activates the components in the brake system, stopping the vehicle. Brake fluid is hydroscopic in nature; when exposed to moisture it will absorb it. When moisture is absorbed into the brake fluid it finds its way to the lowest point in the system and forms rust. That's why it is important to keep an eye on brake fluid for rust and sediment buildup. If this is evident, the system should be flushed out with a pressure brake bleeder and the fluid replaced.

OIL, FUEL, AND AIR FILTERS

Oil, fuel, and air filter changes are absolutely vital for efficient fuel mileage, good drivability, and a healthy engine. Changing filters is inexpensive and has major benefits. Below is a brief overview of the importance of each type of filter. Consult the carmaker's maintenance schedule for replacement intervals.

A typical automotive oil filter: Oil filters come in many shapes and sizes. Oil filter configuration depends on engine compartment space available as well as oil capacity as specified by the engine designer. In addition, oil filters may have check valves built into them to ensure that they stay primed during cold startup. Always make sure to use an OEM-comparable filter to ensure proper filtration.

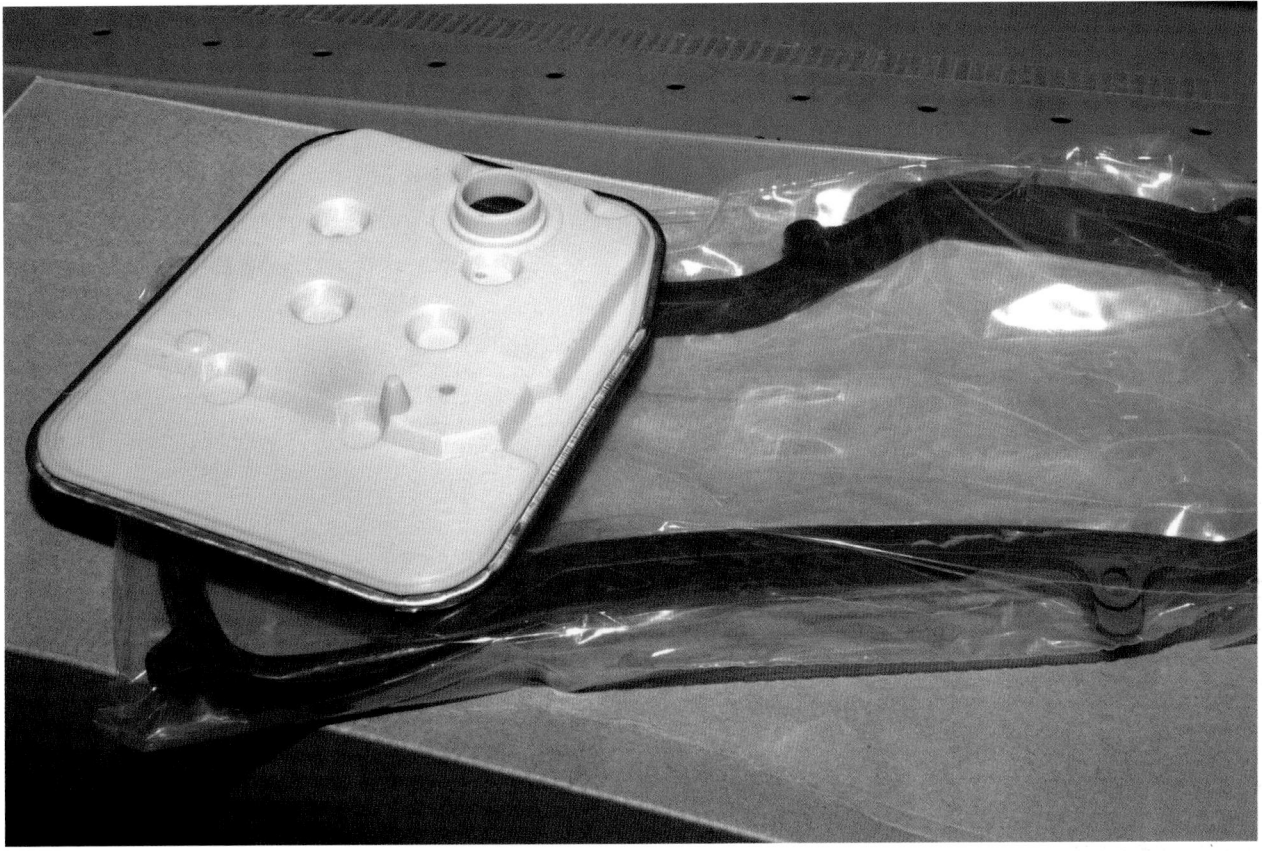

A typical transmission filter: Transmission fluid is nothing more than hydraulic oil designed to produce internal hydraulic pressure and cool and lubricate the unit. Transmissions by their very nature produce wear material that has to be filtered out of the fluid. This is the job of the transmission filter. Whenever a transmission service is done, use an OEM-quality filter to ensure maximum filtration. Transmission filters take various shapes to fit the pan configuration of a particular transmission.

Oil Filter

The oil filter is the storehouse for dirt that gets into your engine's oil. It collects fine dirt and wear-material produced by the engine as well as dirt introduced into the system by the air intake. When changing the oil filter, always make sure to use a high-quality oil filter of OEM (original equipment) quality. Some knockoff and cheap filters omit critical parts such as check valves (which maintain prime on a cold engine) and fine micron filter media (which are capable of filtering out the smallest spec of dirt inside the engine). Remember, you get what you pay for. Change the oil filter every time you change the oil according to the carmaker's maintenance schedule, for severe service every 3,000 miles, for normal service, every 6,000 to 7,000 miles.

Transmission Filter

The transmission filter is the storehouse for dirt in the transmission. Over time, transmissions drop wear material into the pan. This wear material is sucked up into the transmission filter to remove it so it doesn't circulate through the system and cause trouble. Regular transmission service usually falls within the 25,000- to 35,000-mile range. New technologies allow for a complete transmission flush. Old fluid is flushed out and new fluid is pumped in. When performing a complete flush, always replace the filter to ensure that all the dirt has been removed.

Caution: Flushing fluid on transmissions that have been neglected for a long time can result in internal damage. This topic is discussed in the chapter on transmissions and drivetrains.

Air and Fuel Filters

Engines are managed by computers. The engine control module (ECM) directs air-fuel mixtures, fuel pressure, and fuel delivery. It collects data from sensors located throughout the engine, analyzes the data, and sends out engine commands. When an air filter or a fuel filter gets clogged up, things go haywire. Fuel delivery systems make wild adjustments within their operating parameters in order to correct the malfunction of the performance system. This response causes poor drivability, lowers the fuel mileage, and decreases overall performance. That's why it's so important to keep fuel and air filters changed as per manufacturers' recommendations. Rule of thumb: fuel filter replacement every two years or 20,000 miles, whichever comes first; air filter replacement every 12 months or 10,000 to 15,000 miles, whichever comes first. Check your owner's manual to see what your carmaker recommends.

A typical automotive air filter: Because of fuel injection, never before has the air filter been so important to your car's performance and fuel economy. Computer-controlled electronic fuel injection measures airflow and engine operating environments to perfectly mix the air-fuel ratio to deliver maximum fuel economy, performance, and low tailpipe emissions. Replace the air filter according to the manufacturer's specs to realize maximum engine efficiency.

A typical automotive fuel filter: A small yet critical member of the fuel delivery system, the fuel filter has a massive responsibility for proper operation of the system. The fuel filter sifts out dirt and deposits that typically build up in fuel tanks. This operation is critical to proper operation of fuel injectors, small sprayers with orifices just a few thousandths of an inch in diameter that deliver fuel to the cylinders.

ENGINE PERFORMANCE SYSTEM

Today, most cars' ignition systems have far fewer parts than their predecessors. They don't have distributors, and the points, condenser, distributor caps, and rotors are gone. What's left are a few sensors, ECM, ignition module, ignition coil(s), sparkplug wires, and sparkplugs. These systems are highly efficient and tend to run a long time without much maintenance; however, it's a good idea to keep a watchful eye on key parts such as sparkplugs and wires. Have regular maintenance checks done on the ignition system (every 15,000 to 20,000 miles). This process includes removing, cleaning, and re-gapping the sparkplugs. It also includes scanning the system for any trouble codes. This maintenance practice pays high dividends in terms of performance and fuel economy (and that translates into money).

Of course, *always* respond to a check engine light that is lit. It's the engine telling you, "Hey, there's a problem down here!" If you let this warning go unattended, you could face costly repairs down the road. On a side note, if the light is on, there is one simple remedy that you can try: Remove the gas cap and then put it back on securely. A poorly secured gas cap is a common cause of a lit "check engine" light. The reason the check engine light stays on when the gas cap is loose is because fuel delivery systems today are sealed to keep from polluting the atmosphere, when the self-check of the emissions system takes place and it "sees" a leak caused by the loose gas cap, it trips the check engine light to tell you there's a problem with the system. If after you secure the gas cap the light is still illuminated, get it diagnosed ASAP. There's a problem with the emissions system that must be dealt with.

BELTS AND HOSES

The drive belts and hoses on your car degrade over time because they are made of rubber. Healthy belts and hoses can prevent costly problems. So let's take a closer look.

Drive Belts

Drive belts today have a serpentine design, which means one belt runs multiple components. Typically, one belt can drive the water pump, alternator, power steering pump, emissions air pump, vacuum pump, or whatever vehicle configuration exists. The automatic belt tensioner maintains the tension on the serpentine belt. It is a spring-loaded idler pulley that presses against the back of the belt and keeps it properly adjusted. Exposure to extreme temperature changes, contamination from leaking engine fluids, and roadway contaminants contribute to the breakdown of the rubber that makes up the belt. Regular belt inspection is critical to make

A typical serpentine belt with tensioner: The serpentine belt is a long belt that snakes its way through a series of pulleys, idlers, and a belt tensioner. This design eliminates the need for multiple drive belts. An effective cost-cutting design, serpentine belts tend to last much longer than traditional V-belts, usually upward of 50,000 miles.

sure that the components it drives are operating properly for maximum performance. When a crack, rip, or tear in the belt is evident, replace it immediately. Failure of this critical component will leave you stranded on the highway.

Timing Belts

Timing belts are the Rodney Dangerfield of all the belts in your car. *They don't get no respect.* Many of today's cars are equipped with a timing belt in place of the old timing chain. The function of this small yet critical member is to keep your engine mechanically "in time." In a four-stroke internal combustion engine (intake, compression, power, exhaust) the top half of the engine must be synchronized with the bottom half to complete the four-stroke cycle. The timing belt achieves this synchronization by meshing with cogs connected to the crankshaft and camshaft, ultimately producing power in your engine.

The timing belt is made out of rubber and is subject to wear and tear from mechanical and environmental conditions. The environment of the engine is quite hostile. The under-hood temperatures can exceed 500 degrees. Corrosive fluids such as oil, hydraulic fluids, and battery acid are present, and there are mechanical hazards in the form of metal and hard plastics.

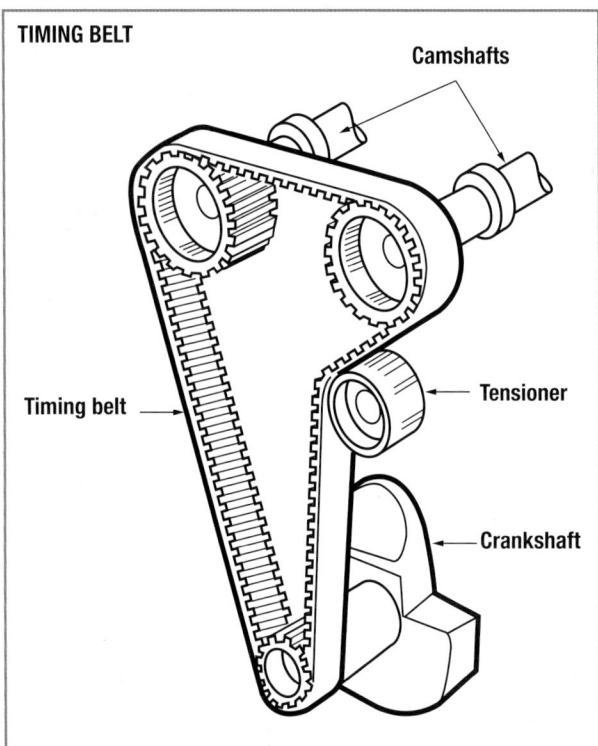

TIMING BELT

Camshafts

Timing belt

Tensioner

Crankshaft

Most timing belt systems are made up of a rubber belt, drive cogs that are bolted to the cam, and crankshafts. On double overhead cam (DOHC) engines there are two cam cogs driven by the belt. Incorporated into the system is a belt tensioner to make sure the belt is properly adjusted. Finally, in most systems, the water pump is also driven by the timing belt.

As you can see, the path that the timing belt must travel is a perilous one, to say the least. Therefore, it is extremely important to check the condition of this important and vulnerable part of your automobile. The bottom line? If you car has a timing belt, check it every 25,000 miles and replace every 50,000 miles, unless specified otherwise in the maintenance schedule.

Telltale signs of a failing belt are cracks, cuts, worn or broken teeth, as well as deterioration from wear, exposure to harmful fluids, and high temperatures. A worn timing belt can affect engine performance. If the belt's teeth are gone, the valve timing can be thrown off, either in excessive advancement or retardation, which results in poor engine performance.

When speaking of engines timed with a timing belt there are two types: interference and non-interference. When the timing belt breaks on interference type engines, the pistons collide with the valves, hence the term *interference.* When this collision occurs, it's usually at highway speed and the result is major engine damage, usually so major that engine replacement is necessary. On non-interference engines, the valves do not collide with the pistons; the engine simply shuts down. Replace the timing belt and you're off to the races again. The average cost of timing belt replacement is $300. The average cost of engine replacement is $3,000 to $4,000. Your choice.

Hoses

The cooling system hoses make up the infrastructure through which coolant flows through the engine, radiator, and heater core. They are subject to extreme heat-up and cool-down. When the engine heats up due to heavy work or a malfunction, the hoses are stretched to their limits. Over time the chemical makeup of the coolant and the adverse effects of high temps degrade the rubber. The hoses become soft, weak, and sometimes brittle. If you stress the engine or overwork it just one time with the hoses in poor condition, there's a good chance they will burst, leaving you stranded. The best way to check hoses is to squeeze them. If they are resilient and rebound when squeezed, then they are okay. If they are too soft or brittle to the touch, they need to be replaced.

CHASSIS LUBRICATION

Your car has lube points throughout the steering, suspension, and driveline. These points must be properly lubricated each time you have a general maintenance workup, which includes an oil and filter change. Steering and suspensions have pivot points and ball and socket joints that, if not lubricated, will wear out prematurely. Driveshafts and driveline plunge joints also have lube points that need periodic lubrication. We'll take a closer look at the importance of regular lubrication for each application later.

So sit back, relax, and let's learn about how to make your car last forever.

SECTION 1
VEHICULAR SYSTEMS

INTRODUCTION TO CHAPTERS 2–9

If you want to make your car last forever, you first have to know *how* to take care of it. And to know how to take care of it, you have to have some knowledge about the nature of the thing itself. And when it comes to automobiles, it means understanding some basic operating principles. Based on these reasonable assumptions, Chapters 2 to 9 are dedicated to teaching you the essential information you should know about the systems of your car. How do they operate? What makes them tick?

Knowledge, confidence, good communication with service providers, good decision-making skills, and a clear mind free of anxiety will help you do what it takes to get the most mileage out of your chariot. Lack of knowledge makes you vulnerable to all the negative stuff going on in the marketplace. So buckle up: We're going for a ride.

Photo credit: Shutterstock

Chapter 2
The Engine

Today there are more powertrain choices on the market than ever before. Because of the high price of oil, carmakers are offering these choices in an effort to appeal to a wider demographic and, more important, to the people who want to save gas and protect the environment. Let's start by taking a look at the different powertrains available today. (We don't want to leave anyone out of the party.) The most popular powertrains are the internal combustion gasoline engines, the diesel engine, the gasoline/electric hybrids, and the EVs (electric motor power).

GASOLINE ENGINES

Most automobiles use a four-stroke internal combustion gasoline engine. How do these engines generate power? They have a four-stroke design, which means that the pistons travel up and down four times in order to complete a power cycle. Vital activity occurs during each stroke, ultimately producing the power required to do the "work" of an automobile engine.

Intake Stroke

On the intake stroke, the camshaft opens the intake valve. At the beginning of this stroke, the piston is at the top position. The fast downward travel of the piston creates a vacuum, which sucks the air-fuel mixture into the combustion chamber and fills it completely. Continuing its rotation, the camshaft then closes the valves and seals the combustion chamber in preparation for the compression stroke. When the piston has reached the bottom of its travel, its new position is called BDC (bottom dead center).

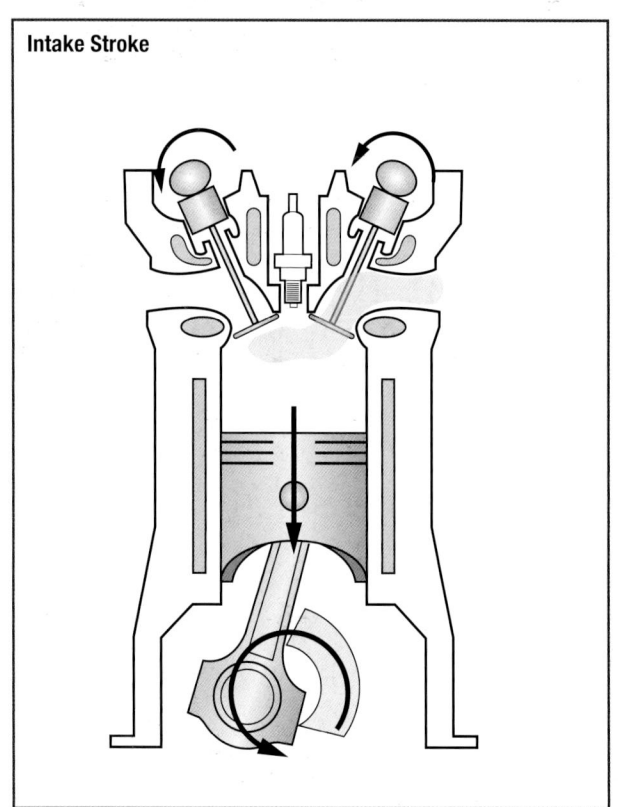

Intake Stroke

The four-stroke cycle begins with the intake stoke. This is where proper timing chain and belt alignment is so critical for all the parts in the upper and lower regions of the engine to operate in sync. Pistons, valves, lifters, cam, and crankshafts all operate in concert to create engine power. If the system is just a few degrees off, the whole thing could self-destruct.

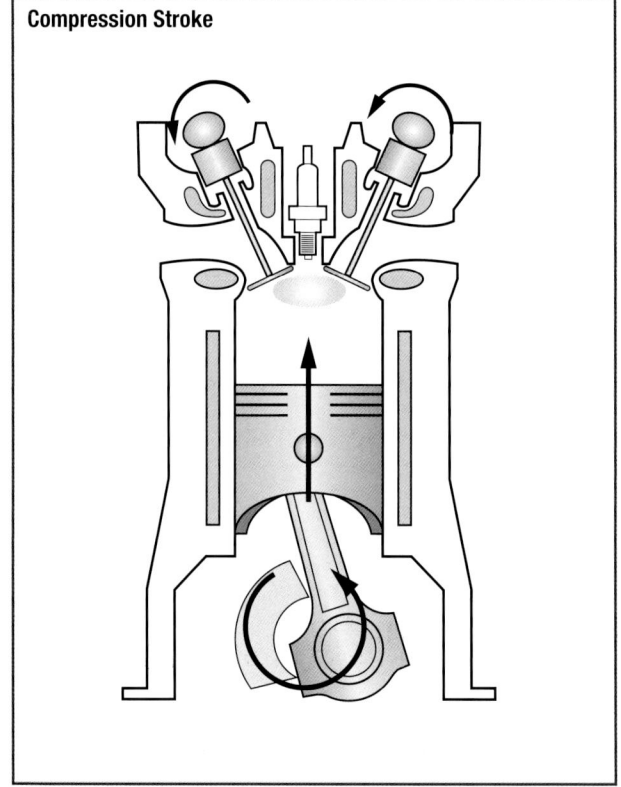

Compression Stroke

The next stroke in the cycle is the compression stroke. The air-fuel mixture fed into the combustion chamber becomes much more volatile and explosive when compressed 8 to 12 times its size. Piston rings and valves must tightly seal the precious air-fuel mixture in the combustion chamber to realize maximum efficiency.

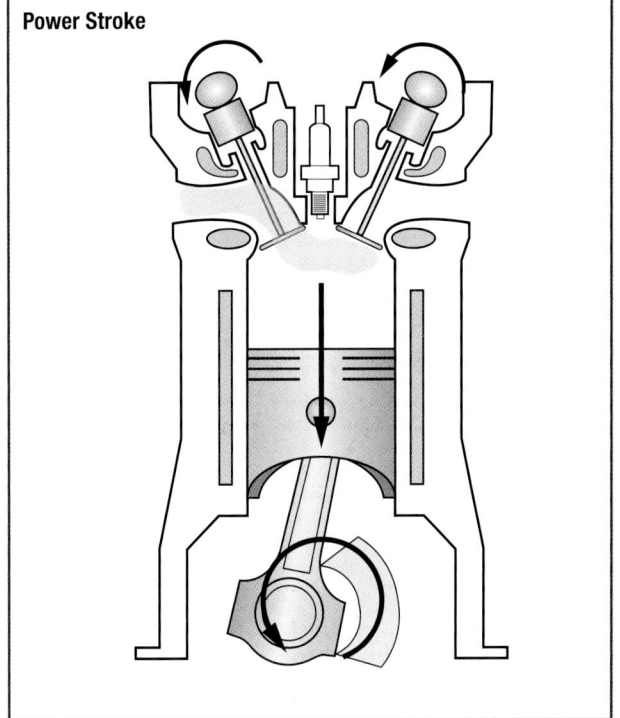

Power Stroke

The previous two strokes have set everything up for the *coup de gras* or power stroke. The air-fuel mixture is at maximum compression and thus volatile, assuming that the combustion chamber is tightly sealed and the proper air-fuel mix has been delivered. All that's needed now is ignition for the downward power stroke of the piston to power the engine.

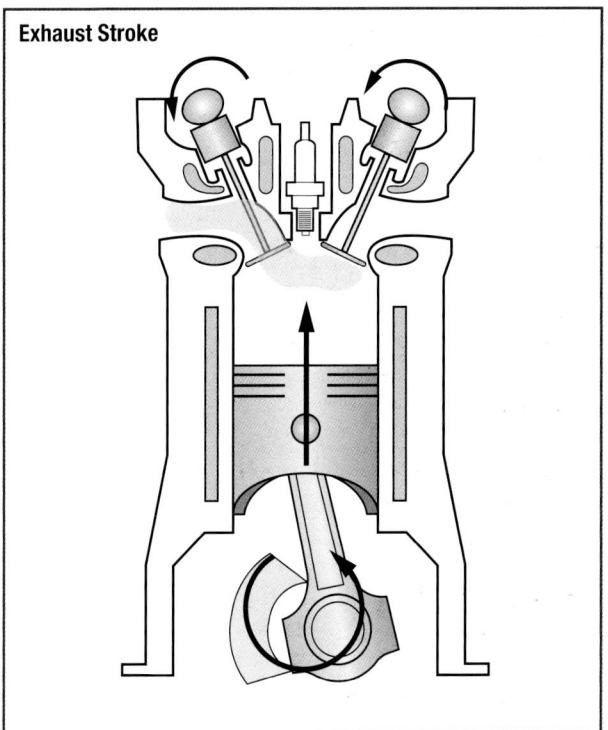

Exhaust Stroke

Now that the power stroke has done its job, there are noxious byproducts in the form of burned gases that have to be removed. The exhaust stroke takes care of this task. Once again, the wonder of exact mechanical timing results in the removal of burned exhaust gas in the combustion chamber. This happens thousands of times a minute in a typical internal-combustion engine.

Compression Stroke

From BDC the piston starts to travel upward, compressing the air-fuel mixture within the sealed combustion chamber. This compression increases the volatility of the mixture. When the piston reaches the top of its travel, which is called TDC (top dead center), the air-fuel mixture is at maximum compression (extremely volatile). At this point the fuel-air mixture is ready for combustion.

Power Stroke

At this point, a spark is generated from the ignition system. The spark jumps the air gap of the plug and ignites the highly volatile air-fuel mixture. The controlled burn of the air-fuel mixture forces the piston downward once again to BDC, thus powering the engine.

Exhaust Stroke

After the air-fuel mixture has burned and provided the energy for the power stroke, there are gaseous by-products that must be removed from the system. As the piston moves upward in the cylinder, the camshaft turns again (opening the exhaust valve) and the waste gases are pushed out of the cylinder and into the exhaust manifold (and eventually out the tailpipe).

Just a side note here, each full revolution of the crankshaft represents four full strokes of the piston, at 60 miles per hour in overdrive, the engine is usually turning at 2,600 rpm. (This is depending on how the drivetrain is geared. It can vary a few hundred rpm one way or another.) That means that the pistons are stroking 10,400 times per minute or 173 times per second. Pretty amazing, huh?

Now that you understand how the engine generates power, let's have a look at the basic parts that make up the engine of your car.

MAINTENANCE TIP

It's vital that you change the oil according to the manufacturer's suggested schedule. If oil changes are not performed regularly, excessive mechanical wear occurs, resulting in a loss of compression due to piston ring wear. The piston rings seal the combustion chamber. The seal keeps compression tight and the power stroke in a controlled downward burn. It also keeps strong airflow into the engine, as well as a steady flow of exhaust gases out the exhaust system. Worn out piston rings cause inefficient combustion, poor fuel economy, loss of power, and premature wear of other engine parts.

The engine block is cast of aluminum or iron. All the necessary holes for internal components such as pistons, camshafts, valve lifters, and bearings are cast into it. In addition, oil galleries for lubrication, water jackets for internal cooling, and mountings for external components are cast into the engine block.

ENGINE COMPONENTS
Engine Block

As you can see by the illustration, the engine block is the housing for the pistons, crankshaft, connecting rods, oil pump, and camshaft (to which everything else is attached).

Crankshaft

The crankshaft is considered the backbone of the engine. It is formed out of steel and shaped into various parts. There are also counter weights (to keep the shaft spinning) and journals (smooth surfaces on which the bearings ride). The pistons are connected to the crankshaft by connecting rods. Consequently, as the crankshaft turns, the pistons go up and down. It's this action that produces the strokes in the four-stroke cycle. The crankshaft rides on bearings that provide a smooth lubricated surface. This surface enables the crank to spin at the high speeds necessary for the engine to function.

Pistons

Pistons are cylindrically shaped metal pieces (plug-shaped) that move up and down in a cylinder. The expanding pressure in the cylinder, produced by the explosion of the air-fuel mixture ignited by the sparkplug, causes this vertical movement of the pistons.

The crankshaft is the mechanical wonder by which rotational movement is translated into the up-and-down movement of the pistons. Crankshafts have journals or smooth surfaces that rod and main bearings ride on. In addition, counterweights are built into the shaft to offset vibration and create centrifugal motion. When built, crankshafts are spun at high speeds on a balancing machine, metal is removed or added to properly balance the shaft, enabling it to spin at high rpm without vibration or coming apart from centrifugal force.

Pistons are made of steel or aluminum. Made in different shapes and sizes, pistons are fashioned for each engine and application. Larger pistons deliver higher compression ratios, which result in a more powerful engine. Each piston has rings tightly fitted to them that seal the intake and exhaust gases as well as the explosion from the power stroke within the combustion chamber. This contributes to maximum engine efficiency.

MAINTENANCE TIP

The signs of negligent maintenance first show up in the cylinders and pistons. It's common to see wear on cylinder walls caused by dry cold starts. This leads to compression loss and, ultimately, diminished power. The primary cause of this wear is viscosity breakdown of the oil. Heat, friction, and chemical contamination cause the engine's oil to lose viscosity (ability to flow and lubricate). Regular oil changes can avoid this problem.

Connecting Rods

As stated earlier, the spinning of the crankshaft causes the pistons to travel up and down in their respective cylinders. One might wonder how the circular motion of the crankshaft can produce an up-and-down linear motion of a piston. The answer lies in the design of the mechanical linkage of the connecting rods that connect the pistons to the crank. The connecting rod connects to the crankshaft journal through the use of a bearing cap. The bearing cap is a separate piece that is bolted to the rod. If you were to remove it, you would see a bearing installed in the rod. This design allows the rod to ride up and down as the crank spins on a smooth lubricated surface.

Connecting rods are cast out of steel or aluminum. Just like the crankshaft, they are weighed and balanced to make sure they operate at high speeds without vibration and wear. Connecting rods vary in length. Depending on the engine application they can be short or long. Shorter rods tend to be found in engines that operate under normal operating conditions. Longer rods tend to be found in engines built for high torque and performance applications.

Oil Pump

In order for all the parts in an engine to move smoothly and effortlessly they must have a strong, steady supply of oil to keep the mating surfaces lubricated and reduce friction and wear. This is the job of the oil pump, which operates off a mechanical drive within the engine. At the bottom of the oil pump is a special tube called a "pickup tube." A screen is attached to the end of this tube that is submerged into the crankcase (the oil pan). This screen strains out wear material and chunks of dirt in the engine.

Oil Pan

Engine oil (for the engine lubricating system) is housed in the oil pan, which is sometimes called the crankcase. The crankshaft and connecting rods spin just above the oil bath, drawing the precious lubricating fluid from its depths. The oncoming rush of air over the oil pan from the forward motion of the vehicle cools the oil as it circulates through the oil pan.

Cylinder Head

The cylinder head sits high on top of the engine block. (There are two heads on engines with two banks of cylinders.) The valves are situated inside the cylinder head. Here's how it all works.

All the parts of the engine must work in sync during the four-stroke cycle. Perfect timing of the moving parts is essential for the engine to function. There are two types of

Oil pumps vary in size, oil delivery capability, and overall design. Typically oil pumps are made of steel, have a gear drive design, are powered by the engine, and are located inside the oil pan or crankcase. Special dry sump oil pumps for high-performance applications are electrically powered and are usually located somewhere inside the engine compartment. The reason for powering such pumps electrically is to take away the mechanical drag of the traditional oil pump from the engine, resulting in higher engine output. The red fluid is assembly lube.

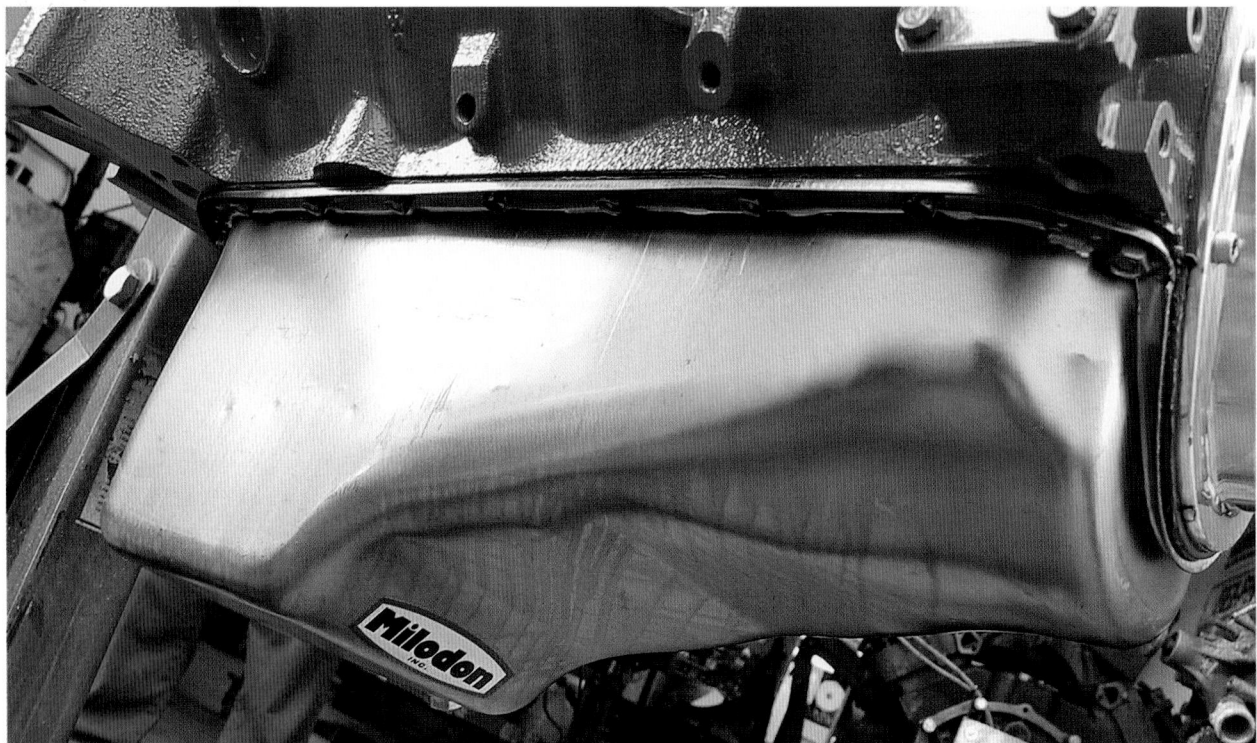

Oil pans are usually fashioned out of steel or aluminum. They vary in shape and size depending on engine oil capacity, engine compartment clearance, and internal design. Internal designs vary depending on application. Some pans require extensive baffling of the oil bath from the crankshaft, others not so much. All this affects the shape and size of the oil pan.

Cylinder heads vary in design based on engine output and design. They are cast out of iron or aluminum. BMW, for instance, builds a lot of performance design into its cylinder heads. Such systems as variable valve timing (VVT) allow for on-the-fly valve timing adjustment based on engine demand. These systems are electronically synced with engine performance systems and deliver high output. Overhead cam designs allow the camshaft to be mounted directly on top of the head and make for a compact engine. Conventional engines like those these V-8 heads belong to, have the cam mounted in the center of the engine and the heads only housing the valves.

mechanical timing drives that control the timing of these parts: a chain drive and a belt drive.

On engines with a chain drive, a timing chain connects the crank to the cam via two gears called a cam gear and crank gear. On engines with a timing belt, a cogged rubber belt connects the crank and cam. This rubber belt meshes with two cogged gears, one for the crank, one for the cam. The cam and crankshafts are perfectly timed mechanically. Thus, when the engine is operating, the valves and pistons are exactly where they are supposed to be during the four-stroke cycle. The crank rotates, causing the pistons to stroke (go up and down). The camshaft simultaneously turns with the crank via the mechanical drive.

Camshaft

When the camshaft is timed properly, it opens and closes the valves at the precise time necessary for the intake, compression, power, and exhaust strokes of the four-stroke cycle. There are lobes (egg-shaped bumps) machined into the camshaft so that, when the shaft turns, it opens and closes valves by virtue of mechanical lift.

The camshaft controls the opening and closing of the valves. Camshafts are made of steel and ride on smooth surfaces called cam bearings. The camshaft is perfectly mechanically timed with the crankshaft via a timing belt or chain. When the camshaft is made, it starts as a solid steel rod and is then ground into a stick that has lobes or bumps on it. These lobes are what raise and lower the valves. Each lobe has built into it a specific lift (height the valve is opened) and duration (amount of time the valve stays open). It is truly a mechanical wonder.

On overhead cam engines, the camshaft is mounted directly above the valves. As the camshaft turns, the valve lifters ride up on the lobes, opening the valves. As the high point of the lobes pass, the lifters ride down the other side of the lobes and the valves close. In pushrod-type engines, the camshaft is located in the center of the engine and valve lifters ride on the lobes. Pushrods are placed on the lifter's seat and fitted into a rocker arm seat at the other end. As the shaft turns, the lifters ride up and down on the lobes and push the pushrods up and down, the rods push on the rocker arms (small see-saw type devices) that push on the valve stems, opening and closing the valves in precise mechanical timing.

There are consequences of neglecting certain maintenance practices. And when it comes to engines, they can be very costly.

Turbo and Super Chargers

A turbocharger is driven by exhaust gas flow to power an air compressor. The compressor portion of the turbo draws fresh

DRIVERS ASK, TOM ANSWERS: ENGINE PROBLEMS SOLVED

Q Tom,
I have a 1992 Ford Bronco full-size with 116,000 miles. It has a 5.0-liter 302 engine. My problem? Oil is getting into the air filter. Can you tell me if this is blowby or a PCV problem? I checked the EGR valve and found that there's a lot of carbon buildup in the intake manifold. Why do you think this is happening? Thanks for your input.

Joe—Buffalo, New York

A Joe,
Beneath the grommet (that the PCV valve pushes into) on the back of the intake manifold is a pellet-style mesh vapor filter. This filter has a tendency to plug solid with sludge. Once plugged, the crankcase does not properly ventilate. The resulting pressure forces the oil-laden engine vapors backward through the air cleaner hose and fills the air cleaner housing with oil. Replacement of the filter screen beneath the PCV valve will take care of this problem in the majority of cases.

Good luck.
Tom

Q Tom,
I have a '79 Dodge van with 98,000 miles. When I start the engine it runs a little rough, but when I put it in gear and try to move, it splutters, pops, and stalls. I wondered whether I was just out of gas because I don't use the vehicle very often, and I suspected the gas gauge was lying. So I put a couple of gallons in, but it didn't seem to make any difference. Someone suggested the timing chain sprocket (which I understand is nylon) is worn and needs replacing. If it is the sprocket, can I replace it without having to reset the timing? Any suggestions would be much appreciated. Thanks for your help.

Geoff—Fresno, California

A Geoff,
If you need to replace the timing chain sprocket you *will* have to reset the ignition timing. I suggest you check the number one cylinder in reference to TDC (top dead center). This will verify if the cam sprocket (nylon gear) has jumped a tooth in timing. If this sounds over your head, then take it to a shop and have it diagnosed. This should cost you roughly one to one and a half hours of diagnostic time at the shop's labor rate. Good luck.
Tom

Q Tom,
I had the front and back main seals replaced on my Jeep Cherokee two weeks ago (it has a straight six-cylinder engine). Both seals are leaking again! What could be causing the problem—from a mechanical point of view?

Sam—Dallas, Texas

A Sam,
What other point of view might you expect from me? Metaphysical? Psychological? Lie down on a couch and tell me about your seal problem . . . ommmmmm . . .

All kidding aside, I would make sure it is the same leak. A great way to make absolutely sure is to conduct an oil leak dye test. During this procedure, the technician adds a fluorescent dye to the engine oil, and the engine is then run for a few days. At this point, the vehicle is put up on a lift and the questionable area is exposed to an ultraviolet light. The leak can easily be located, as it will show up in a bright yellow color under the light. Another possibility could be that either the PCV valve or the crankcase ventilation system is not operating properly due to sludge plugging it up. This problem can cause excessive crankcase pressure and oil seal leakage.

If the vehicle is of high mileage, check the crankshaft surfaces upon which the front and rear main seals ride. Make sure there isn't any excessive wear or scoring, as this would result in leakage as well. If wear on the front of the crank is evident, there are sleeve kits that can be installed to take up the gap from the wear, restoring the sealing surface, and most important, averting replacing the crank.
Tom

Q Tom,
I bought a used '98 Neon with 80,000 miles. It now has 108,000 miles and needs a head gasket. I plan on replacing it myself. Is the dealer the best place to get the head gasket? Also, has the gasket been redesigned to *really* fix the problem? What about using an aftermarket timing belt (or should I stick with the OEM)? Should I have the head milled? New head bolts? New water pump? Any tips? Also, should I see if Chrysler would pick up some of the tab?

Thanks,
Steve—Rochester, New York

A Steve,
First off, forget about Chrysler picking up anything. This is not a safety recall, thus freeing the carmaker of any liabilities. You can try, but I doubt you'll get anywhere.

Buy a Chrysler gasket set, because these gaskets have been re-engineered specifically for this problem (they are laminated). Also, you must use a special sealant from Chrysler, use new head bolts (because the old ones stretch), and yes, have the head checked with a straightedge and milled if necessary (straight, clean surfaces seal better than crooked ones). Make sure you effectively clean the block and head, and check the block plane with a straightedge too. While you are inside, replace the timing belt with a new OEM replacement.

As for the water pump, if it has the same mileage as the rest of the engine, replace it. Ask a Chrysler technician who works on these engines about head gasket replacement and what else you should do; however, I think I've covered it. I wish you success.
Tom

air from outside and forces it into the air intake of the engine, increasing the engine output. Turbocharged engines benefit greatly from using synthetic motor oil, more on this in the chapter on lubrication.

A supercharger is driven by a pulley driven by the engine. It also draws fresh air from outside and like the turbo, forces it into the air intake of the engine increasing engine output.

A turbocharger is nothing more than a small turbine driven by the flow of exhaust gas from the engine. The turbine inside the turbocharger force-feeds more air and fuel into the engine, thus increasing horsepower. Turbochargers are usually located close to the exhaust manifold where maximum exhaust gas flow is realized to drive the turbine within the turbocharger and boost the air-fuel flow into the engine. *Shutterstock*

Q Tom,
My Honda Accord needs additional oil every 1,000 miles. Is it possible to change oil less often since I have to add it at such a fast rate?
Jack—Brooklyn, New York

A Jack,
The questions you should be asking are: "Where is the oil in my engine going? Why does the engine lose enough oil that I have to add it every thousand miles?" Have the engine diagnosed for an oil leak or internal consumption. If you leave it alone, it will get worse and could result in engine damage.
Tom

Q Tom,
Our 2003 Chrysler Sebring has a DOHC sign on the engine. What does this stand for?
Gabbie—Montreal, Quebec

A Gabbie,
This stands for double overhead cam. Your engine has two camshafts, one for each cylinder head. Each camshaft controls the valvetrain on each cylinder head.
Tom

Q Dear Tom,
Can you help me understand how it happened that I drove my 2000 Toyota Camry to a quick lube for a simple oil change and came out needing a water pump? I had to have it towed home and then towed to a repair shop where they said I need a new engine. You might ask if I maintain the service on my car and the answer is yes, every six months.
Barbara—Philadelphia, Pennsylvania

A Barbara,
Wow. There are too many variables here to accurately assess your situation. What do you mean by "I maintain the service on my car every six months"? What service? Oil changes? Tire rotation? Sparkplug replacement? This information is too vague for me to help you. That said, I would go through the maintenance records to see what exactly has been done in recent months to determine what happened. Sounds to me like the car had a bad water pump, causing the coolant to leak out, which caused the engine to overheat and blow the head gasket. This, in turn, caused engine coolant to mix with the engine oil, damaging the engine's road and main crankshaft bearings and necessitating engine replacement. That's the best I can offer. Sorry for your woes.
Tom

WHAT HAPPENS WHEN YOUR ENGINE ISN'T LUBRICATED

Your car's engine will operate efficiently and last longer if you change the oil and filter regularly. When you neglect oil and filter changes, the moving parts of your engine are not lubricated adequately. Proper lubrication of bearing and mating surfaces is essential to the life of your engine. Over time, dirt and internal wear material clogs up the oil filter. In addition, a phenomenon called "sludging" occurs. During this process, overheating and oxidation causes the oil to lose its ability to lubricate and a cake-like substance called sludge builds up inside the engine. As the process continues, this sludge soaks up the engine's oil and builds on itself. As a result, decreased lubrication causes friction that produces heat between bearing and mating surfaces. The friction and heat wear down the metal surfaces, ultimately resulting in catastrophic engine failure.

MAINTENANCE TIP

A lways follow the manufacturer's suggested maintenance schedule. If you're not sure, err on the aggressive side and follow the severe maintenance schedule. Then you know for sure that the engine is always operating with fresh, clean oil and that you will get the maximum life out of it. For those of us who want to keep our cars a long time, this approach saves us big bucks.

USING THE WRONG ENGINE OIL OR FILTER
Engine Oil

A few years ago, a frantic woman called me during my national radio show. Her husband, a mechanic from the "old school," refused to use the oil that was suggested by the manufacturer in her new Ford Taurus. The car had a high-performance V-6 engine (double overhead cam). This design required 5W20 semi-synthetic oil. The husband had used "straight 30 weight" oil for years successfully in his vehicles, and he wasn't going to pay the high price for "new fangled" oil. At 25,000 miles, the engine had developed a faint knocking sound at idle that escalated under acceleration. The dealer determined that the engine had a rod knock caused by using the wrong engine oil. Although the car was still within the warranty period, the claim was denied and the elderly couple was faced with a $5,000 bill to replace the engine in their one-year-old Taurus. Don't be pennywise and pound foolish. Take care of your car's engine by giving it a healthy diet of the recommended oil.

Oil Filter

Not all oil filters are created equal. Always buy OEM (original equipment) quality or better. Cheap knockoff filters often lack check valves to ensure proper prime when starting a cold engine and fine micron filter media to trap very small particulates. Just because it may look like the old one and it screws onto the engine doesn't mean it's what your vehicle needs. Spend a little money now; save a lot of money later.

> ### MAINTENANCE TIP
> When changing the oil, always use oil and oil filters as recommended by OEM specs to ensure your car's engine is getting maximum lubrication and filtration. Skimp in this area and you could skimp yourself right out of a warranty claim.

TIMING BELT BREAKAGE

On engines equipped with a timing belt, it must be inspected regularly and replaced at the prescribed interval. When it comes to engines with timing belts, there are two types: interference and non-interference. These terms refer to what happens when the timing belt breaks and the valves are "out of time" with the pistons. The valves on interference engines come so close to the pistons that they will collide if they are out of mechanical time with each other. This collision usually occurs at highway speeds; hence, the collision between the valves and pistons is often violent. Catastrophic engine failure always occurs, and either the engine needs major work or it has to be replaced.

> ### MAINTENANCE TIP
> Follow the manufacturer's suggestions for timing belt inspection and replacement. And always replace the timing belt with OEM quality or better.

DIESEL ENGINES

When Rudolph Diesel applied for the patent on his revolutionary new engine, he was granted Patent No. 67207 for a "Working Method and Design for Combustion Engines, . . . a new efficient, thermal engine." The diesel engine achieves combustion by injecting diesel fuel into a combustion chamber filled with highly compressed, super-heated air. That's why the patent office described Diesel's engine as a "thermal engine."

The diesel engine uses a four-stroke cycle just like a gasoline engine; however, there is no electrical ignition system used to achieve combustion, and the compression ratio is much higher than in a gasoline engine.

Intake Stroke

The intake valve opens, letting in air. The piston travels down, drawing the air into the cylinder. At BDC the valves close, sealing the combustion chamber in preparation for the compression stroke.

Compression Stroke

The piston travels back up to TDC, tightly compressing the air in the cylinder.

Power Stroke

As the piston reaches the top of its travel (TDC), fuel is injected at the height of the compression. When air is super compressed, it gets hot because there is an increase in molecular collisions and friction. It's so hot that it ignites the fuel. The expanding explosion of the fuel-air mix forces the piston downward, creating the power stroke.

Exhaust Stroke

The exhaust valve opens, the piston moves back to the top (pushing out the exhaust gases created by combustion of fuel), and the cycle repeats itself.

Key Differences Between Gasoline and Diesel Engines

- Gasoline engines take in a mixture of gas and air, compress it, and then ignite the mixture with a timed electrical spark. A diesel engine takes in only air and compresses it to a compression ratio that produces high combustion chamber temperatures. The fuel is injected into the chamber at the height of compression and the heat from the compressed air ignites the fuel spontaneously, generating the downward power stroke of the piston.

- A gasoline engine compresses air and fuel at a ratio of 8:1 to 12:1 (on average), while a diesel engine compresses at a ratio of 14:1 to as high as 25:1. The higher the compression ratio of the diesel engine, the better the combustion efficiency. Why? Because as the combustion ratio increases, the temperature increases, and the diesel fuel is burned more completely and efficiently.
- Gasoline engines generally use either carburetion (in which the air and fuel is mixed long before the mixture enters the engine cylinder), or fuel injection (in which case the fuel is injected at the intake stroke, outside of the cylinder). In contrast, diesel engines use direct fuel injection. The diesel fuel is injected directly into the engine's cylinder when the piston is at the top of the compression stroke (TDC).

Diesel Fuel vs. Gasoline

Those of you who have compared diesel fuel and gasoline know that they are quite different. They smell differently, and diesel fuel is heavier and oilier. Diesel fuel has a higher energy density than gasoline. A quick chemistry lesson illustrates this fact:

- 1 gallon (3.8 liters) of diesel fuel contains approximately 155×106 joules or 147,000 btu of energy.
- 1 gallon of gasoline contains 132×106 joules or 125,000 btu of energy.

In short, you get more bang for your buck out of a gallon of diesel fuel than you do from a gallon of gasoline.

MAINTENANCE TIP

Follow the manufacturer's suggested maintenance schedule for your diesel vehicle. *Always* use suggested oil for diesel application.

HYBRID POWERTRAINS

A hybrid electric vehicle (HEV) combines the use of a low-emission internal combustion engine with the battery and electric motor of an electric vehicle.

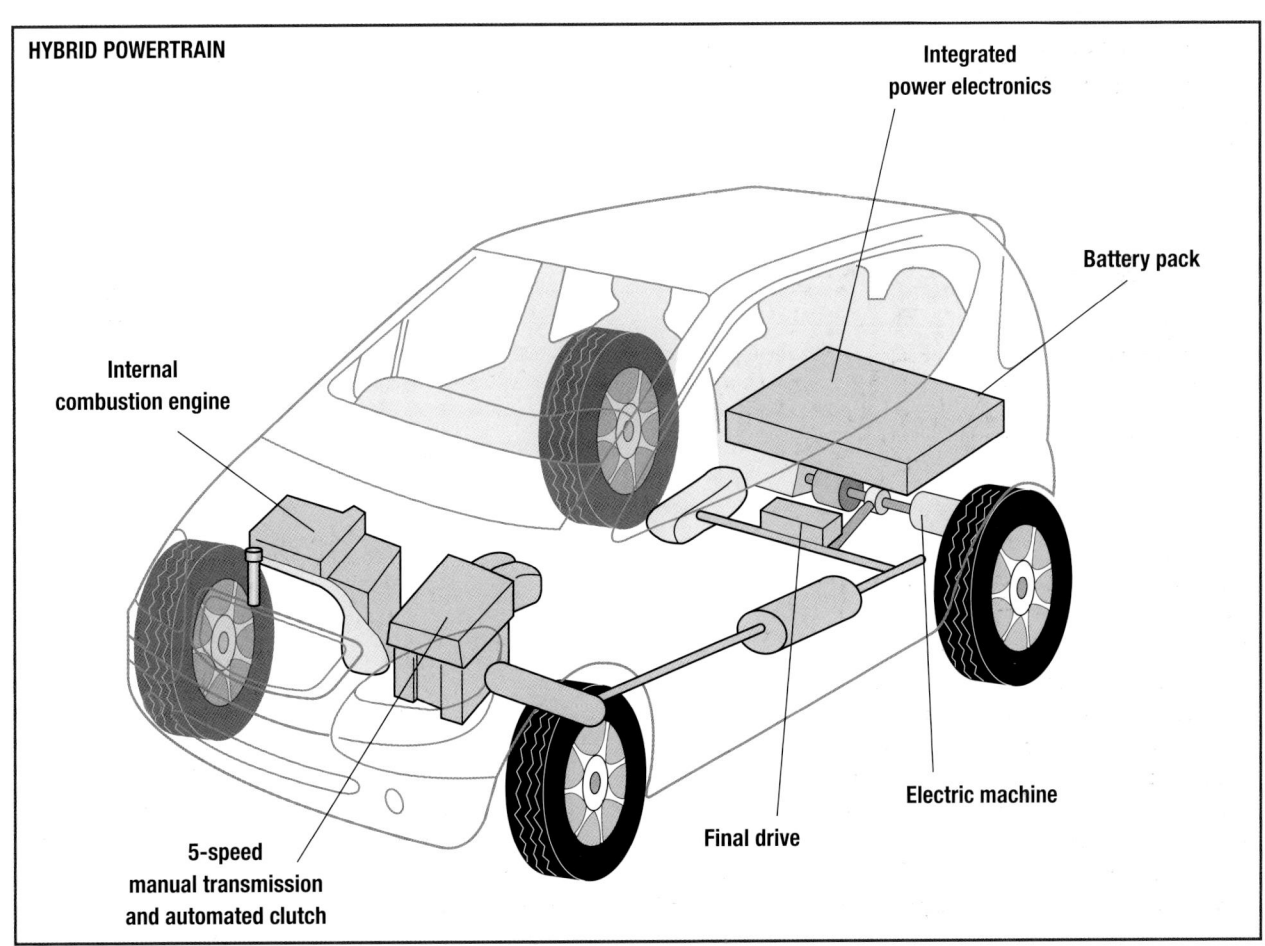

HYBRID POWERTRAIN

Integrated power electronics

Battery pack

Internal combustion engine

Electric machine

Final drive

5-speed manual transmission and automated clutch

ELECTRIC POWERTRAIN

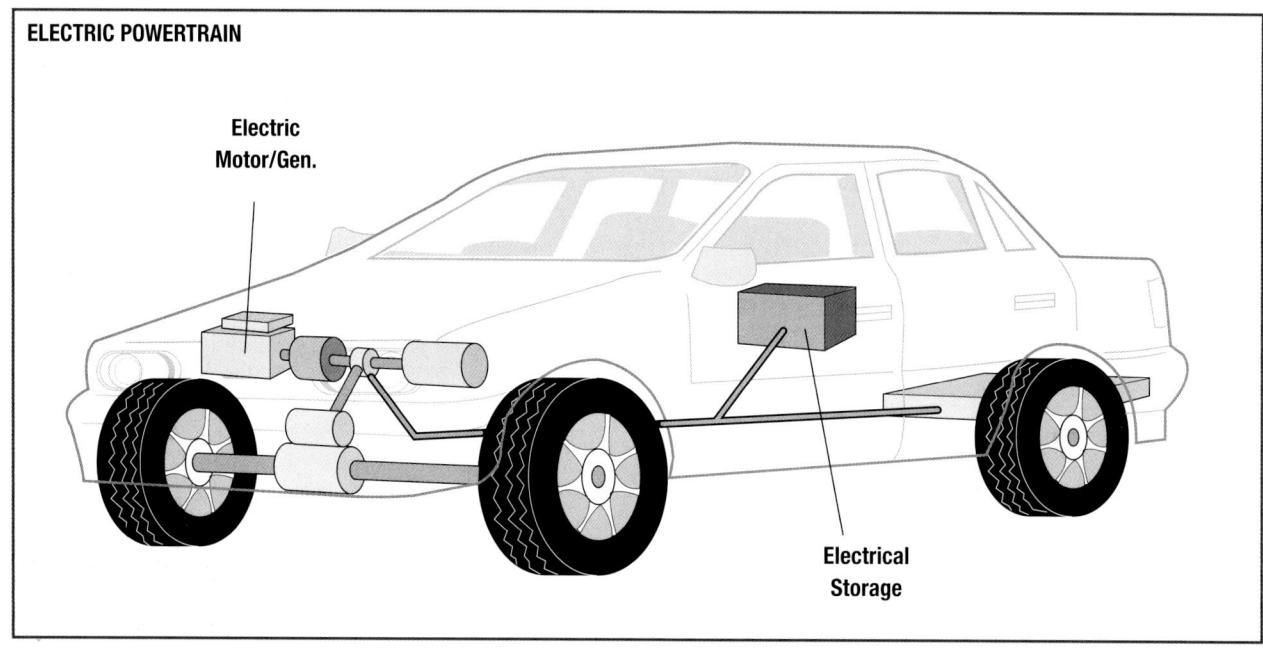

Electric
Motor/Gen.

Electrical
Storage

A typical HEV system consists of:

- **Electric traction motors and controllers**, which drive the wheels when the engine is not driving them
- **Electric storage systems**, such as batteries, ultra capacitors, and flywheels, which store the electricity needed for powering the electric motor
- **Hybrid powerplants**, such as spark ignition engines or diesel engines, which share the responsibility of powering the vehicle with the electric motor
- **Specially designed fuel systems** for the hybrid powerplants
- **Unique transmissions** designed for hybrid power

When driving a hybrid vehicle, the powertrain switches seamlessly between the internal combustion engine and electric motors, constantly seeking to deliver the best fuel economy. Typically, when you come to a stop, the gas engine shuts off. The vehicle is powered by the electric motors at low speeds. When you need to accelerate hard, both the electric drive and gas engine kick in to get the vehicle to the desired speed. When braking, a generator activated by the brake

> **TIP**
>
> Always be extremely careful when jump-starting a hybrid vehicle. Typically, the electrical system is high voltage. If you make contact with the jumper cable while jumping the vehicle, it can stop your heart.

system recharges the hybrid battery, ensuring that the battery stays charged at all times.

ELECTRIC POWERTRAIN

The powertrains of electric vehicles are simple. They consist of a battery pack, electric motor (or motors, in applications where more than one motor is used), and a transmission, differential, or gearbox of some sort to transfer power to the drive wheels.

The mileage range for electric vehicles varies, depending on the type of battery technology used. In recent years, lithium ion batteries seem to offer the greatest range. Tesla, an EV manufacturer, boasts an up-to-200-mile range on a charge. Other EV makers typically quote up to 70 miles. The range will increase as battery technology evolves.

PROJECT 1
Check Oil

 Time Required: 5 minutes

 Tools Required: Paper towel or rag

Skill Level:

 Cost Estimate: $0

 Tip: Check your oil at every fill-up or at least once a month. If the oil level is low, it will get dirty faster and accelerate engine wear.

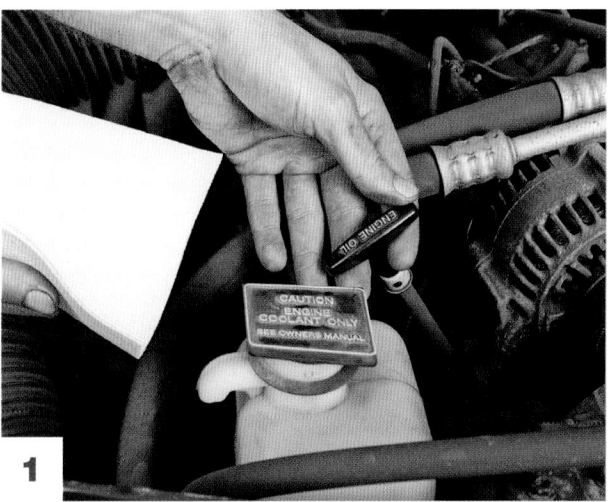

1

Pull engine oil dipstick in engine bay.

2

Wipe the dipstick clean with a paper towel or rag.

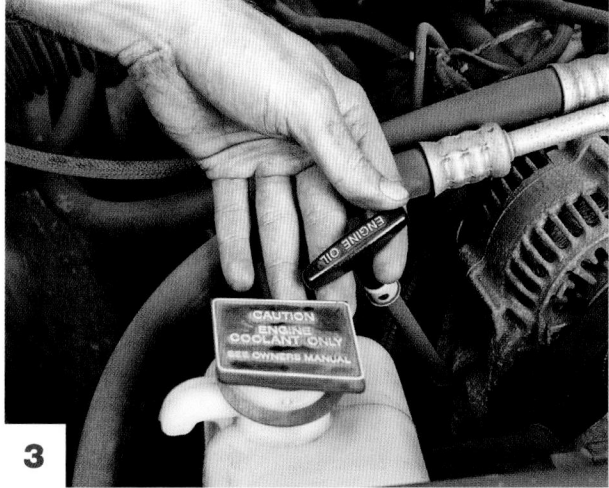

3

Reinsert the dipstick until the handle sits in its fully inserted position.

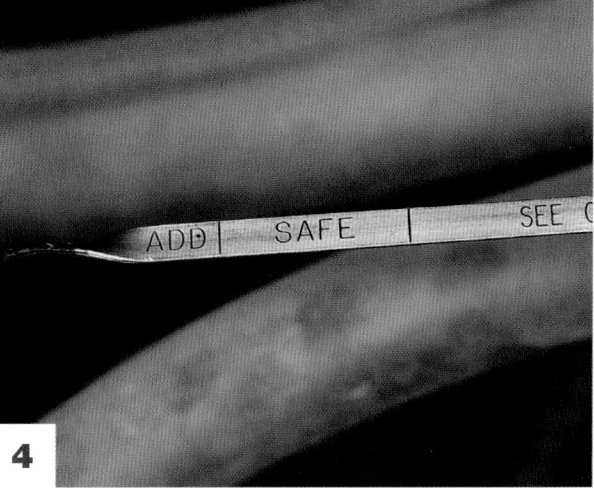

4

Pull the dipstick again and check the markings on the end for your engine oil's level. This engine's oil is fresh, so it is a translucent gold color. The streak of oil ends in the safe zone on the dipstick, indicating that the level is okay.

PROJECT 2
Change Oil and Filter

 Time Required: 30 minutes

 Tools Required: Funnel, drain pan, wrench, possibly an oil filter wrench

 Skill Level:

 Cost Estimate: $15–$20

 Tip: Stand the dirty filter threaded-side up in the filter box to prevent it leaking as you install the new one and add oil.

1

Changing your oil and oil filter regularly is essential to long engine life. Recommended intervals are included in your owner's manual. Oil is held in the oil pan on the bottom of the engine. The oil filter is located at left in this photo

2

With the engine warm but not hot, remove the drain plug from the oil pan. Turn counterclockwise. Allow the oil to drain into a pan. Tip: The plug is about ½-inch long. Don't let it drop into the drain pan.

3

Turn the oil filter counterclockwise to loosen. You might be able to free it by hand, but more likely you'll need an oil filter wrench, which any auto parts store and many convenience stores will carry. Some oil will drip when you loosen the filter so position your drain pan accordingly. Allow the oil to drain from the pan and filter area for a few minutes.

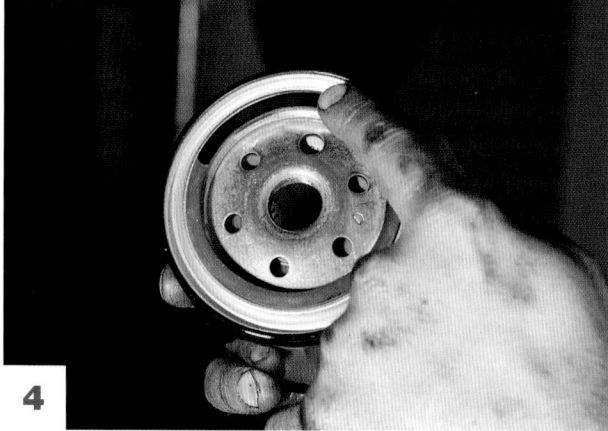

4

Wet the rubber seal on your new oil filter with fresh oil and thread it on. Snug the filter with the filter wrench, generally three-quarters to one full turn after the rubber gasket contacts the engine surface. Replace and fully tighten the oil drain plug. Note: Be careful threading in the drain plug, as your pan will leak if you mess up the threads. Don't put the drain plug in with an air wrench; tighten it with a hand wrench.

The oil filler cap will be on top of the engine and labeled. Unscrew it and set aside.

Insert a funnel in the fill hole.

Pour in the number of quarts prescribed in your owner's manual and replace the filler cap. Run your engine for a few minutes, then turn it off and check for leaks at the filter or filler plug. Recheck the oil level to make sure it's full. Note: Make sure you properly recycle your old oil and filter. Many auto shops accept used oil and filters. Even many cities/counties will accept used motor oil and filters for recycling. Check with your local city offices.

Chapter 3
Transmissions and Drivetrains

The transmission and drivetrain are responsible for powering your vehicle forward. The transmission translates the power produced by the engine into forward motion. The drivetrain is a series of gear-driven components powered by the transmission. It is typically made up of driveshafts, axles, differentials, and transfer cases or auxiliary gearboxes. Configurations vary with vehicle design and equipment.

It's important that you have a basic understanding of how each of these systems work. This knowledge will drive home the importance of maintaining your car so that you can get the most mileage out of it. In addition, this information will help you identify a problem and communicate it effectively to your technician.

TWO BASIC TRANSMISSIONS DESIGNS: MANUAL AND AUTOMATIC

Below is a typical manual transmission setup that is usually found on four-wheel-drive and rear-wheel-drive vehicles.

Case and Related Parts

The following is a typical manual transmission setup that is usually found on front-wheel-drive vehicles.

As you can see, there are a lot of parts that make up a manual transmission. Configurations vary with vehicle year, make, and model; however, the basic design of multiple gears, shafts, and bearings make up the underlying theme. You achieve motion through meshing one or more gears via the manipulation of the shifter and clutch in concert with vehicle speed and load.

To the right is a typical automatic transmission setup.

The difference between the manual and automatic transmissions lies in how they achieve forward motion.

The manual transmission achieves forward motion through a mechanical medium. During the process, gears mesh one to another and, at the same time, a clutch disc is pressed tightly to a smooth-faced device called a flywheel. The flywheel is bolted directly to the back of the engine's crankshaft. This connection transfers the power of the engine

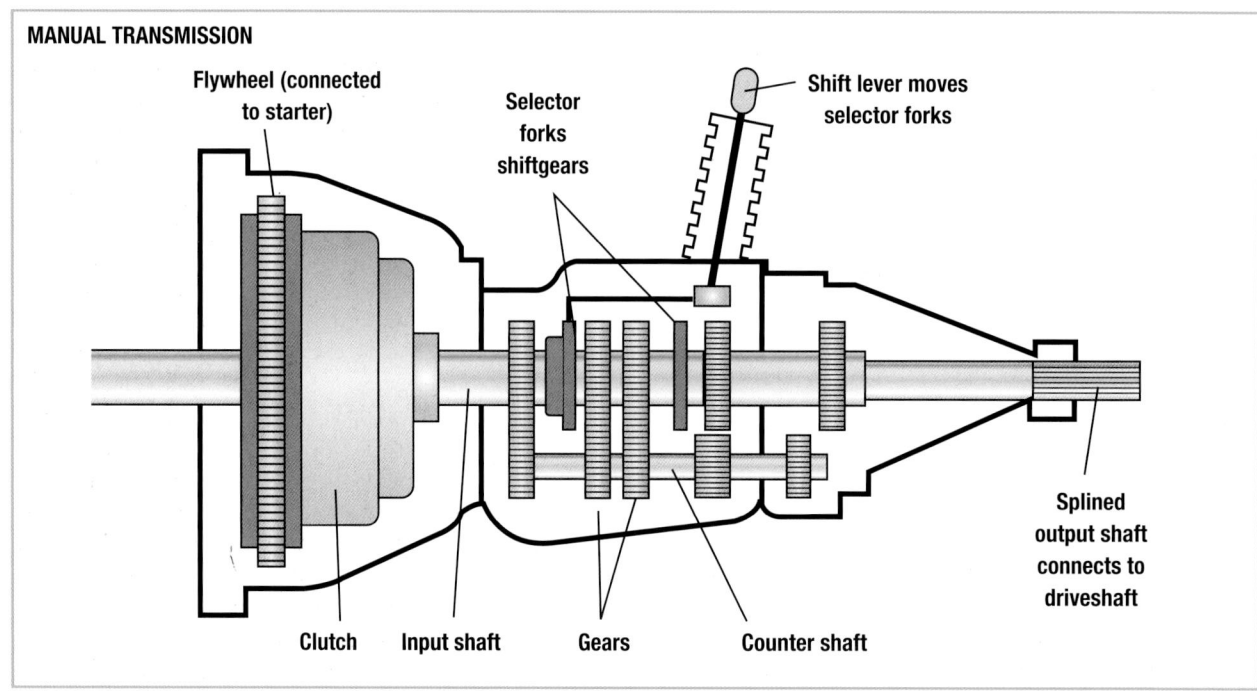

MANUAL TRANSMISSION

Flywheel (connected to starter)

Selector forks shiftgears

Shift lever moves selector forks

Splined output shaft connects to driveshaft

Clutch   Input shaft   Gears   Counter shaft

As illustrated here, there are many parts that make up a manual transmission. Gears, cogs, syncro rings, shafts, and bearings all come together to complete the picture. Gears and most of the internal parts are made of extremely hard heat-treated steel for long-lasting service. Manual transmission cases are either made of cast iron or aluminum.

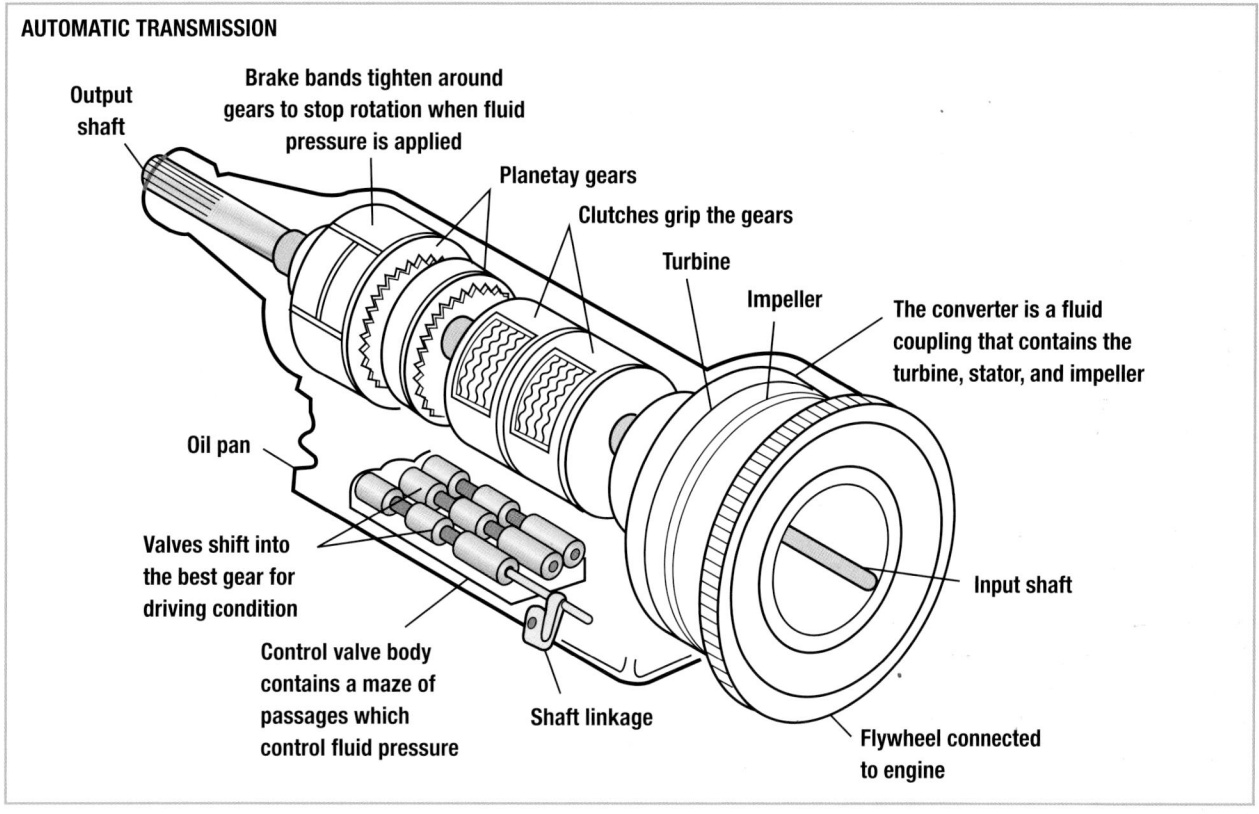

AUTOMATIC TRANSMISSION

Output shaft

Brake bands tighten around gears to stop rotation when fluid pressure is applied

Planetay gears

Clutches grip the gears

Turbine

Impeller

The converter is a fluid coupling that contains the turbine, stator, and impeller

Oil pan

Valves shift into the best gear for driving condition

Control valve body contains a maze of passages which control fluid pressure

Shaft linkage

Input shaft

Flywheel connected to engine

Automatic transmissions are complicated. They have many more parts than manual transmissions. The reason for the complication is because an automatic transmission operates all by itself. All you have to do is select "drive," and a series of hydraulic and electronic commands and functions take over. The result? Sending you off without having to depress a clutch or shift gears.

MAINTENANCE TIP

For the most part, typical maintenance on manual transmissions involves checking and maintaining the lubricant level. In days gone by, most manual transmissions used 90-weight gear oil as the standard for lubricant. In the last decade this has changed dramatically. Carmakers use synthetic gear lube, motor oil, automatic transmission fluid, and gear oil (and not necessarily 90-weight). The best way to determine what lubricant your vehicle's transmission takes is to check your owner's manual. Or maybe you should let your professional technician add the fluid to your manual transmission. On transmissions with external gearshift linkage, check the adjustments and adjust as necessary. Make sure there are no leaks and, if there are, tend to them immediately. The loss of transmission lubricant can result in major damage and a lot of expense.

through the transmission throughout the drivetrain and ultimately to the drive wheels.

The automatic transmission achieves forward motion in a completely different way. When a gear is selected, oil (transmission fluid) is routed under pressure (created by its internal pump) through the valve body. The valve body is the brain of the transmission, controlling up and down shifting through hydraulic pressure and electronic commands from the vehicle's performance system. The valve body directs the flow of transmission oil to where it is needed in order for the transmission to perform a function (such as the application of "passing gear," reverse, first, or second gear). Oil is then forced through the torque converter at high pressure. This action creates a fluid coupling between the engine and the transmission. The torque converter changes hydraulic pressure within an automatic transmission to mechanical torque, which drives the driveshafts and, ultimately, the wheels of your car.

In design, the torque converter is similar to a turbine engine. Fluid is forced under pressure through small passages called fins. These passages vary in size and flip flop in direction. As fluid is forced through the fins (which get smaller in size), a strong, almost solid "fluid coupling" is created. This is what powers the driveshafts and wheels. The fluid coupling effect is similar to what happens when the clutch is applied on a standard transmission. The applied clutch connects the engine to the transmission, and the torque converter does the same thing through the fluid coupling.

TORQUE CONVERTER ASSEMBLY

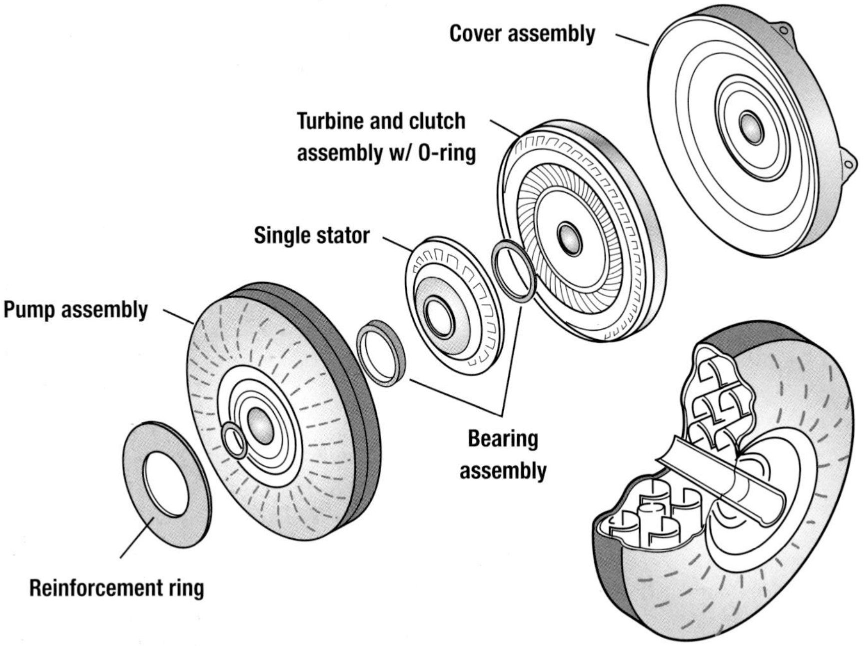

Cover assembly

Turbine and clutch
assembly w/ O-ring

Single stator

Pump assembly

Bearing
assembly

Reinforcement ring

BELT DRIVE CVT

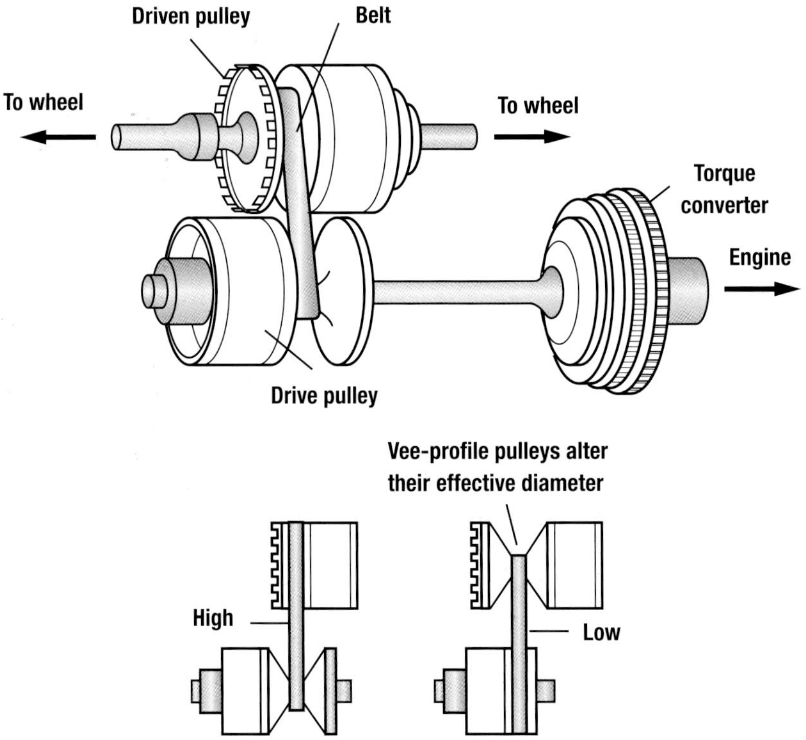

Driven pulley

Belt

To wheel

To wheel

Torque
converter

Engine

Drive pulley

Vee-profile pulleys alter
their effective diameter

High

Low

Now that we have a fluid linkup, how do we accelerate forward and shift gears? The gears are applied by a series of mechanisms called servos and bands that are controlled by engine electronics and hydraulic pressure. For example, when the gas is depressed, the engine control module (ECM) senses the need to shift, so an electronic signal is sent to the transmission to downshift into passing gear. Electrical switches called solenoids are tripped and valves within the valve body divert the flow of oil to the bands or servos, which in turn apply or disengage gears. Just like magic, the transmission shifts.

Constant Variable Transmission

In recent years carmakers have created a transmission design called the constantly variable transmission (CVT). In this design, the transmission gear ratio is constantly changing in order to produce maximum torque, regardless of the speed of the vehicle. Additional benefits include elimination of harsh shift points and improved fuel economy.

There are a few different types of CVTs on the market. They include the following:

Belt Drive System

In this system, the belt rides up and down inside the pulley grooves. The closing and opening of one of the pulleys produces different gear ratios. As the belt rides up and down, turning at different speeds, gear ratios are changed. This action results in a constantly variable gear ratio.

Toroidal CVT

Although the Toroidal CVT system appears to be drastically different than the belt drive, the operation of all the components of this system lead to the same results, a continuously variable transmission delivering a constantly variable gear ratio.

In this transmission, one disc connects to the engine. This is equivalent to the driving pulley in the belt drive system. Another disc connects to the drive shaft. This is equivalent to the driven pulley: rollers (or wheels), located between the discs act like the belt, transmitting power from one disc to the other.

Both the belt-drive CVT and the toroidal CVT are examples of frictional CVTs that work by varying the radius of the contact point between two rotating objects. There are CVTs that use a different design, however.

Hydrostatic CVTs

The Hydrostatic CVT uses variable-displacement hydraulic pumps to vary the fluid flow into hydrostatic motors. In this type of transmission, the rotational motion of the engine operates a hydrostatic pump on the driving side. The pump converts rotational motion into fluid flow. Then, with a hydrostatic motor located on the driven side, the fluid flow is converted back into rotational motion, which results in powering the vehicle.

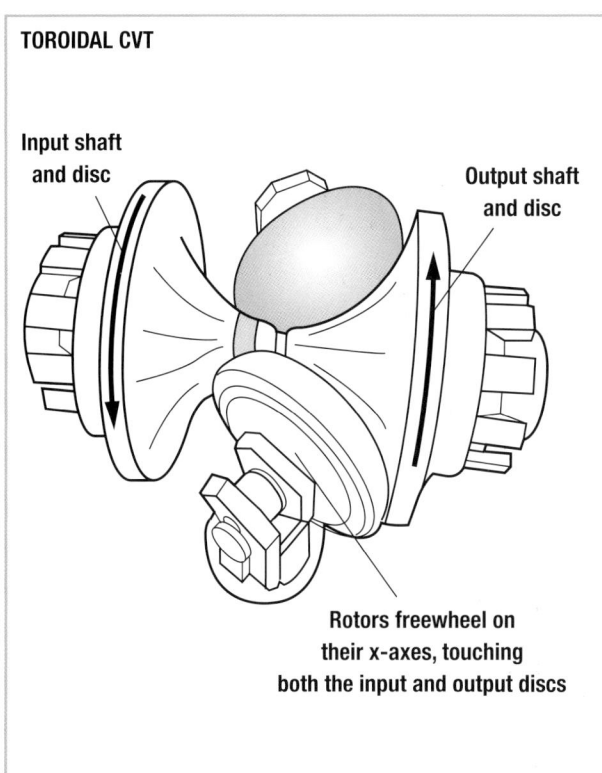

TOROIDAL CVT

Input shaft and disc

Output shaft and disc

Rotors freewheel on their x-axes, touching both the input and output discs

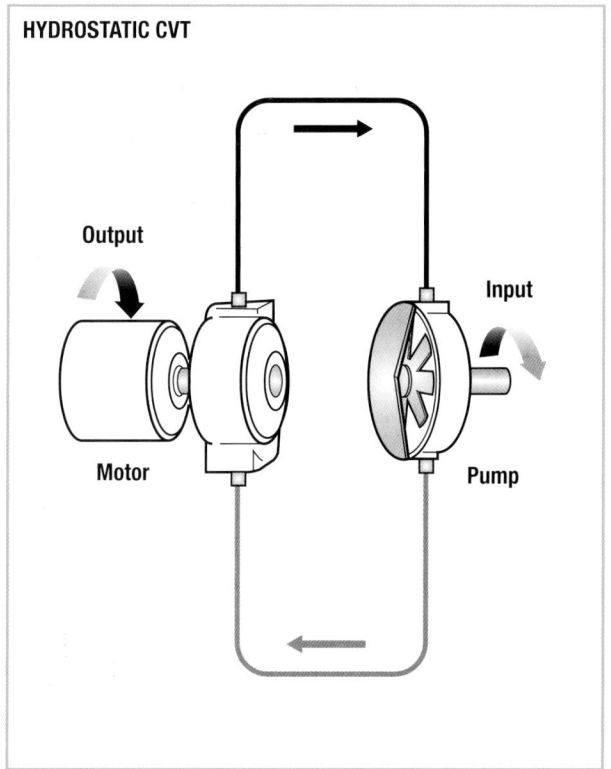

HYDROSTATIC CVT

Output

Input

Motor

Pump

DRIVETRAIN CONFIGURATIONS

Now that the basics of manual, automatic, and CVT transmissions are behind us, let's take a look at the different drivetrain configurations. It can be confusing when you consider all the offerings, which include four-wheel drive (part-time, full-time, and permanent), all-wheel drive, front-wheel drive, and rear-wheel drive. What does all this mean?

Four-Wheel Drive

There are three different configurations to four-wheel drive (4WD): part-time, full-time, and permanent.

Part-time 4WD is the most basic of all 4WD systems. With this setup, the driver can choose when to drive in two-wheel drive or 4WD. In addition, it offers the choice of either a high or a low range in which to operate the system. At first this sounds pretty good—look at all the choices we have!—until you realize that you can't engage the 4WD on pavement unless it's very, very slippery. Why? Because when you engage 4WD with this system you lock the front and rear wheels together through the transmission and transfer gearbox. This is great for straight-ahead traction on slippery surfaces. However, on dry pavement it makes for odd driving, cornering, and handling characteristics. Also, you can harm the drivetrain components by driving in 4WD for extended periods of time on dry pavement because there's insufficient slippery surface to let the wheels slip against each other. This causes the driveshafts to twist up and exposes the transfer case to extreme mechanical stress.

So why would anyone want to choose part-time 4WD? Three reasons:

1. It's less costly to build and therefore to buy.
2. It's durable under the heavy stress of driving off-road or in snow, ice, mud, or under other slippery road conditions.
3. When you don't need 4WD you can disengage it.

Full-time 4WD is the most commonly used system on the market. Full-time 4WD offers a two-wheel-drive mode for summertime driving or dry-road conditions and an automatic 4WD mode for changing road conditions. It also offers 4WD high and 4WD low modes for when the going really gets tough. The automatic 4WD mode is a convenience for many drivers. In addition to the transmission and transfer gearbox, a center differential is used to couple the front and rear wheels. The center differential allows the front and rear wheels to turn at different speeds as needed, letting the full-time 4WD work automatically. Very simply,

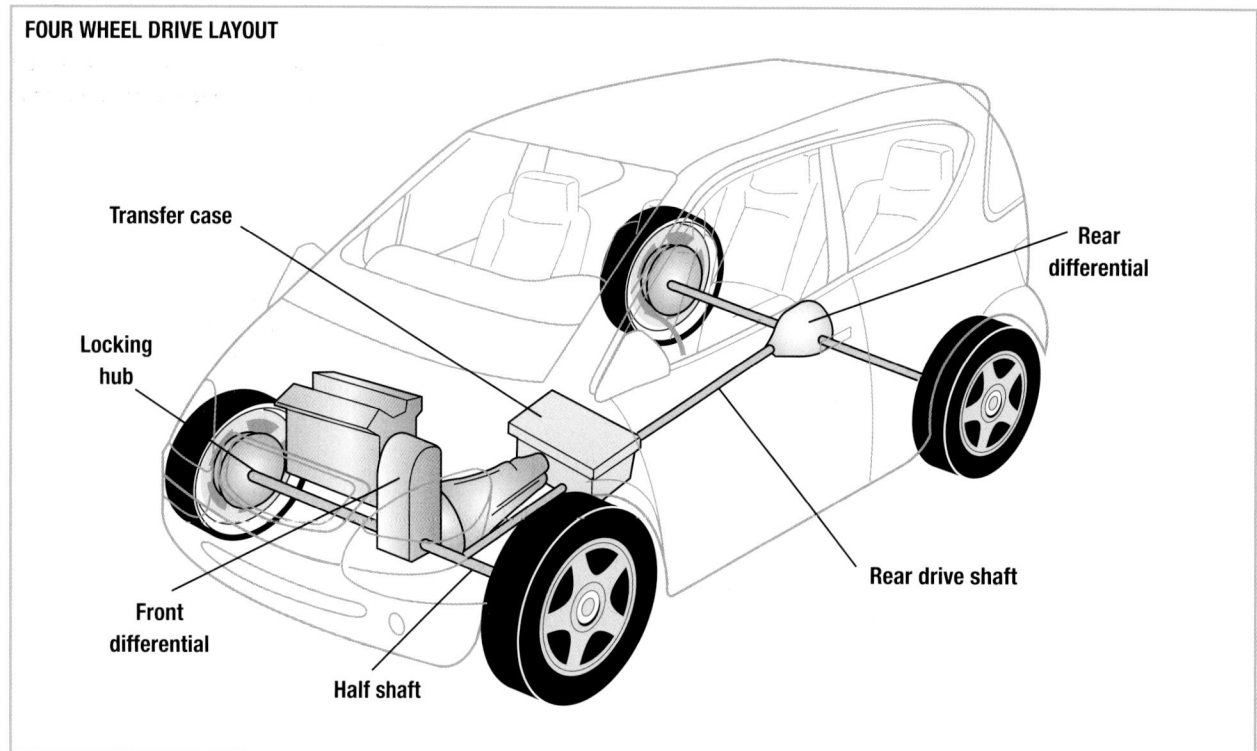

FOUR WHEEL DRIVE LAYOUT

Transfer case

Locking hub

Front differential

Half shaft

Rear differential

Rear drive shaft

Part-time four-wheel-drive (PT 4WD) is a system that only gets used when the roadways are slippery. I recommend you engage the system occasionally during the off-season just to make sure system components get lubricated and stay operational. If you leave PT 4WD unused during the dry seasons, system components can and do freeze up from corrosion and non-use. Hub covers loosen up from vibration, allowing road dirt, grime, and weather elements to get into the hubs and cause problems. A simple check of the hubs and engaging the system for short runs while driving in a straight line will ensure the system stays operating reliably all year long.

when engaged in automatic 4WD on a dry straight road, the system operates in two-wheel drive. When the wheels start to spin due to slippery road conditions, the system reacts to wheel-spin by progressively locking the front and rear wheels together to optimize traction. This system is limited because it requires the driver to determine when to engage it.

Permanent 4WD is similar to full-time 4WD, but it has no two-wheel-drive mode. The vehicle is always in 4WD, so you don't have to determine whether conditions are right to engage it. We still have transmission, transfer gearbox, and center differential coupling the front and rear wheels. The only difference is that torque (or power) is constantly being applied to all the wheels, giving maximum traction in all weather and road conditions. Current systems have high and low modes for when the going gets tough. Most important, the system does the thinking for you. It automatically applies as much lock up (to all the wheels) as needed for maximum traction.

All-wheel drive is used on a lot of cars where a high-low range is not needed. Think of the all-wheel-drive system as a permanent 4WD system without the two-speed transfer gearbox. There is no high and low range and the system is always in automatic four-wheel drive. If your idea of "off-road" is a smooth, level dirt road, then all-wheel drive may be all you need. But for serious rock climbing, towing in mud and snow, or even slopping through heavy, deep, unplowed snow and forging new roads, a two-speed gearbox coupled with the ruggedness of a heavy-duty 4WD system, whether it is part time or full time, is a must.

4WD DRIVE TERMS DEFINED

Locking differential: Locks both wheels on the axle, forcing them to turn together to deliver maximum traction.

Limited-slip differential: Detects slippage in one wheel and sends torque to the other wheel that is not spinning. Its operation is automatic.

On-the-fly-shifting: This term means that the 4WD can be engaged while driving the vehicle. A lot of systems require that you stop the vehicle before engaging the 4WD.

Automatic hubs: Some systems require that you manually "lock in" the front wheels in order to drive in 4WD because they freewheel when the 4WD is not engaged. On vehicles equipped with automatic hubs, the only thing you have to do to "lock in" the front wheels is to flip a switch.

TRANSFER CASES

The transfer case is an auxiliary gearbox connected to the back of the transmission that allows the driver to select high and low drive range. Transfer cases are unique to 4WD vehicles only. Power is directed from the transmission through the transfer case to both ends of the vehicle through two separate driveshafts. The transfer case is attached to the rear of the transmission and gets its input directly from the transmission. Power is directed from the engine through the transmission and then through the transfer case to either the rear wheels or both the front and rear wheels, depending on what drive mode the driver selects.

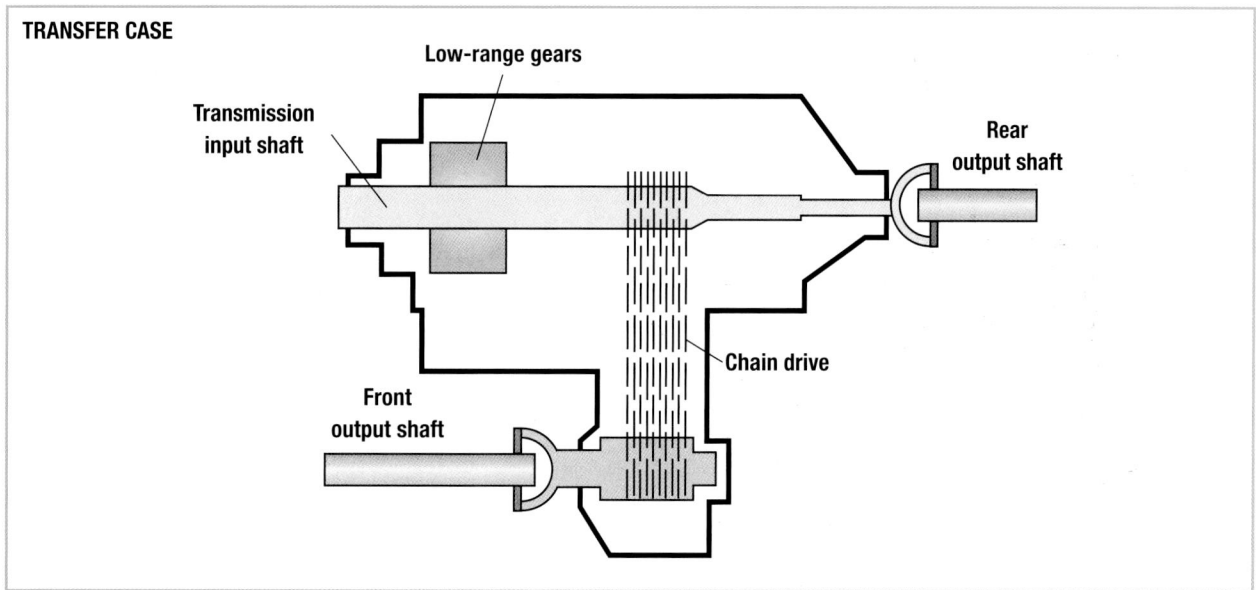

TRANSFER CASE

Low-range gears

Transmission input shaft

Rear output shaft

Chain drive

Front output shaft

A caveat here with respect to transfer cases and tires on 4WD vehicles: Based on personal experience, I have seen people install two different sized tires on their 4WD vehicle to give the appearance of the vehicle being "jacked up," using larger diameter tires on the rear and smaller diameter tires in the front. Bad move. The two sizes will result in the front and rear driveshafts turning at different rpm. This will stress the transfer case to the nth degree because the front and rear driveshafts are turning at different rates of speed, essentially creating "twist" within the transfer case. I have seen transfer cases vaporized because of this move. All four tires on 4WD vehicles must be the same overall diameter.

DRIVERS ASK, TOM ANSWERS: TRANSMISSION PROBLEMS SOLVED

Q Dear Tom,
I'm having a problem with my '97 Pontiac Grand Prix (3800 engine). I have to add transmission fluid to it over a long period of time, about a gallon or more in 25,000 miles. I cannot find any fluid residue under the car. What could be causing this loss of fluid?

John—LaGrange, Georgia

A John,
Check to see if the transmission is equipped with a vacuum modulator valve. This valve operates off engine vacuum to smooth out the transition between shifts. If the valve had a pinhole in the diaphragm, transmission fluid would be sucked up into the intake manifold and burned in the engine. Also, a small leak at the cooling lines will drip onto the highway while driving or be burned off on the exhaust pipe. Finally, the transmission oil cooler in the radiator tank may be leaking a small amount over time into the engine coolant. Check to see if the coolant has a milky, oily, strawberry color look and feel to it. If it does, the oil cooler is leaking into the radiator. Get it into a transmission shop and have it checked out to pinpoint the cause of fluid loss.

Good luck.
Tom

Q Tom,
My '94 Olds Cutlass with a six-cylinder engine overheated the other day. Upon inspection of the coolant system, I noticed a thick strawberry milkshake-like substance. Also, the automatic transmission fluid was low. I have since replaced the radiator and now have the daunting task of flushing the milkshake out of the coolant system. Any suggestions?

Casper—Anchorage, Alaska

A Casper,
The strawberry milkshake in the radiator indicates the transmission oil cooler in the old radiator burst and the transmission oil mixed with the engine coolant, hence the strawberry milkshake-looking substance in the radiator. This is not good because the transmission will eventually fail. Seals will swell, hydraulic pressure will be lost inside the unit, and internal wear of the transmission will accelerate.

Flush the cooling system and have the transmission rebuilt. Sorry for the bad news.
Tom

Q Dear Tom,
I own a '96 Toyota Camry with 133,000 miles. The local Toyota dealer says that it's way overdue for a transmission flush, but when I go to local quick lube shops they all refuse to do it because of the mileage on the vehicle. The transmission operates perfectly now, but the transmission fluid is a dark brown. Is it wise to have the dealer do the work and risk having trouble after the job? Or should I just keep driving and hope for the best?

Mary—Washington, D.C.

A Mary,
The answer to this question is a tough one. On high-mileage vehicles, transmission fluid change is a crapshoot because one has no way of knowing the extent of internal wear. When the old fluid is overheated it loses its lubricating and cooling properties and, most important, its ability to act as a hydraulic pressure medium. The transmission experiences excessive internal wear. This wear causes the unit to heat up. Heat causes the rubber seals to harden and the glue on the clutches to become brittle and crystallize. When new fluid is introduced into the unit, the high detergency of the new fluid scrubs the old glue away from the back of the clutches, rendering the transmission useless. As for the rubber seals, the fluid leaks by them because they have shrunken from the heat. Take it to the dealer and have the dealer drop the pan to try to get a handle on the extent of internal wear before flushing the transmission. Then you can make an informed decision on whether to proceed with the flush. Good luck.
Tom

DIFFERENTIALS

The power from the engine is ultimately directed through the transmission to the drive wheels by means of the differentials. Differentials also allow the drive wheels to turn at different rates of speed, making for ease of turning. Some performance cars and 4WD vehicles have a Posi-Traction, or lockup differential. It is designed specifically for locking the drive wheels together for maximum traction on acceleration.

Differential Locations in Different Vehicles
Front-wheel drive is used on most passenger cars today. This design weighs less, eliminates the need for a driveshaft and transmission tunnel (creating more interior space), and places the engine over the drive wheels (maximizing tire traction).

Rear wheel drive is often chosen for its simplicity and good handling characteristics. Placing the drive wheels at the rear allows ample room for the transmission in the center of the vehicle and easy access for service. Traction in inclement weather is a problem because there is virtually no weight over the rear wheels. To counter this effect, people put sand bags in their trunks during the winter. In performance cars with high-output engines, this design is desirable because the extra weight in the rear of the car (coupled with setting up the rear suspension to transfer vehicle weight downward on the rear wheels) results in better drive wheel traction on hard acceleration off the line.

RECOMMENDED DRIVETRAIN MAINTENANCE FOR DIFFERENT SYSTEMS
Automatic Transmissions
Just like the oil in your car's engine, the transmission oil (usually referred to as fluid) is subject to degradation from dirt, friction, and heat. Breakdown of the fluid can cause premature failure of the transmission. Close to nine out

Q Tom,
I own a '97 Town and Country minivan with more than 140,000 miles. The dealer told me that I might need a new transmission, and it will be a few thousand dollars to replace it. At this time I don't have the money to buy a new car, and I'm not sure if it's worth paying that much for a transmission for my current vehicle. I could take it to an independent person who said they could do it cheaper than the dealer. He said he would give me a free quote. I asked him if I should just get new transmission fluid and filter, and he said that was not good enough. I have to go the whole nine yards. Is this true?
Thank you,
Lydia—Escondido, California

A Lydia,
I find it interesting that the second shop advised you that "You need the whole nine yards" without even looking at the transmission. Wow! What a diagnostician! How did he do that? Frankly, Lydia, I would stay away from that shop and find one trustworthier to have it evaluated before embarking on such a costly repair. When transmissions have high mileage on them and they have been neglected over their life (that is, not changing the fluid and filter for the entire life of the transmission), there's nothing you can do other then rebuild or replace them.

If the vehicle has that kind of mileage on it and the transmission is toast, and you're on a limited budget but need the vehicle, try to find a used low- to mid-mileage transmission for your vehicle. It will be cheaper than rebuilding your old unit. Call your local junkyard and ask if they have a transmission for your vehicle.

Your vehicle is built on the Chrysler minivan platform; Voyagers and Caravans will interchange with your vehicle.
Tom

Q Tom,
I own a beautiful 2006 Mustang GT with a manual transmission and hydraulic clutch system. I have been told that, with a cable clutch system, it is not good to leave the clutch engaged when stopped because it causes excess wear on the clutch system. Is this true? Does it apply to hydraulic clutches as well? Also, do you have any other advice that might save wear-and-tear on the clutch and transmission?
Jeannette—Boise, Idaho

A Jeannette,
This is a fallacy! Clutches, throw-out bearings, and clutch plates are designed to be engaged and disengaged rigorously over their lifetimes (usually about 60,000 to 90,000 miles, depending on how you drive). Go ahead and hold your clutch pedal down at the stoplight any time you feel like it. As for how to make the clutch last as long as possible, don't ride the clutch when taking off from a stop. Make sure it is completely engaged (foot *off* the pedal) before accelerating from a dead stop. And don't "hill-hold" with the clutch. Use the brake instead and learn how to engage a clutch from a stop on a hill. Enjoy your beautiful Mustang.
Tom

Q Dear Tom,
I own a 2002 Jeep Grand Cherokee. The transmission doesn't shift to higher gears unless I rev it up to 4,000 rpm. Why is that?
Kelly—Detroit, Michigan

A Kelly,
You need to get the vehicle to a shop and have the system scanned for codes for transmission malfunction. These vehicles are noted for pressure solenoid failures, causing the symptoms you described. The fluid pressure solenoid controls oil flow based on electrical commands it receives from the ECM. If it malfunctions, erratic shift patterns occur. Good luck.
Tom

DIFFERENTIAL

Differentials are gearboxes just like transfer cases and manual transmissions, and they require regular maintenance. I like to check fluid level every oil change just to make sure there are no leaks. In addition, a visual inspection of the entire unit is smart to make sure there are no axle leaks or loose axle bearings. Differentials can use gear oil or special lubricants depending on the type of differential used. Also when checking the fluid, make sure the fluid is not a milky color. This indicates water contamination, which will accelerate internal damage.
Photo credit: Shutterstock

of ten transmission failures are due to fluid contamination and overheating, according to the Automatic Transmission Rebuilder's Association. Automatic transmissions require regular maintenance. The rule of thumb? Replace the fluid and filter every 30,000 miles or every 12 months, whichever comes first. A complete transmission transfusion (or flush) is recommended because this procedure exchanges all the old fluid for new. There is one caveat here. On vehicles with a poor transmission service history you should seek the advice of a professional before doing a complete fluid exchange. A "poor transmission service history" refers to a transmission with burnt fluid (evidence of overheating) or a transmission with fluid that's been in the unit more than 80,000 miles.

Why could a complete flush cause problems in these transmissions? There are many documented cases of high-mileage transmissions failing shortly after having a complete fluid exchange. Why? If the unit has overheated (evident by burnt fluid), the glue on the back of internal clutches has crystallized. When it is soaked in a bath of fresh high-detergency transmission fluid, the glue on the clutches dissolves, rendering the clutches, and thus the transmission, useless. Therefore, on units with high mileage, it might be wise to change only the filter and the fluid in the pan.

CVT Transmissions

Maintenance varies with the type of CVT. The best advice is to follow the maintenance schedule dictated by the carmaker.

Standard Transmissions

Standard transmissions are not quite as touchy as the automatics; however, it's a good idea to have them checked every oil change. Standard transmissions use one of three lubricants: automatic transmission fluid, 30W motor oil, or gear oil. When checking the fluid be sure to check the level, the presence of moisture (which renders the fluid a milky color), or the presence of wear particles. A small amount of wear material is acceptable, but excessive wear material can indicate a problem. The maintenance change interval for transmissions that use automatic transmission fluid and 30W motor oil is every 50,000 miles. For gear oil the recommended interval is 80,000 miles. Follow the carmaker's maintenance schedule because some can and do vary.

4 × 4 MAINTENANCE

In addition to a transmission, all 4 × 4 vehicles have a transfer case, locking hubs, and front and rear differentials. Some have an additional center differential that is part of the 4 × 4 drivetrain system. The maintenance of the transfer case is usually the same as the standard transmission (check your owner's manual just to make sure). Maintenance of the locking hubs is extremely critical, however. Locking hubs come in two forms: automatic and manual. Both forms of hubs must be inspected for wear and disassembled, cleaned, and lubricated regularly (every 24,000 miles or 24 months). Snow, ice, water, salt, and mud find their way into these mechanized units and render them useless, costing the owner big bucks. Do yourself a favor and keep the locking hubs in good working order.

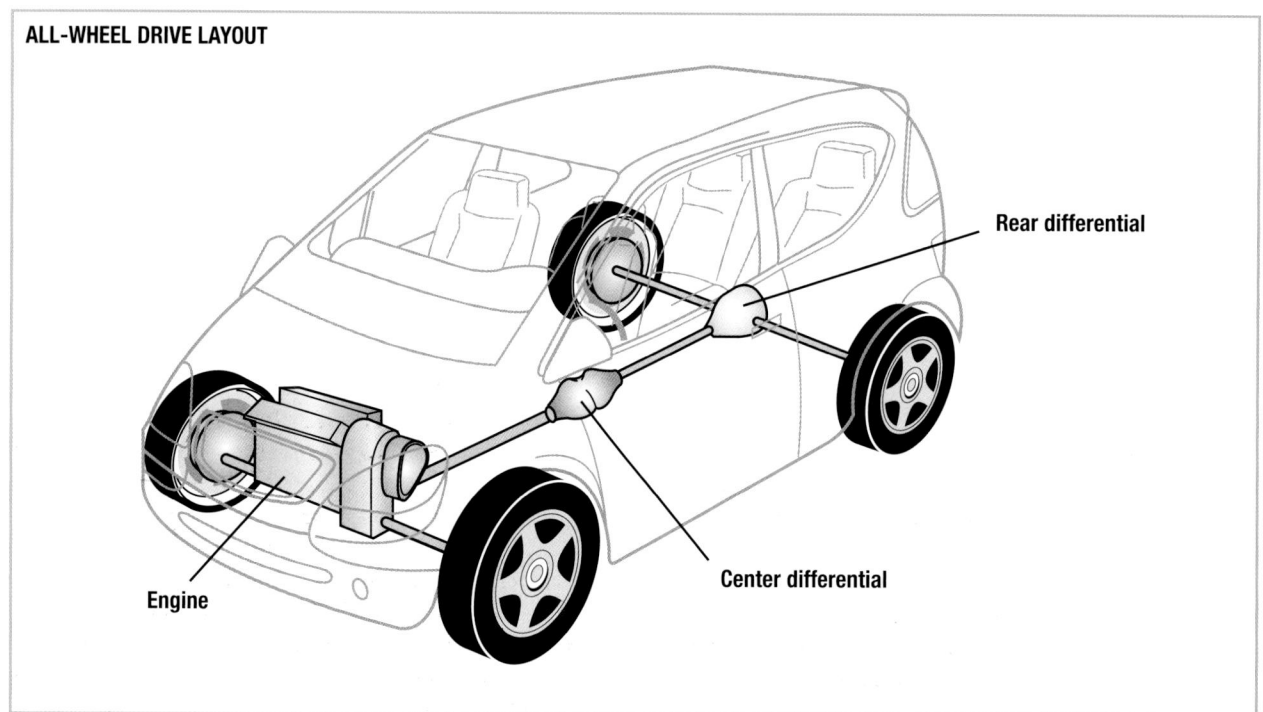

ALL-WHEEL DRIVE LAYOUT

Rear differential

Center differential

Engine

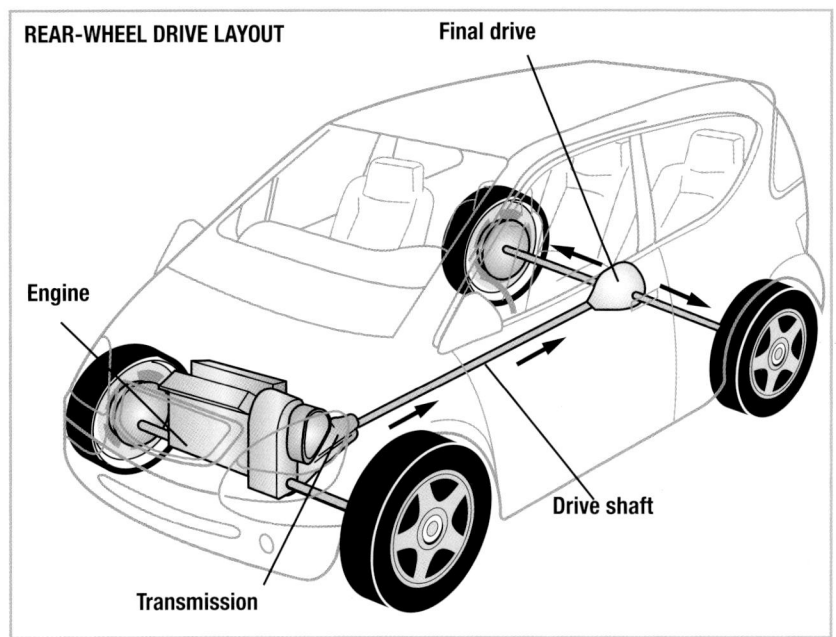

REAR-WHEEL DRIVE LAYOUT

Final drive

Engine

Drive shaft

Transmission

Rear-wheel drive is now the standard of old. Easy to maintain, rear-wheel drive required the use of a driveshaft that spanned a good portion of the undercarriage. A tunnel was built into the underside of the vehicle to keep the shaft tucked up close and away from the roadway. Rear-wheel drive tended to be ineffective in inclement weather like winter or excessive rain because of the lack of weight over the rear wheels resulting in poor traction.

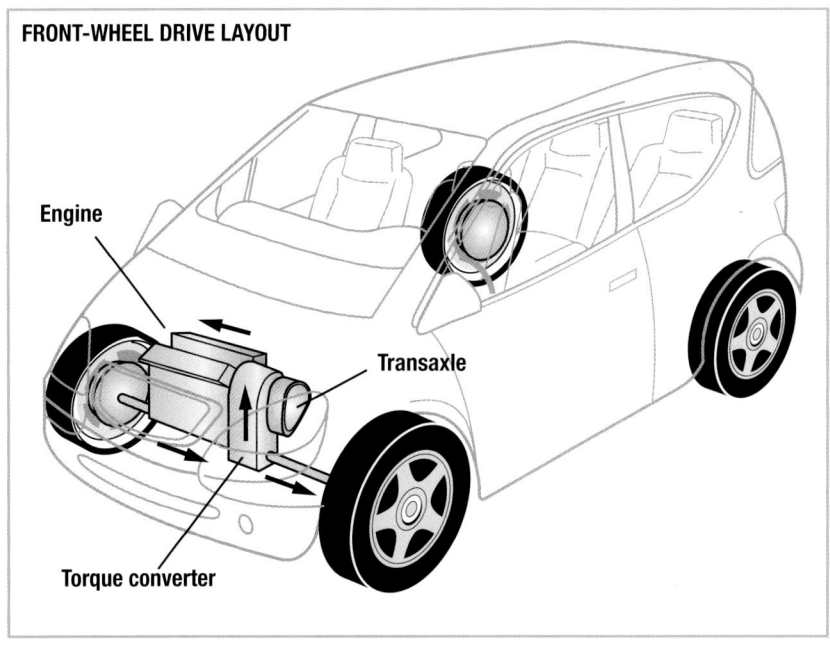

FRONT-WHEEL DRIVE LAYOUT

Engine

Transaxle

Torque converter

Front-wheel drive is pretty much standard for most passenger cars today. The compact design makes for more interior room and less major components and marrying of the differential with the transmission. This is why it is sometimes referred to as a "transaxle." Because the transmission and differential are combined, they take the same fluid. whether it is motor oil, gear oil, or special synthetic gear lube. This basic design has proven to be long lasting, durable, and reliable.

DIFFERENTIAL MAINTENANCE

Cars with rear-wheel drive or all-wheel drive and 4 × 4s have differentials as part of the drivetrain system. The only maintenance required for the differentials is to check the fluid level every oil change. The technician should check the gear lubricant for proper level, color, and consistency. Low lubricant level indicates a leak, a milky color indicates moisture in the lubricant, and the presence of metal indicates mechanical wear. Check your owner's manual for the recommended fluid change intervals for your particular vehicle.

FRONT-WHEEL DRIVE MAINTENANCE

Vehicles with front-wheel drive have half shafts, which must be checked every oil change for wear and dents. These shafts must be perfectly balanced and aligned in order to turn "true" while driving the front wheels. There will be vibration in the drivetrain if they are out of balance from dents or misalignment. This vibration causes additional wear on related components such as transmissions, differential components, seals, tail shafts, CV joints, and so on. In addition, keep an eye on the CV joint boots. When

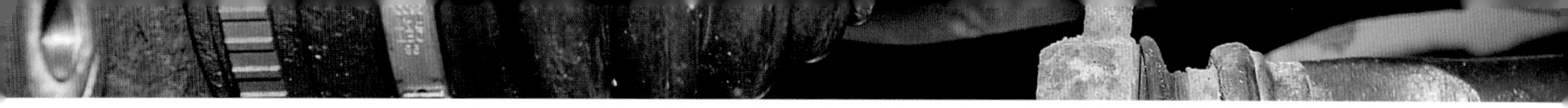

Pictured here is a typical CV joint boot. Note the clamps at each end of the boot, one on the axle and one on the joint. Lubricant is packed inside this boot to ensure the CV joint is properly lubed. Boot inspection is a critical part of regular vehicle maintenance. Whenever the car is in for an oil change, make sure the tech looks at the CV joint boots and replaces them if cracking or tearing is evident. If a bad CV joint boot is caught early enough, the joint may be saved, preventing a costly boot replacement.

these crack or split, the combination of centrifugal force and drive force throws the lubricant out from the boot, exposing the CV joint to the weather and road elements and accelerating wear. Have the wheel bearings checked for up-and-down as well as side-to-side play, and replace as necessary.

MAINTENANCE OF REAR-WHEEL DRIVE DIFFERENTIALS

Rear-wheel-drive differentials require minimal maintenance. Regular checks of the fluid for level, color, and consistency are recommended. Every oil change is sufficient. A low level, the presence of metal in the lubricant, or change of color of the lubricant could be an indication of trouble. A check of up-and-down and side-to-side play of the wheel bearings will bring to light any potential problems before they get to "pocket-draining" levels.

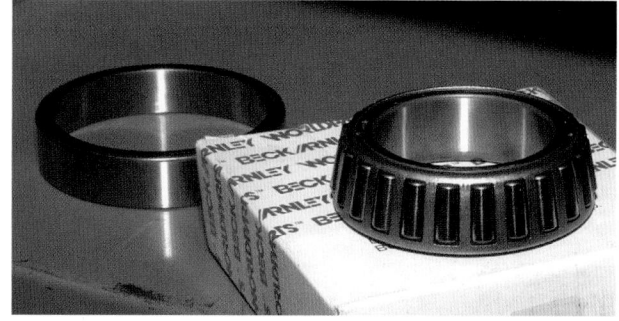

Wheel bearings come in many different shapes and sizes, but they all do the same thing: provide a smooth surface for the wheels to ride and roll on. Wheel bearings are comprised of a set of rollers, a race (the face on which the rollers ride), and an encasement. When bearings wear out from lack of lubrication of just plain mechanical wear over time they make a roaring or groaning noise. A simple way to determine which side is bad is to turn the steering wheel right and left while driving slowly to shift the weight of the vehicle from one side to another. Whichever side the roaring noise is louder on is the side that has the bad bearing.

PROJECT 3
Check Transmission Fluid

 Time Required: 5 minutes

 Tools Required: Dipstick

Skill Level:

 Cost Estimate: $0

 Tip: Vehicles don't burn transmission fluid; if it's low, you have a leak that should be fixed.

1

Check the transmission fluid with the engine fully warmed up and running. The transmission fluid dipstick will be in the engine bay and may be labeled with words or a symbol. Your owner's manual will identify its location, markings, and the transmission's fluid capacity.

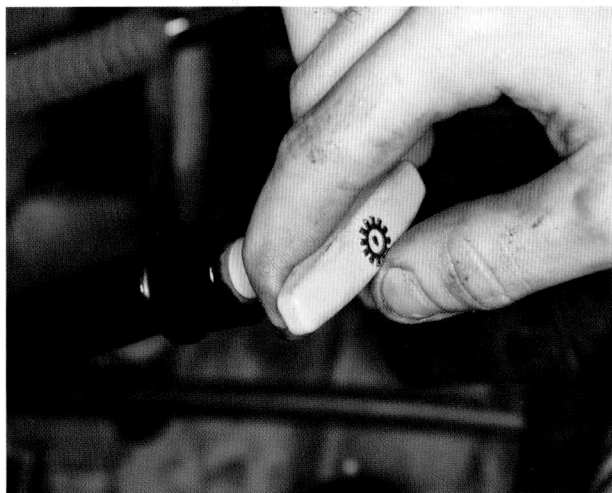

2

Pull the dipstick and wipe it clean with a cloth or paper towel.

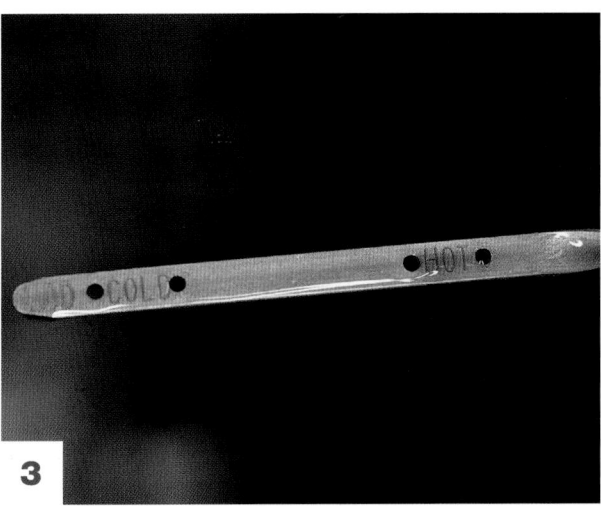

3

With the engine warm, the fluid should reach the full/hot mark on the dipstick. This late model Dodge Dakota has the appropriate fluid level.

Chapter 4
Steering, Suspensions, and Wheel Alignment

What suspension and steering systems do the carmakers most often use? What are the most common problems with these systems? And what can you do to maintain them in order to avoid these problems? These are the kinds of questions addressed in this section, but first we'll take a look at the basic parts and the jobs they do.

Most cars today use an independent strut suspension and a rack-and-pinion steering system. However, heavy-duty and medium-duty trucks often use a conventional suspension and steering system. How do these systems differ in design?

SUSPENSION SYSTEMS
Conventional Suspension Components
- **Shock absorbers or struts** dampen spring oscillation. They aid in ride control by keeping the tires down on the road and preventing them from bouncing after hitting a bump. Without the shock absorbers or struts, your car or truck would ride like a bucking bronco.
- **Springs** support the vehicle's weight and absorb road shock. There are three designs: coil, bowed leaf (flat), and torsion bar (twisted spring steel rod).

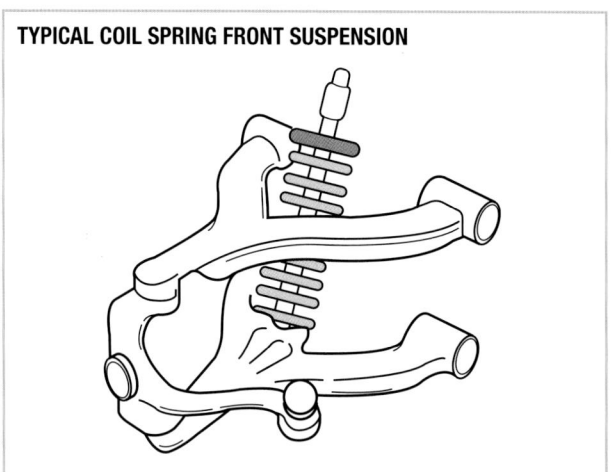

TYPICAL COIL SPRING FRONT SUSPENSION

As you can see in the illustration, many parts make up a conventional coil spring suspension system. The green parts are the upper and lower control arms. These connect to the vehicle's frame via the use of rubber and steel bushings. The purple part is the steering knuckle. This connects the control arms via upper and lower ball joints. The orange part is the coil spring, and the yellow part is the shock absorber. With so many parts that make up this system, it's no wonder that wear is a fact of life, and alignment angles go out from constant road jostle.

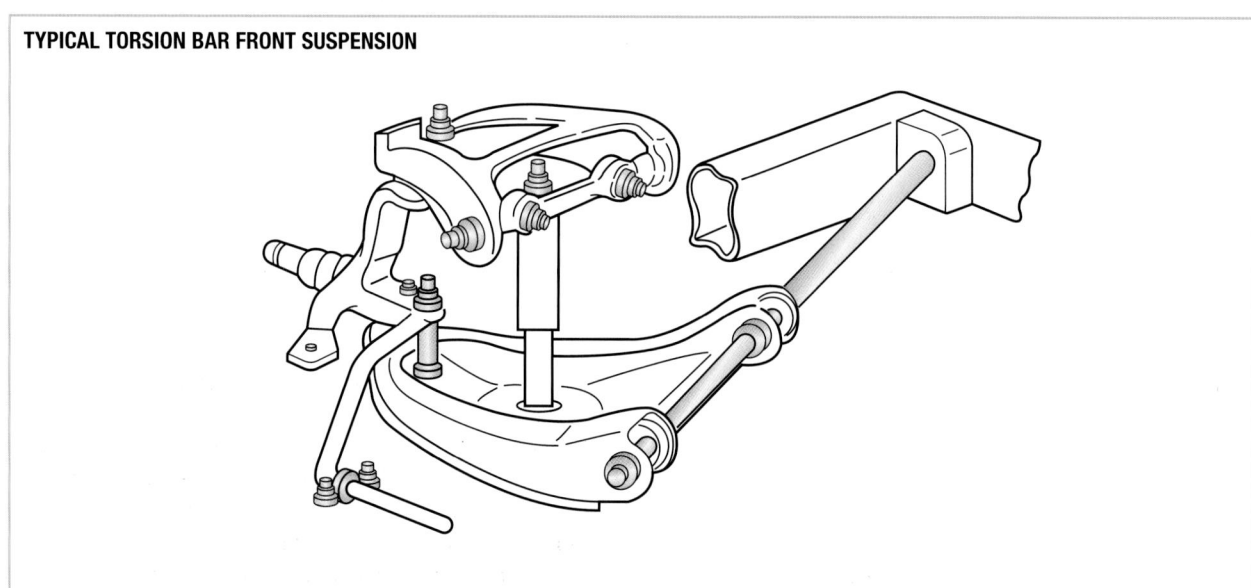

TYPICAL TORSION BAR FRONT SUSPENSION

The torsion bar suspension pictured here is basically the same in design as the coil suspension. The only exception is the use of a torsion bar to act as a spring. With this system, a spring steel bar is secured to the control arm, and then secured at the other end to an anchor welded to the vehicle frame. Then the bar is twisted via a tensioner. This raises or lowers the vehicle body.

TYPICAL COIL SPRING REAR SUSPENSION

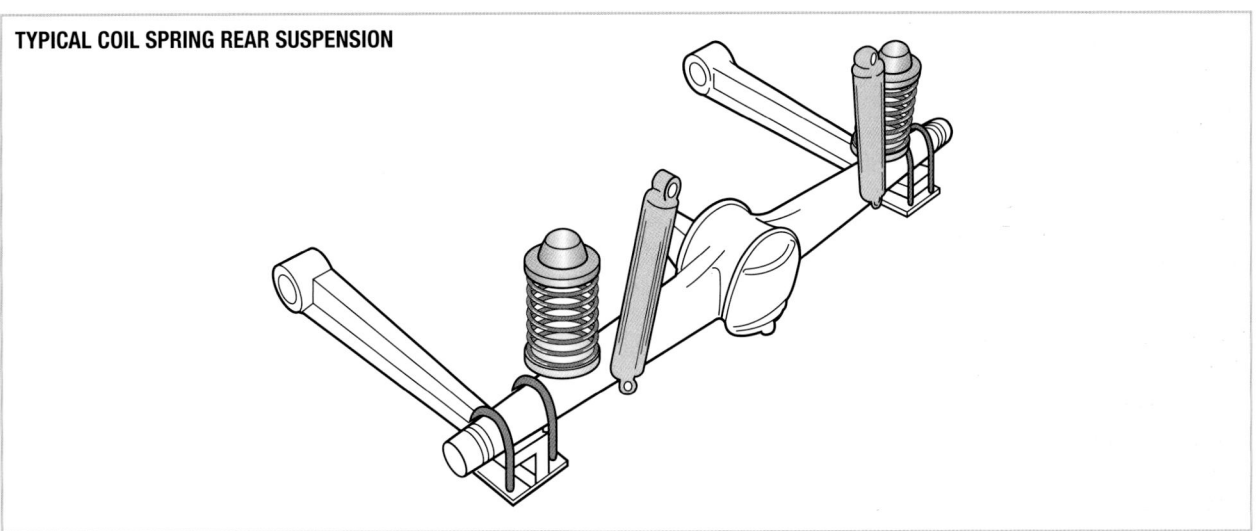

Here is a typical coil spring suspension. The red parts are the coil springs, yellow the shock absorbers, and gray the axle and control arms. The axle is connected to the vehicle's frame via the use of the control arms and shock absorbers. The vehicle sits on the springs. This is what supports its weight. Shock absorbers dampen the spring oscillation as the vehicle rides down the road.

TYPICAL LEAF SPRING REAR SUSPENSION

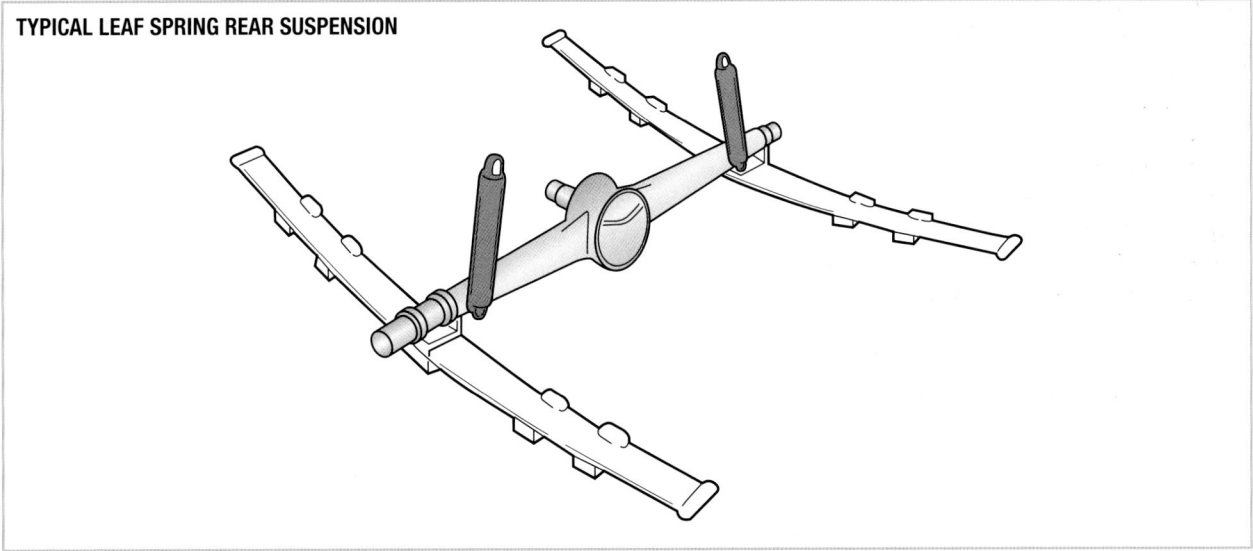

This is a leaf spring suspension. Leaf springs (red) are flat spring steel bars that are heated up and arched, then left to cool off. Once cooled, the multiple-arched bars (now called leaves) of different lengths are bolted together with shackles creating a spring stack. The bottom bar has eyelets at each end that rubber bushings are inserted into. These are then bolted to the underside of the vehicle's frame, then to the axle. They support its weight. The yellow parts are shock absorbers that also connect to the underside of the vehicle.

- **Upper and lower control arms** are connected to the vehicle's frame at one end using rubber or steel bushings. At the other end, ball joints bolt to the steering knuckle (to which the wheels are attached). This allows for turning right and left and for up and down movement (roadway jostle).
- **The steering knuckle** allows for turning and up-and-down movement. In addition, the wheel's hub rides on bearings that ride on the spindle portion of the knuckle. The wheel bearings are sealed and packed with grease (for lubrication and cooling) on the spindle.
- **Ball joints** provide the moveable link that connects all the parts of the system, allowing for turning and road movement.
- **Sway bars** stabilize the vehicle's body when making a turn. The sway bar is a spring steel bar that spans the width of the vehicle's undercarriage. It is secured to the bottom of the frame and attaches to the control arms via the use of sway bar links. Sway bars prevent the vehicle's body from dipping when turning.

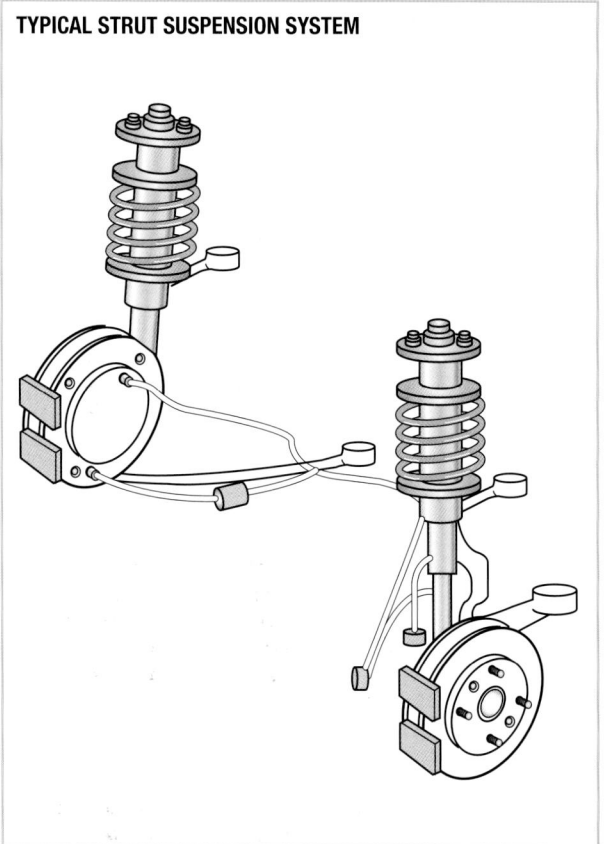

TYPICAL STRUT SUSPENSION SYSTEM

What a brilliant design the McPherson strut suspension is. Shock absorber, coil spring, and lower ball joint are all incorporated into one assembly. Upper control arms and ball joints are gone. Plus, because of the removal of these components, the vehicle weighs less and, because of less moving parts, there's less going out of the alignment angles. Finally, this suspension makes cornering and handling much easier and more responsive.

Strut Suspension Components

In a strut assembly, the lower ball joint, steering knuckle, spindle, shock absorber, and coil spring are incorporated into one unit. This type of suspension design does not need upper control arms and upper ball joints. An upper strut mount and bearing are used to connect the top of the strut to the vehicle. This design allows for right and left turning and provides a cushioned attachment to the vehicle's frame via a strut tower.

A lower control arm connects the strut to the frame of the vehicle.

Two Types of Suspension Designs: Conventional and Independent

With conventional suspensions, each front wheel has its own separate suspension parts, thus it interacts with the road surface independent from the other wheels. In contrast, the rear wheels are connected to a straight axle and operate as a unit. So when one rear wheel responds to the road surface the other is affected. The quality of the ride and handling of the vehicle is somewhat compromised by this design.

With independent suspensions, all four wheels have their own separate suspension parts and thus interact with the road surface independently of each other. This results in a better ride and improves the overall handling of the vehicle.

STEERING SYSTEMS
Conventional Steering System Components

- **Tie rods** "tie" the steering linkage together. Both an inner and outer rod is used, and they are connected by a threaded sleeve. This sleeve allows for the adjustment of the toe angle (alignment characteristic).

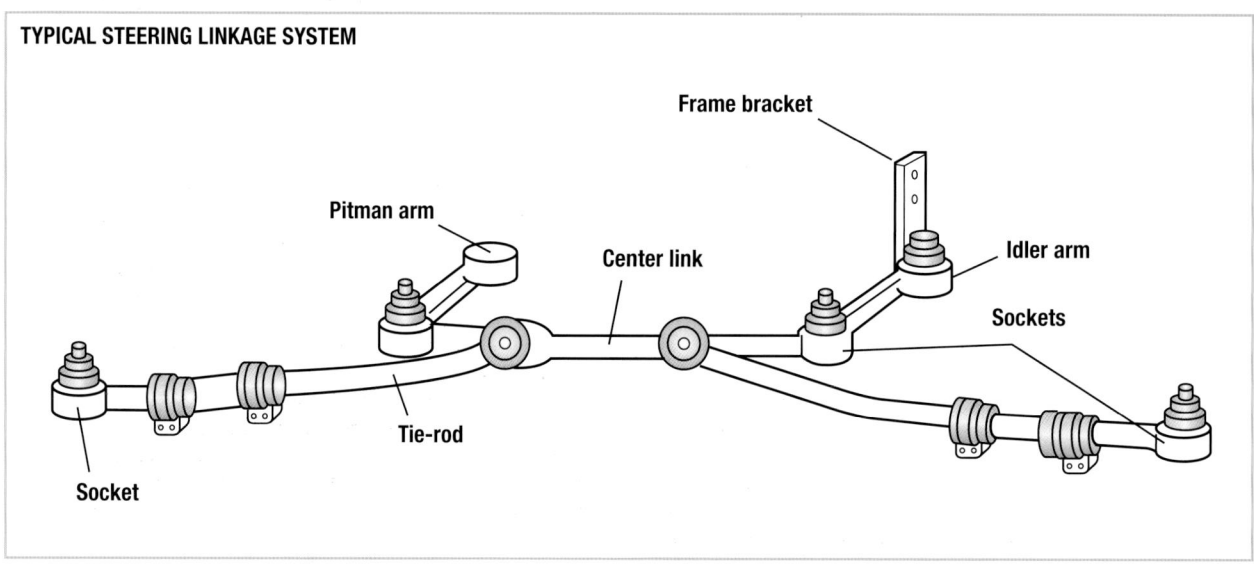

TYPICAL STEERING LINKAGE SYSTEM

Frame bracket

Pitman arm

Center link

Idler arm

Sockets

Tie-rod

Socket

Look at all the parts that make up a conventional steering system. While the system works well when properly aligned with good parts, just one worn tie rod or ball joint will knock the whole steering alignment out of whack. Because of the many moving parts in this system it is imperative to keep on top of alignment and component wear as an out-of-alignment system due to a bad part or worn parts needing alignment will wear tires out in a hurry.

DRIVERS ASK, TOM ANSWERS:
STEERING AND SUSPENSION PROBLEMS SOLVED

Q Tom,
I recently had a four-wheel alignment done on my '92 Lexus SC400. The car still doesn't track well. The technician said that the car veers in the direction of the road pavement. When I oversteer to correct it, the steering returns back to the veering direction. He thought that the suspension looked okay, but opined that there might be something wrong with the power steering. The power steering works fine, but the steering wheel will not hold steady no matter how flat and straight the roadway is. Can you suggest a cheap fix?
Collin—Eastman, Ohio

A Collin,
No cheap fix here. Sounds like either the rack is loose internally, rack mounts are loose, ties rods are loose, cradle mounts are loose, or you have low tire pressure, a worn rag or u-joint at the rack, or a worn u-joint in the steering coupler between the rack and steering wheel. Someone is not doing their job in finding the problem; find another shop that's competent in steering and suspension work.
Tom

Q Dear Tom,
I own a 2003 Mustang. I think it has a problem with the rack-and-pinion bushings. How do I verify this?
Martha—Kalamazoo, Michigan

A Martha,
Worn rack bushings usually cause the vehicle to wander left and right while driving down the road. You would find yourself constantly trying to correct the vehicle's path with the steering wheel. What's happening? The rack is floating left and right within its mounting brackets, causing the vehicle to drift. If you suspect bad rack mount bushings then get it into a shop immediately, because this could be dangerous. The vehicle would be hard to control if the rack comes loose from its mounting brackets. Good luck.
Tom

Q Tom,
I just bought a used '96 Chevy Sport Van G-30. I knew the front end needed some work, so I took it to my mechanic. The idler arm and sway arm bushings were bad, so he replaced them and aligned the front end. The settings are within the specs, but the van doesn't drive well. I have to keep sawing the wheel to keep it on the road. It feels like it still has loose parts, but I know it doesn't. My mechanic and I have talked about the problem, and he has moved the settings around a few times, but it hasn't solved the problem. What do you think is wrong? Thanks for any help you can offer.
Brian—Peoria, Illinois

A Brian,
Have your technician check the steering box. It sounds like the box is loose, either internally or externally. The external mounting bolts can loosen due to vibration, which would cause the steering box to flop around when the steering wheel is turned right or left. If the steering box is secure, then there is a gear adjustment that can be done internally to take up slop if it is found to be loose internally. Also check the small joint at the bottom of the steering shaft where it connects to the steering box. It could be loose. Finally, check the tire pressure; low tire pressure will cause wandering also.
Tom

Q Tom,
I own a '96 Dodge Stratus. Every time I hit a bump or turn corners, I hear a loud creaking noise coming from the front driver's side. Also, when I turn the wheel the steering wheel makes a really loud squealing sound. The power steering fluid is full. What could it be?
Charlene—Jamestown, New York

A Charlene,
Check the front lower control arm bushings and ball joints. It sounds like a bushing or ball joint is worn. Also, check the upper strut mounts; it could be a bad bearing plate. Finally, the cause of the squeal when turning the steering wheel could be a worn or maladjusted serpentine belt; also, a bad power steering pump would act like this as well. Good luck.
Tom

Q Tom,
I own a 2000 Ford Ranger with 64,000 miles. I hear a noise when the front-end bounces (squeaking). I inspected the front end and found no loose parts. Ball joints and tie rods are fine. I used a grease gun with a needle fitting to inject grease into the ball joints' rubber boots since they don't have any grease fittings. The noise went away. Does this mean the ball joints could still be bad?
Tony—New York City

A Tony,
Yes, the vehicle might have a bad ball joint. You need to get it up on a lift, unload the suspension, and properly check for looseness of the ball joint, which involves shaking the wheels right and left and up and down. If there's excessive back and forth or up and down play when you check it, then the ball joint socket is worn out and it should be replaced.
Tom

Q Dear Tom,
I purchased a '98 F150 4WD. The torsion bars have been cranked up to raise the front end. There is extensive side-to-side play in the front wheels, with the center link, tie rod ends, and idler arm all moving. Do you know where I can find the factory torsion bar settings? Also, will I have to replace all of the mentioned parts?
Keith—Tallahassee, Florida

A Keith,
Regarding the torsion bars, there are factory specifications for adjusting them. It involves measuring the clearance between the lower control arm and the jounce bumpers on the frame of the truck. There are a few different specs depending on what suspension is in your truck as well as body length. Once the torsion bars have been lowered to the correct height and the steering system has been shored up, the vehicle will need an alignment because torsion bar adjustment along with steering linkage part replacement changes the alignment angles. When checking the steering linkage, there should be no side-to-side movement at all. Start with the idler arm. If this component is loose, replace it as it could cause a lot of slop in the steering linkage to begin with. If you find loose ball and socket joints in any other steering linkage component, replace that component too.
Tom

45

- **Drag link** is a long bar that provides a connection between the tie rods to form one big moveable linkage system. It's called a drag link because it "drags" the whole steering linkage from right to left.
- **The idler arm** provides support for the linkage system by connecting to the drag link and the vehicle's frame. The pitman arm is connected to the drag link and the steering box. The pitman arm commands right and left movement of the linkage system, causing the vehicle to turn right or left.
- **The steering box** converts the turning motion of the steering wheel into right and left movement of the steering linkage. This is achieved through an internal gearing system specifically designed to convert circular motion to right and left motion. Sometimes referred to as the "steering gear," the steering box is mounted to the vehicle's frame just above the pitman arm.

Rack and Pinion Steering System Components

- **Steering rack and tie rods:** The rack contains special gearing to convert the turning motion of the steering wheel to right and left. This design eliminates the need for the steering box, threaded adjustment sleeves, drag link, pitman arm, and idler arms.

So how do we keep our tires from wearing out as they roll down the road? Regardless of what types of suspension and steering system in your car, with all the parts that make them up and all the movement going on, there is going to be wear and tear, and parts will simply wear out. Worn out parts cause misalignment of wheels, and this results in tire wear.

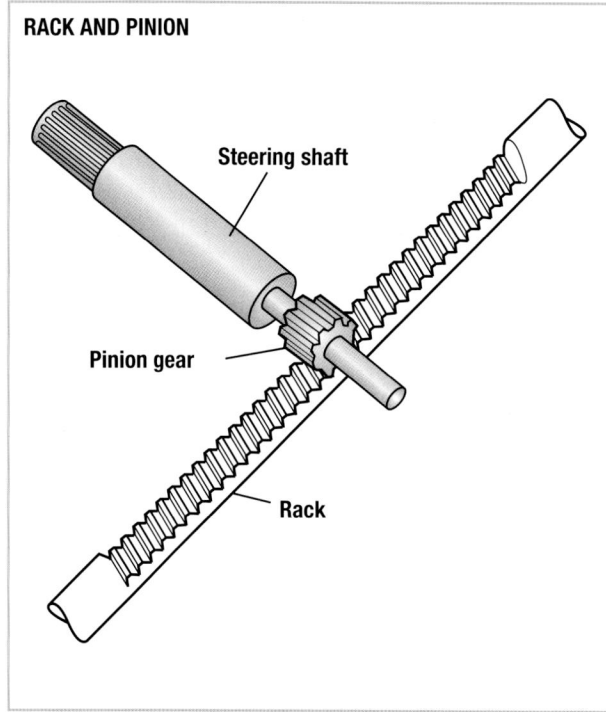

RACK AND PINION

Here we have the basic theory on which the rack and pinion steering system works. The steering shaft comes down from inside the vehicle cabin; sometimes a flex joint is used to clear engine compartment obstructions, and then the shaft attaches to the input shaft of the rack unit. The input shaft has a small gear called a pinion gear attached to the bottom of it. The pinion gear meshes with another gear inside the unit called the rack gear. It is long and flat and has teeth on one side of it. As the steering wheel is turned right and left, the pinion gear meshes with the rack gear and moves the tie rods, which are connected to the steering knuckles and ultimately the wheels—both right and left—resulting in steering the vehicle. Brilliant!

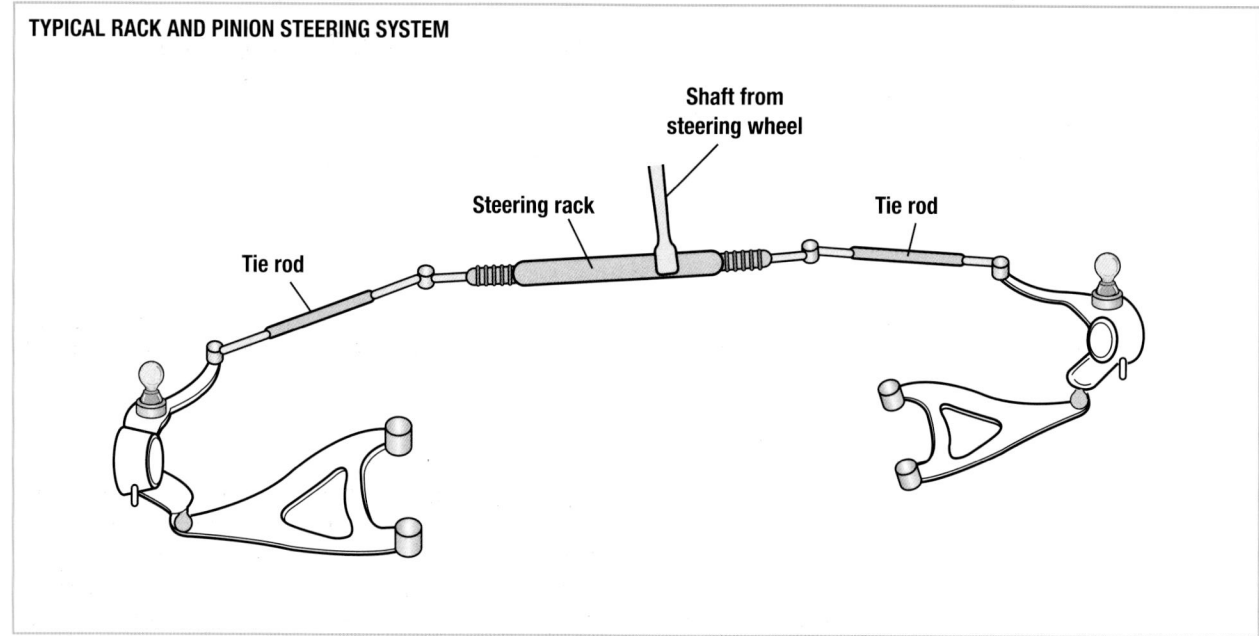

TYPICAL RACK AND PINION STEERING SYSTEM

Rack and pinion steering is another great design. With one fell swoop, the designer removed the steering box and threaded adjustment sleeves for the tie rods, drag link, pitman arm, and idler arms. So much potential for worn parts and misalignment was removed. This steering design is much more responsive to cornering and handling.

CONVENTIONAL STEERING AND SUSPENSION

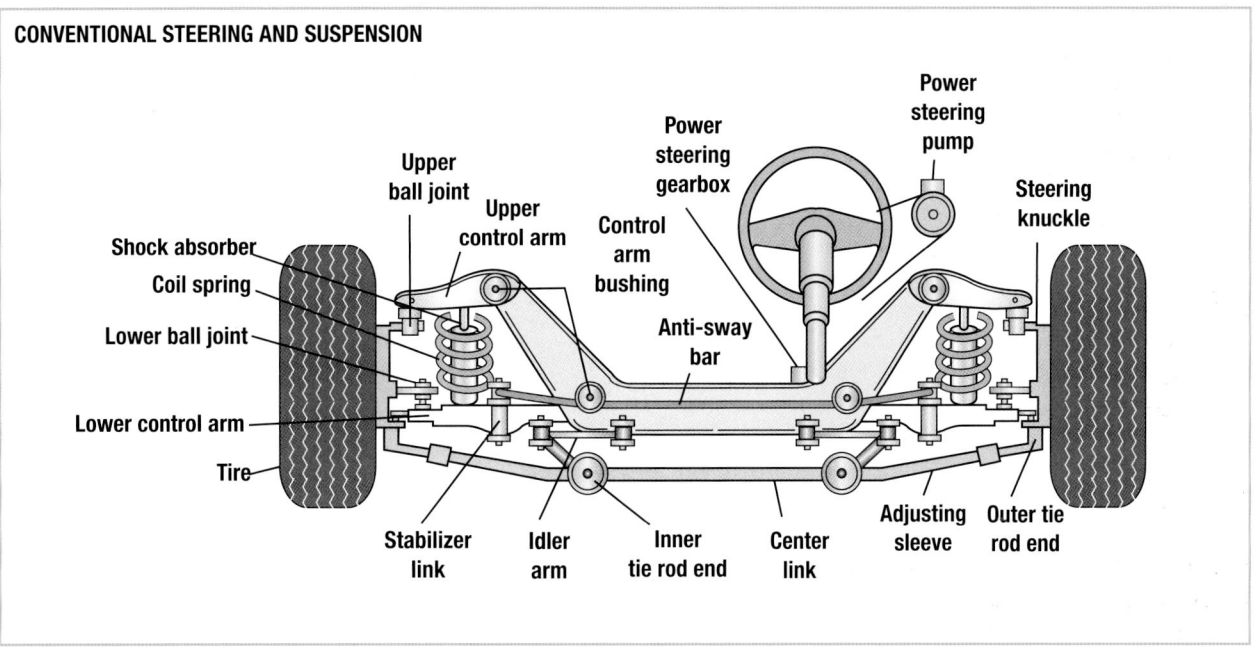

RACK AND PINION WITH MCPHERSON STRUTS

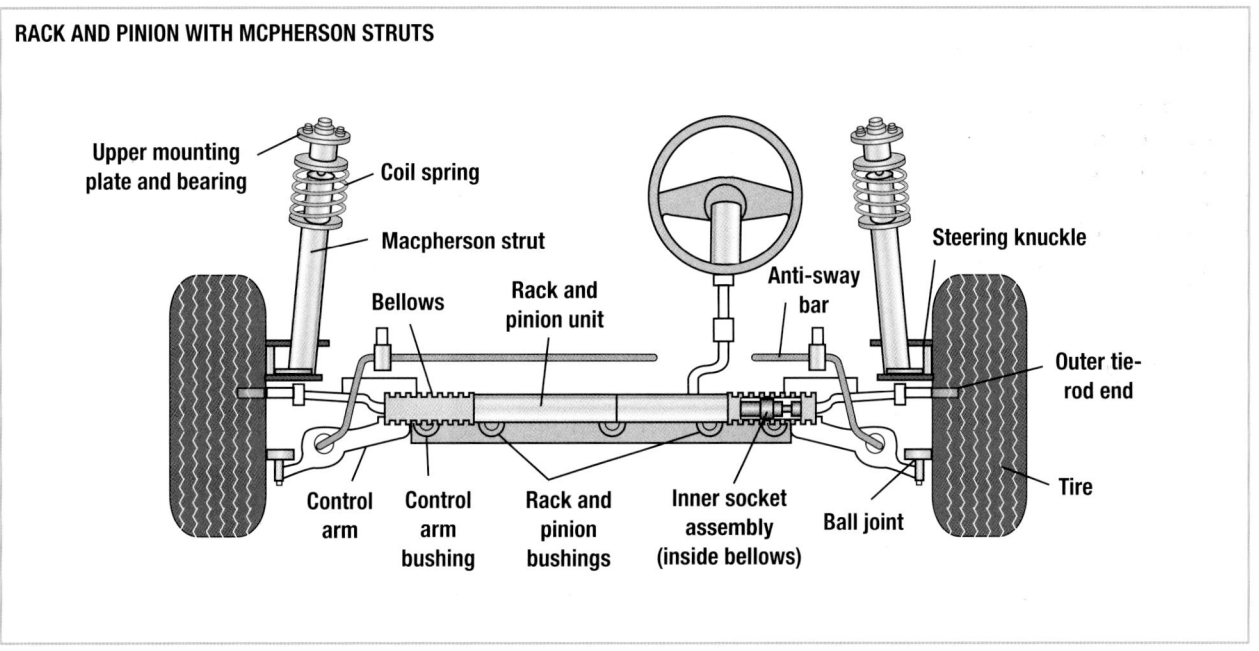

Here we have an illustration of a conventional steering and suspension system as compared to a rack and pinion steering and McPherson Strut suspension system. Note the difference in the number of parts used in both systems. There are many more in the conventional design. Plus, there are more alignment adjustment points in the conventional system than in the rack and strut system.

Carmakers, in their infinite wisdom, realized that in order to minimize tire wear, they had to build adjustments into the steering and suspension systems to compensate for the effects of worn out parts. Otherwise, when you hit a pothole the size of the "Sea of Tranquility," you would knock out all the perfect factory-set alignment angles and cause unsolicited tire wear.

How do you get the most life out of your tires? Long tire life depends on four things: The condition of the suspension system, the condition of the steering system, accurate wheel alignment, and proper tire maintenance with respect to maintaining proper inflation, rotation, and rebalance. These four elements work together to create the environment necessary for maximum tire life.

Wheel Alignment

Vehicle steering and suspension systems wear out over time. Rubber bushings, metal joints, and parts that make up these systems get jostled from regular use over hill, highway, and dale. This wear results in the alignment angles going out of spec. This is why alignment adjustment points are built into the systems, to compensate for this wear which causes misalignment of steering and suspension parts.

The three adjustable alignment angles include camber, toe, and caster.

These angles affect tire wear and the handling characteristics of your vehicle.

Camber

The term *camber* refers to the angle of wheel alignment that measures the tilting in or out relative to the top of the tire. If a car's camber angle is too positive the top of the tire is tilting outward. If the camber angle is too negative the top of the tire is tilting inward. Conditions that cause excessive camber include worn ball joints, control arm bushings, strut bearings/mounts, or excessively worn wheel bearings. These parts must be tight (not sloppy) before the camber angle can be adjusted accurately.

A tire affected by negative or positive camber exhibits smooth even wear on the outside rib (positive camber) or inside rib (negative camber). Mechanical adjustments will correct both positive and negative camber unless the parts affecting the camber angle are worn beyond adjustment within factory specs. If this is the case, the parts need to be replaced and the tires re-aligned.

Toe

The best way to explain how *toe* affects wheel alignment is to look down at the tops of your feet. Imagine that you're hovering above the hood of your car and you can see through the body of the vehicle. Your feet represent the tops of the tires. Now slowly turn your feet inward to an excessive degree. That's what your tires look like when they're toed-in too far. Now turn your feet outward excessively. That's what your tires look like when they're toed-out too far

When the toe angle is out too far or in too far, tires wear out quickly. This angle also affects whether or not your car's steering wheel is straight. When the toe angle is way out of alignment, the steering wheel is crooked. Excessive toe is caused by worn tie rods, loose rack mounts, worn idler arms (some vehicles have two), pitman arm, drag link assembly, or a worn rack or steering box. Before you can accurately set the toe angle, the steering linkage parts must be tight. You can adjust the toe alignment angle by either lengthening or shortening a steering linkage part called a tie rod (found in both conventional and rack and pinion steering systems).

A tire affected by excessive toe-in or toe-out exhibits a scalloped wear pattern, also known as "wipe pattern." The best way to describe this pattern is to consider how a man's face feels when he has a five o'clock shadow. If you run your hand over his face, it's smooth one way and rough the other way. If you run your hand across a tire that has scallop wear, it will feel smooth one way and rough the other. When the toe angle is misaligned, the tires are scrubbed or pushed down the road and rubber is scraped off as they roll.

Caster

The *caster* angle is best illustrated by a bicycle experience of your childhood youth. Remember when you rode your bike with no hands? Remember how the handlebars returned to the straight-ahead position when you leaned right or left to turn a corner? This is an expression of the caster angle. The caster angle of your car expresses itself when the steering wheel returns to the straight-ahead position after making a turn. It also expresses itself when the car tends to wander right or left.

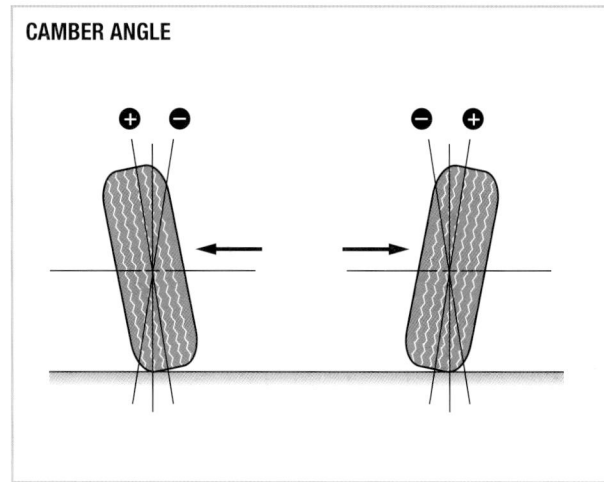

CAMBER ANGLE

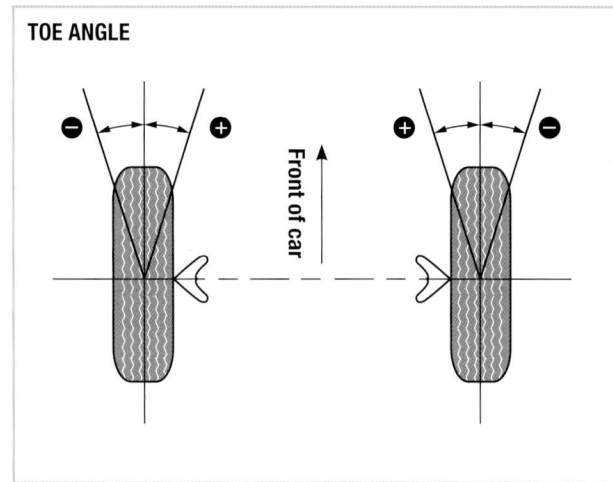

TOE ANGLE

Front of car

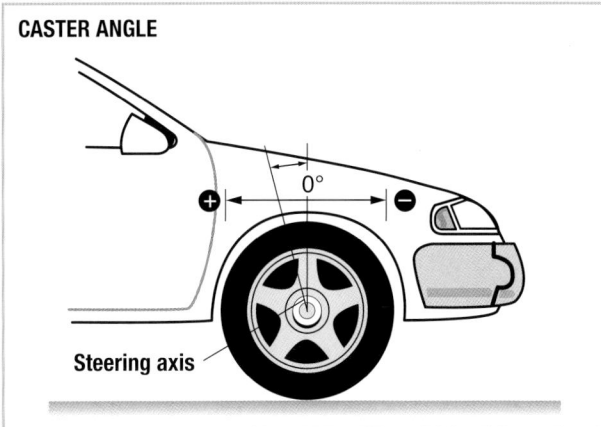

CASTER ANGLE

Steering axis

Back to the bicycle example, what happened when you turned the handlebars backwards and let go? The wheel returned violently to the straight-ahead position and sent you flying over the handlebars because of the extremely positive caster angle created by turning the handlebars backwards.

Excessively positive or negative caster causes the vehicle to track right or left. Failure of the steering wheel to return to the straight-ahead position after making a turn is another indication of caster misalignment. Also, maladjusted caster causes the vehicle to wander while driving down the road. In extreme cases on front-wheel-drive vehicles, excessively negative caster on one side will cause a condition called "torque steer." In this condition, when you accelerate quickly from a stopped position, the vehicle will pull hard in the direction of the negative caster angle. Quite often adjusting the caster angle will eliminate "torque steer." Caster angle is corrected by either mechanical adjustment or by bending a suspension part.

Four-Wheel Alignment

For most of today's cars, the alignment angles can be adjusted on all four wheels to gain maximum vehicle control and tire longevity. In a four-wheel alignment, the angles on all four wheels are measured and then compared to manufacturer's specifications. Adjustments are made by mechanical adjustment. When a car capable of four-wheel alignment is adjusted properly, the vehicle tracks straight, handles better on the road, and the tires last longer. On vehicles with a rear straight axle, the adjustment is limited to caster and camber. On vehicles with independent suspensions, often the toe angle is also adjustable via adjustable trailing arms.

MAINTENANCE TIP

Check the tire wear and suspension and steering components whenever the car is on a lift, either for an oil change (every 3,000 to 5,000 miles) or tire rotation (every 6 months or 6,000 miles). This way, if a negative tire-wear pattern crops up, you can correct it immediately. As a rule of thumb, carmakers suggest an alignment check every 12 months or 12,000 miles, whichever comes first.

PROJECT 4
Check Power Steering Fluid

Time Required: 5 minutes

Tools Required: Dipstick

Skill Level:

Cost Estimate: $0

Tip: Dipstick may be marked for hot and cold check levels—use appropriate mark.

1

The power steering fluid reservoir is usually clearly marked. It should be near the front of your engine, or opposite the transmission, where the power steering pump is driven by a pulley.

2

With the engine off and relatively cool, turn the cap counterclockwise and remove.

3

This dipstick shows the level cold. Some power steering dipsticks have markings for cold and hot. If the level is low, top up the system with the proper power steering fluid. Check your owner's manual for the specific fluid recommendations. Tip: Vehicles don't consume power steering fluid. If yours is low, check for signs of leaks in the system and on the ground.

Chapter 5
Tires

Most people take their tires for granted. We don't give them a second thought. Often, the only time we notice our tires is when they go flat, blow out, or when they have to be replaced because they're worn out. Yet choosing the right tires for your car, your driving habits, and your geographic location will give you a safer, more effective driving experience as well as save you money.

How do you select the tires that best suit your needs? Should you buy all-season tires, truck tires, or highway tread? What characterizes an all-season tire? What does it mean to "up-size" your tires? How many snow tires should you use on a four-wheel-drive vehicle? A two-wheel-drive vehicle? What can you do to get the maximum life out of your tires? Tire knowledge pays off, so let's get a little under our belts.

HOW TO "READ" A TIRE SIZE

People ask me all the time to explain the numbers and letters found on the sidewalls of tires. Here's a typical description commonly found on a sidewall and an explanation of what it means:

P185/75R14

- "P" stands for the service description. In this case, it is a passenger car tire. "LT" stands for Light Truck, and a "Z" rating means it's a performance tire.
- The number 185 is the width of the tire measured in millimeters (sidewall-to-sidewall, inflated at the correct inflation level and mounted on the right rim size).
- The number 75 is the aspect ratio of the tire (the ratio of height to width). In this case, the height of the tire is 75 percent of 185 millimeters or 138.75 millimeters.
- The "R" means it is a radial tire. If the tire is a high-performance tire, there will be a "Z" designation here. The size will read P185/75ZR14.
- The number 14 is the measurement of the rim diameter.

If you want to be confident about choosing the best tires for your needs, learn how to read the Uniform Tire Quality Grading System (UTQGS). The UTQGS information is molded into the sidewalls of the tires. This system grades tires on three factors: tread wear, traction, and temperature resistance.

Tread wear grade gives a comparative rating based on the wear rate of a tire when tested under carefully controlled conditions. For example, a tire graded at 200 should have its useful tread twice as long as a tire graded at 100. Obviously, tire life (in miles) varies depending on actual driving conditions.

Variation in driving habits, service applications, attention to proper maintenance (that is, rotation, wheel alignment, maintaining air pressure), and road conditions all contribute to tread wear.

Traction grade reflects the tire's ability to stop on wet pavement under controlled conditions on asphalt and concrete. The traction grades from highest to lowest are: "AA," "A," "B," and "C." A tire graded "AA" may have relatively better traction performance than a tire graded "A," "B," or "C," based on straight-ahead braking tests. The grades do not consider cornering or turning traction performance of the tire.

Temperature resistance grade reflects the tire's resistance to heat, as well as its ability to dissipate heat. Sustained high temperatures can decrease tire life and can cause sudden tire failure. The grades from highest to lowest are: "A," "B," and "C." "C" grade represents the absolute minimum federal standards. This grading system is based on the proper

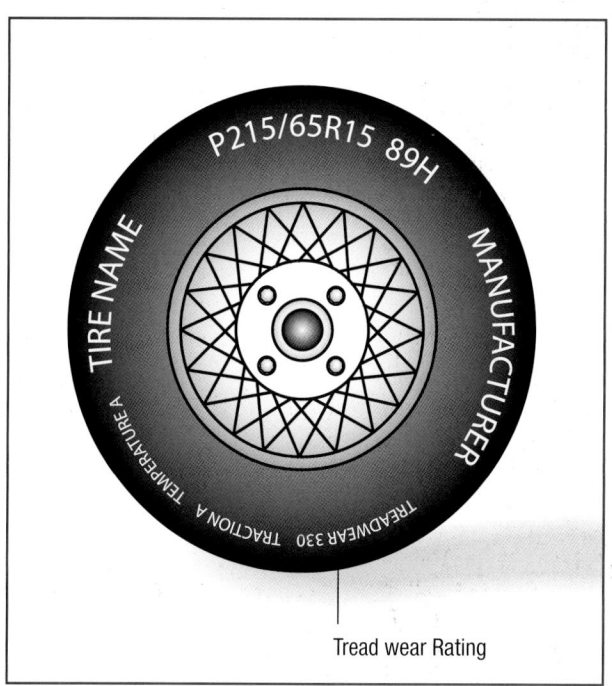

Tread wear Rating

The tread wear rating gives an indication of how long the tread of a particular tire will last on a vehicle. Now the estimated tread life given is assuming the alignment angles are kept perfect, tire rotations are done every 6,000 miles or six months, inflation is kept up according to the sidewall specs, and steering and suspension components are replaced and realigned when worn. Of course this is not real world unless you are meticulous when it comes to tire maintenance. Most people are not.

Traction Rating

The traction rating is supposed to tell you how the tire gains traction in several roadway conditions, that is rain, snow, ice, mud, and so on. These tests are based on each individual tire maker's criteria and not federal standards. That's the problem with the Uniform Tire Quality Grading System (UTQGS): There are no standards that tire makers have to follow. They pretty much make up their grading system based on their own criteria.

Temperature Rating

The temperature rating measures how well a tire resists as well as dissipates heat while in use. Tires generate heat when in use. Friction buildup from rolling resistance causes the tire body (or carcass) to heat up. How well a tire resists and dissipates heat is critical to its service life and, most important, its safe operation. This is a critical rating to your safety.

inflation of the tire, the proper mounting on the rim, and the assumption that the tire's load is within its capacity. Excessive speed, under inflation, and overloading (separately or in combination) can cause excessive heat buildup and possible tire failure.

For more information on the UTQGS, check out this link:

SIPING (NON-SKID DESIGN)

All-season and winter tires have a unique tread design called *siping* (a non-skid design). Siping is the semi-segmenting of a tread lug, which means that the lug is cut an additional 50 to 70 percent of its depth. Because of this cut, the tread lug can open and close as the tire rolls down the road. The opening and closing of the tread lug creates a pumping action that clears water, slush, mud, and other materials from under the tire. In addition, tread siping creates a squeegee action, clearing the road surface as the tire rolls along the road surface.

HOW TO DETERMINE WHAT TIRES TO BUY

What tires you buy depends on the type of vehicle and on your driving patterns. For example, if you drive a sedan on highways all year and live in a climate where there is little or no winter weather, a long-lasting all-season tire that does not have an aggressive tread design will fit the bill. A tire of this nature delivers good traction in moderate weather, wears 40,000 to 50,000 miles (assuming that the alignments and tire rotations are performed), and offers a relatively quiet ride.

If you drive a pickup truck that is used for work, however, obviously you should purchase truck tires. They are made with a heavier carcass (body) and with multiple plies (sometimes steel plies). The construction of truck tires tends to vary with load range; the heavier the load range the tougher the tire construction. Also, truck tires tend to have stronger sidewalls to resist impact breaks, and deeper tread with a heavier rubber compound. Usually, the tread design is aggressive, providing greater traction in mud and snow. On the down side, truck tires are often quite noisy and offer a stiff, hard ride.

Let's say you drive a collector car only in good weather. In this situation a highway tread would work well. The tread

THE FEDS' TAKE ON TIRES

The federal government has collected ratings on more than 2,400 lines of tires for you at this website. Not only that, but there's tire maintenance information and information on inflation rates and load-carrying capacities, how to read the sidewall labeling, tire defects, tire pressure monitoring system, and much more. Go to http://www.safercar.gov/portal/safercar/menuitem and click on "tires" in the left-hand column.

is ribbed, and straight even grooves are cut into the rubber evenly around the circumference of the tire. This type of tire delivers a smooth, quiet ride. If you were trying to pull through snow with a highway tread, however, it would be like trying to climb a mountain in high heels. Impossible! So the rule of thumb when buying tires is this: Determine the service needs and fit them.

Finally, when buying tires, before leaving the tire store, there are a few things to consider:

- **Road hazard protection:** This is a policy that protects you against road hazards that would destroy the tire and not normally be covered under the tire warranty. Items such as twisted metal, nails in sidewalls, and impact breaks from slamming into a curb or a nasty pothole— essentially anything that brings about the demise of the tire will be covered under this plan. The way the price of the replacement tire is determined is by pro-rating based on the amount of tread remaining at the time of the tire failure. If 50 percent of the tire tread has been used, then the replacement will cost 50 percent of the original price.
- **Mileage warranty:** Some tire makers warranty their tires to last a certain amount of mileage providing proper tire maintenance can be proven if the tire fails prior to its stated mileage. The important thing to keep meticulous maintenance records in the event you need to make

a claim to replace a failed tire before its time. Once again, replacement price is based on the percentage of tread used.

- **Nitrogen filling:** A lot of tire dealers offer nitrogen filling of tires. What are the benefits of this? Nitrogen drastically reduces oxidation on the rim and inner-liner of the tire because oxygen is almost totally eliminated from the mix. Air is made up of about 78 percent nitrogen, 21 percent oxygen, and 1 percent argon as well as other inert gases. The more oxygen you replace with nitrogen, the less oxidation takes place inside of the tire. Nitrogen-filled tires hold their air longer than oxygen-filled tires because nitrogen is comprised of fatter molecules than oxygen; therefore, it diffuses through tire walls more slowly because it has larger molecules. The temperature of nitrogen gas doesn't fluctuate, which helps the tire pressure stay more consistent. As a result, the tire runs cooler because it remains properly inflated. This is one of the reasons that aircraft and racing tires use nitrogen. In short, nitrogen keeps the tire properly inflated longer than air, which leads to less rolling resistance, which leads to greater fuel economy and extends tire life.
- **Lifetime balance and rotation:** Some tire dealers offer lifetime rotation and rebalance of tires once you initially pay for the tire balance. Ask about this because it is a huge savings and ensures tire longevity.

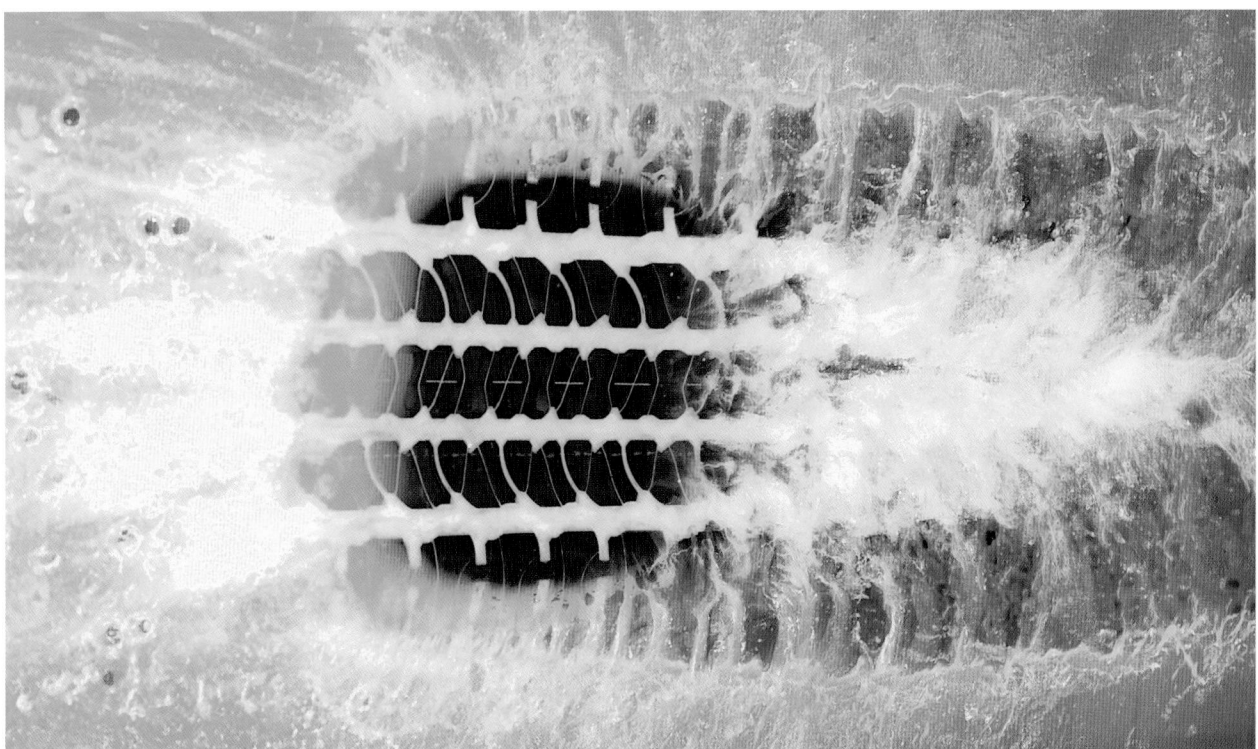

Siping or non-skid is always built into the lugs. Note the superimposed image of the semi-segmenting of each lug. This allows the tread to self-clean and squeegees the road surface while rolling. *Photo courtesy of the Goodyear Tire and Rubber Company. Used with permission.*

TIRE DESIGNS

There are many tire designs on the market today. What are the most popular designs? What distinguishes one design from another?

All-Season Tires

All-season tires have two unique characteristics: Their tread design disperses weather elements out from under the footprint of the tire, and they are made of a rubber compound that doesn't freeze.

Their tread design disperses rain, snow, slush, and mud out from under the footprint of the tire. If you were to observe a typical all-season tread design under a slow-motion camera as it rolls down the road, you would see two actions. It squeegees the road surface, and at the same time it pumps water, snow, and slush out from under the tire. This dual action provides maximum tire-to-road traction.

The rubber compound that is used for all-season tires does not freeze when temperatures reach 32 degrees Fahrenheit or 0 degrees Celsius). This characteristic is essential for the pumping and squeegee actions described above.

Touring tires characteristically have a tread designed to give a smooth, quiet ride. Note the straight center tread. This makes for a comfortable ride. Also built into this tread design are small shoulder lugs on the outside rib, which improves cornering traction and makes water course out the side as the tire rolls through water. *Photo courtesy of the Goodyear Tire and Rubber Company. Used with permission.*

Touring Tires

Tires that fall into this category are designed to give superior ride and handling out on the open road at highway speeds.

Touring tires typically have a straight rib tread design that is not aggressive, offering a smooth, quiet ride. "Water coursing" is built into the tread design, but these tires don't do well in winter weather.

Touring tires are made of a rubber compound that lasts a long time. However, unlike all-season or winter tires, the rubber tends to freeze at low temperatures and become stiff, resulting in poor traction in inclement weather.

Performance Tires

These tires have a tread design that provides superior cornering, handling, and traction in aggressive driving conditions at low and high speeds. They also tend to hold up well under prolonged driving at high speeds. Tread lugs are typically larger and have little or no siping. Shoulder lugs are larger, a feature that gives maximum traction on cornering.

All-season tire tread designs vary by tire manufacturer. They all have one thing in common: The tread disperses water and weather elements from under the footprint of the tire while rolling down the road. Tread designs vary in aggressiveness. Some use large cleated lugs for maximum ice traction. Others use a less aggressive tread with smaller lugs for a quieter and smoother ride. *Photo courtesy of the Goodyear Tire and Rubber Company. Used with permission.*

DRIVERS ASK, TOM ANSWERS: TIRE PROBLEMS SOLVED

Q Tom,
I own a 1994 Taurus. It has new front brakes, rotors, and tires. The car pulls to the left quite significantly if I let go of the wheel. The tires seem to be wearing normally (they've been on the car since November). I have been told that it could be the CV joint in the front end. Is it possible that a CV joint can make the car pull one way or another?
Ann—Albuquerque, New Mexico

A Ann,
I would start by switching the front tires from side to side. If the pull goes to the right when you switch the tires, you'll know it's a tire problem. If the pull still goes to the left the vehicle will need at least some time on a lift and perhaps an alignment machine. So many things can cause a vehicle to pull, from the tires, to worn front-end parts, to a shifted drivetrain cradle. A good shop should be able to identify the cause. Good luck.
Tom

Q Tom,
The tires on my 2005 Chevy pickup have been replaced and the wheels aligned; however, at 60 miles per hour the steering wheel starts to shake. What's wrong?
Walt—Burlington, Vermont

A Walt,
Take the truck back to the shop that replaced the tires and have them re-check the calibration of the wheel balancer and your tires for proper balance. They probably got it wrong when they balanced the new tires. This is common as wheel balancers should be recalibrated for every new set of tires and wheels. Imbalanced tires cause shaking. If the tires are okay, then check the steering linkage and suspension for worn parts.
Tom

Q Tom,
I have seen advertisements that promote filling tires with nitrogen instead of air. They claim better mileage and less air loss (air pressure maintained). I own a 2006 Jeep Grand Cherokee, and I am considering having this done. My vehicle also has special valve stems that Jeep calls "tire pressure monitor and warning signal." Will it affect that system? I talked to the Jeep dealer, and they were not sure about the advantage of using nitrogen. What do you think? Is it worth it?
Jack—New Brunswick, New Jersey

A Jack,
Filling the tires of your Jeep Grand Cherokee with nitrogen will not have a negative effect on the tire pressure monitoring system. I received a service bulletin from GM stating their position on filling tires with nitrogen. They are of the opinion that it has no ill effect on GM vehicles at all. So if it's good enough for the General, it's good enough for me!

Nitrogen is an inert gas that is moisture-free. It does not expand and contract (within the range of temperature changes experienced in tires) like air does, so tire pressure does not fluctuate significantly. In addition, its molecules are fatter than that of oxygen; therefore, it doesn't tend to bleed out of the tire's rubber carcass over time, making for much more stable tire pressures. Maintaining more stable tire pressures should result in better fuel mileage. You ask me, is it worth it? It isn't a necessity; it doesn't make your vehicle any safer, but if you want to maximize tire life and gas mileage, this is one more step you can take. Go for it!
Tom

Q Tom,
I have a 2001 Chevy K2500HD pickup truck. The tire sidewalls say to inflate from 45 psi up to 80 psi. Why such a wide inflation range? It's my understanding that running underinflated tires is dangerous, so why would I run them at 45 psi when they can be inflated up to 80 psi?
Richard—Butte, Montana

A Richard,
Inflation rates are wide and vary with the weight of the load being hauled on truck tires. If you are using load range "E" tires and are hauling a full truckload regularly, then 60/80 psi (depending on how heavy the load) would be the correct inflation level. If you drive most of the time with the truck empty, then 45/45 psi would be just fine. At 45/45 psi, you just won't get the max load-carrying capability and the tires will flatten with a full truckload. If you carry a lot of weight all the time, then I would set the psi at the max recommended levels (60/80). Hope this clears things up for you.
Tom

Q Tom,
The Yokahama tires I put on my '97 Jaguar XJ6 have begun to whine after about 5,000 miles of driving. What causes tires to whine?
Gary—Hinckley, Tennessee

A Gary,
Providing the wheel bearings are okay and not worn, negative wear pattern on the tires due to misalignment or worn steering or suspension parts or improper wheel balance can cause the tires to whine. Check the tread for a negative wear pattern, which includes high-low choppy wear or a wipe pattern. This is characterized by tread that feels smooth one way and rough the other when you run your hand across the face or the tread. If you find the tires to have a negative wear pattern, determine the cause, correct it, and rotate the tires. With any luck, they will correct themselves after a few thousand miles of running.
Tom

Q Dear Tom,
I own a 2004 Cadillac Escalade, and there is a picture of the truck displayed on the dash panel showing the left front tire only. What does this picture mean?
Carolyn—Washington, D.C.

A Carolyn,
The tire pressure monitoring system detects low air pressure in the left front tire. Check the tire with a pressure gauge, and compare the reading with the other tires on the vehicle. I suspect you have a leak in that tire. A small nail, a cracked valve stem, a bad valve stem core, or a rim bead leak can causes a tire leak. Let's assume that there's no nail and the valve stem is good. The only other possibility is a bead rim leak. This type of leak is common on vehicles equipped with aluminum or alloy wheels. Water gets in between the tire bead and bead seal area on the wheel. Corrosion sets up and an air leak ensues. The best way to solve this problem is to clean the rim of corrosion using a corrosive buffing wheel. Next, clean the tire bead area with a tire solvent. Then apply tire glue to the rim bead area and inflate the tire. The glue creates a moisture barrier and thus stops corrosion, and the tire leak is fixed.

I have witnessed extreme examples of porous aluminum wheels that leaked air in the body of the rim (due to poor casting of the aluminum or alloy metal) and had to be replaced. Sometimes epoxy application can stop a leak of this nature. I hope this helps.
Tom

Performance tires tend to have a wide, smooth face designed to grip the road surface. They also have heavy shoulder lugs on the outside rib built into them for good traction during aggressive cornering. The V-styled patter is effective in coursing water from under the tire's footprint. Finally, performance tires are made of softer rubber that bites into the road surface, giving the vehicle great traction. The down side is that they tend to wear out faster than conventional tires. *Photo courtesy of the Goodyear Tire and Rubber Company. Used with permission.*

Truck tires are designed to deliver longer mileage and heavier duty service than passenger car tires. The reason for the long durable service under extreme conditions is because truck tires are built heavier. The carcass is usually built of steel or heavy-duty synthetic materials. The rubber compound is usually much harder and therefore lasts longer. Load-carrying capacity is higher, but ride quality is poor due to the stiff, durable construction. *Photo courtesy of the Goodyear Tire and Rubber Company. Used with permission.*

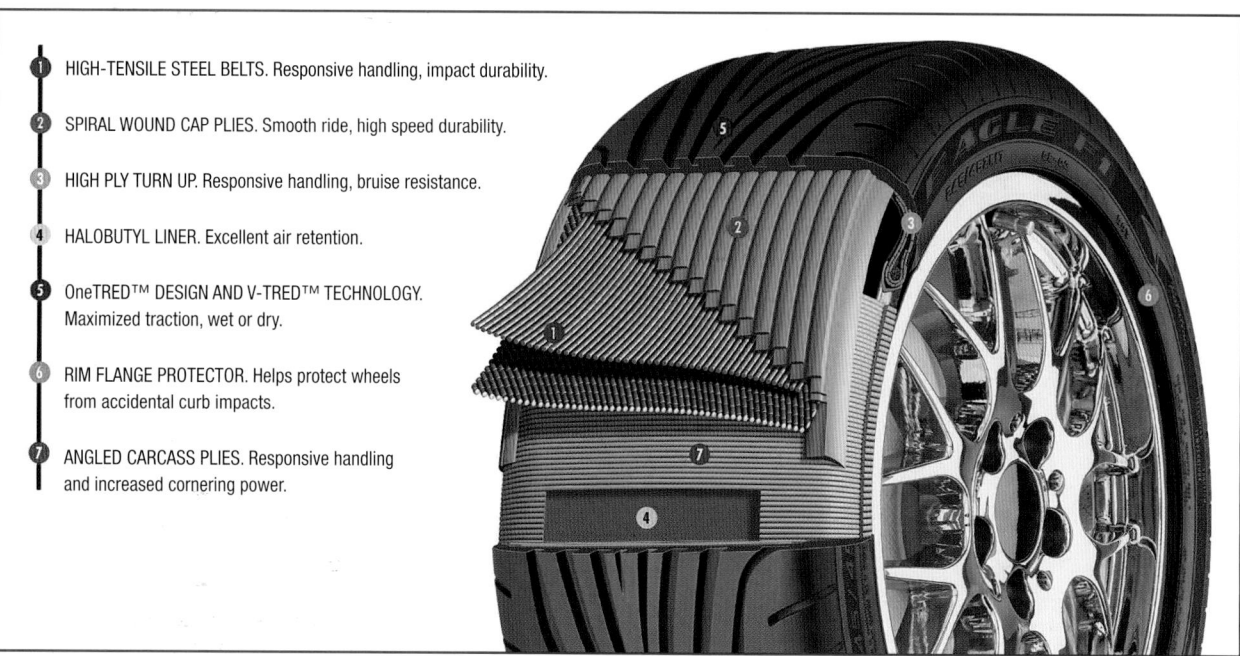

1. HIGH-TENSILE STEEL BELTS. Responsive handling, impact durability.

2. SPIRAL WOUND CAP PLIES. Smooth ride, high speed durability.

3. HIGH PLY TURN UP. Responsive handling, bruise resistance.

4. HALOBUTYL LINER. Excellent air retention.

5. OneTRED™ DESIGN AND V-TRED™ TECHNOLOGY. Maximized traction, wet or dry.

6. RIM FLANGE PROTECTOR. Helps protect wheels from accidental curb impacts.

7. ANGLED CARCASS PLIES. Responsive handling and increased cornering power.

Whoever came up with the nylon overlay was brilliant. It makes perfect sense. High-performance tires tend to get hotter than conventional tires by virtue of how they're used: aggressively. The high roadway speeds and resulting centrifugal force would naturally try to blow the tire apart. By tightly wrapping the belt package with nylon, the higher the tire temps go, the tighter nylon gets from shrinkage, keeping the whole thing together. Once again, brilliant! *Photo courtesy of the Goodyear Tire and Rubber Company. Used with permission.*

Performance tires are made of a softer rubber compound that maximizes traction during aggressive driving. They are designed to dissipate heat more effectively, since more heat is generated from aggressive or high-speed driving. Also, at high speeds centrifugal force tries to throw the tire apart. To overcome this force, there is a nylon overlay in the tire's belt. When the nylon heats up from the friction of driving, it shrinks. This action pulls the belt package tighter together and, ultimately, keeps the tire from coming apart.

Light Truck Tires

The design of light truck tires allows them to work effectively under heavy loads, as well as to operate in heavy-duty environments such as construction work sites and off-road conditions.

The tread design of light truck tires varies. They can have a highway tread for over-the-road work or aggressive lug patterns that provide maximum traction in rough terrain.

The rubber compound in light truck tires is hard, which makes them more durable. Steel or tough plies are woven into the carcass, providing a tough body that resists breakage on impact and punctures from projectiles.

Winter Tires

Winter tires provide the best weather traction to those of us who experience severe winters.

The tread design on winter tires is unique. The lugs are multi-siped, maximizing traction on snow and ice. Often the lugs have sharp-edged cleats that bite into the ice and snow as the tire rolls along the road surface. Finally, this specific tread design channels water out from under the footprint of the tire.

The rubber compound in winter tires remains flexible in all seasons, especially when it gets cold outside. This characteristic allows the tread to clean itself. In short, the tread lugs open and close as the tire rolls. This pumping action channels and flushes out the weather elements, as well as creates a squeegee action on the road surface, resulting in maximum traction.

If you want maximum traction in snow, install snow tires at all four corners of the vehicle. This move will give you maximum traction in all winter conditions. If you install snow tires only on the front of a vehicle with front-wheel drive, you will find that the rear of the vehicle will fishtail when you corner (the rear tires won't have the bite that the winter tires have). On a rear-wheel drive vehicle the opposite

Here we have an aggressive truck tire tread design. Tread like this delivers great traction in mud and inclement weather. You usually find this type of tread on the traction tires of a truck. *Photo courtesy of the Goodyear Tire and Rubber Company. Used with permission.*

Here's a great winter tire example. Note the large aggressive lug design. This tire will work great in deep, unplowed snow as well as off-road conditions. The treads are siped heavily so the tire will deliver a quiet, smooth ride. *Photo courtesy of the Goodyear Tire and Rubber Company. Used with permission.*

A high-quality winter tire will give great winter traction as well as a smooth, quiet ride on snow-covered roadways. The rubber compound stays soft and pliable even though it gets cold outside. Where conventional tires stop self-cleaning in extremely cold weather, winter tires tend to continue self-cleaning and biting, providing winter traction. *Photo courtesy of the Goodyear Tire and Rubber Company. Used with permission.*

is true. The front will have a tendency to slide one way or another. In the spring, remove the snow tires, the reason being that snow tires are made of rubber that is softer and more pliable than regular tires. This allows them to stay soft and movable in the wintertime, which is necessary for the tread to self-clean. If you run snow tires on hard pavement in dry weather, they will wear out in short order, costing you unnecessary replacement dollars.

PLUS SIZING YOUR TIRES

The big craze today is plus-sizing tire and wheel combinations. The combination of hot looks and increased cornering and handling performance is the reason why automotive enthusiasts do this. "Dub" is the urban street term assigned to large rim and tire combinations. As a matter of fact, a magazine dedicated to vehicular modification has named itself *Dub Magazine.* The reason for increased cornering and handling performance when shortening the aspect ratio (or sidewall) is because there's much less flex in the sidewall, which makes for a more responsive steering wheel-to-tire response. The vehicle takes on a sports car feel in cornering and handling. It's commonly referred to as installing "dubs."

A typical dub application might entail changing from a 17-inch tire and wheel combo to a 22-inch setup. The new setup allows you to move to a wider tire with a shorter aspect ratio (sidewall) and a larger diameter rim (usually quite flashy or with spinner hubcaps).

There are two factors to consider when plus sizing your tires and wheels:

- Make sure the new tire is not too wide. If the tire is too wide, then it might not clear critical suspension and steering components. In addition, the tire could rub or scrape against body panels, damaging your very expensive dubs. Carefully measure before installing. Measure and re-measure. It might take a little extra time, but it could save you lots of dollars.
- Make sure the overall diameter of the new tire and wheel combo is very close to the original spec (ideally, it should be exact). If the change is too drastic, the speedometer and vehicle performance computer will be thrown out of kilter. The computer receives critical wheel speed information from these sensors that is used by the performance computer to work out fuel delivery, ignition, and transmission shift strategies.

TIRE MAINTENANCE

You spend a lot of money on tires, so you want them to last. What should you do to get the most mileage out of them?

Plus sizing allows you to go with a wider, shorter sidewall tire. This move makes for a customized look while maintaining the same overall tire and wheel diameter, which is critical to proper operation of vehicle speed sensors, speedometers, and performance computers. Another consideration when plus sizing is tire and wheel width. Always make sure you have sufficient steering, suspension, and body clearance or tires and or wheels will interfere with one or the other. *Photo courtesy of the Goodyear Tire and Rubber Company. Used with permission.*

TIRE TIP NO. 1

Rotating and re-balancing your tires every 6,000 miles or six months will maximize tire life and minimize wear to the shocks and struts.

Rotation and re-balancing is a simple service that can dramatically extend the life of your tires. Tires are made out of rubber, and they naturally wear with use. Each tire has a different wear factor, depending on its mounted position on the car. Rotating the tires every 6,000 miles or six months gives each tire equal time at each position on the car, minimizing wear. It is important to re-balance the tires every time they are rotated. When the tire is new, it is balanced based on the mass of rubber present at that time. As the tire wears down, the rubber mass diminishes, throwing off the balance. This causes a "tramping" (or bouncing) effect as the tire rolls down the road at highway speeds. This motion creates a choppy wear on the tread, causes tire noise, and escalates wearing (not to mention that it causes premature wear of the shocks and struts!).

TIRE TIP NO. 2

Regular alignment checks and adjustments every year or 12,000 miles will maximize tire life.

Wheel alignment: Have your wheels checked for alignment every year or 12,000 miles (whichever comes first). The alignment angles in your car's front and rear end change as parts wear and poor road conditions jostle the steering and suspension. On cars with four-wheel independent suspension or front-wheel drive, get a four-wheel alignment. Why? Because these cars have adjustable alignment angles at each wheel that are affected by the same forces mentioned above. When the rear or front wheels get out of alignment, the tires want to track against each other. This causes pulling, drifting, dog tracking (the rear of the car tries to pass the front), and excessive tire wear.

TIRE TIP NO. 3

Regular air pressure checks and adjustments will maximize tire life.

Air pressure: Improper air pressure causes tires to wear. When a tire is under-inflated, the center of the tread "bows" inward, causing excessive wear on both sides of the outside of the tread area. When a tire is over-inflated, the center of the tread "bows" outward, causing wear on the center of the tire's tread. Air pressure varies with temperature and poor tire condition. In addition, excessive weight requires more air in the tires. This is the reason why tire makers offer an inflation range with a maximum air pressure. If you must carry additional weight, check the tire manufacturer's recommended air pressure adjustments.

TIRE TIP NO. 4

Keep the steering and suspension systems in good working order to maximize tire life.

Suspension and steering components: Worn suspension and steering parts cause tires to wear. When you have the vehicle aligned, have them checked for integrity and replace worn parts immediately. An alignment is only as good as the parts you're aligning. A technician can spend all day setting a front end to perfect specifications, but if the parts are worn, the alignment is worthless.

TIRE TIP NO. 5

Keep fresh shocks and struts on your car to maximize tire life.

Shocks and struts: The purpose of the shock absorbers and struts are to dampen spring oscillation. Without them the wheels would bounce merrily down the road, wearing out your poor tires prematurely (not to mention the wear and tear of suspension components).

The right tires for your vehicle produce a safe, effective, and comfortable ride. Maintaining those tires results in less wear and tear on many of your car's other parts. Ensure you and your family a safer ride and keep more money in your pocket by paying attention to your tires.

PROJECT 5
Check Tire Pressure

 Time Required: 10 minutes

 Tools Required: Pressure gauge

 Skill Level:

 Cost Estimate: $2–$10

 Tip: Tires lose 1 psi per month on average, so check and top up regularly for long, safe service.

1

Air pressure should be measured when the tire is cold, that is, before driving on it. Recommended inflation pressures in your manual and on the tire's sidewall apply to a cold tire. Remove valve stem cap.

2

Press the tire pressure gauge onto the valve stem so that the gauge's receptacle engages squarely.

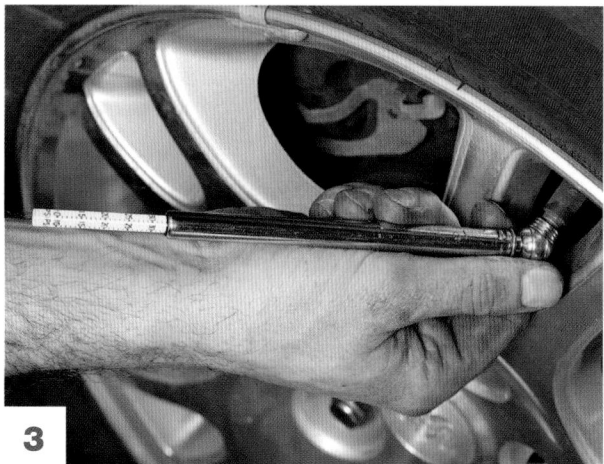

3

The pressure within the tire will force a graded stick out the back of the gauge on this type. You can also purchase a gauge with a round dial where the psi is indicated by a needle. Your best choice is a digital tire pressure gauge.

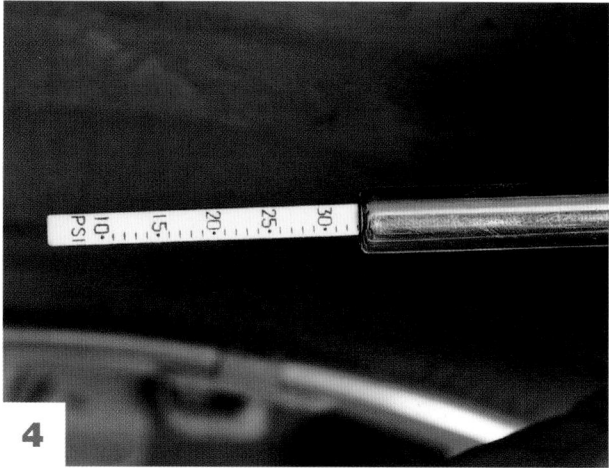

4

Remove the gauge and read it in good light. Tip: Remember to check and inflate your spare tire, too, so that it's ready if you need it. Check tires once a month and maintain proper pressure for safe handling and long tire life.

PROJECT 6
Assess Tire Wear

 Time Required: 10 minutes

 Tools Required: Penny or tread-depth gauge

 Skill Level:

 Cost Estimate: 1 cent to $8

 Tip: Wear should be even over the tread surface. If not, the tire has been improperly inflated, or there is an alignment or suspension problem.

1

Telling a good tire from a worn one isn't always easy by sight alone. The tire on the right is good; the left tire is ready to be replaced.

2

An old standby for measuring tire wear is the penny test. Insert a penny into the tread with Lincoln's head pointed down and facing you. If you can see the top of his head, the tire is ready for replacement.

3

A new tire has considerably more tread depth. That depth provides channels through which rain, snow, and mud can escape so the tire doesn't ride up on them. When tread gets too thin, traction drops off dramatically.

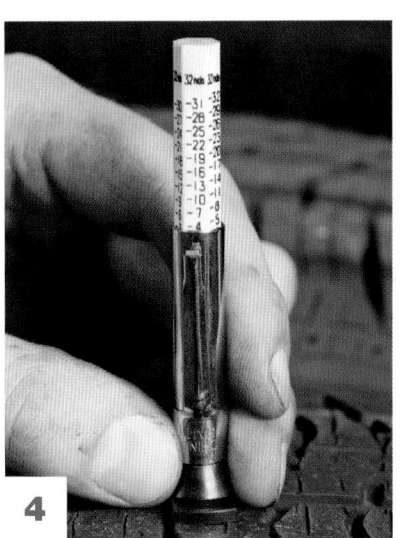

4

A tread depth gauge is an inexpensive tool. This one shows depth in $\frac{1}{32}$-inch increments. The more worn of our two tires shows only about $\frac{3}{32}$ inch of tread depth, meaning it's due for replacement.

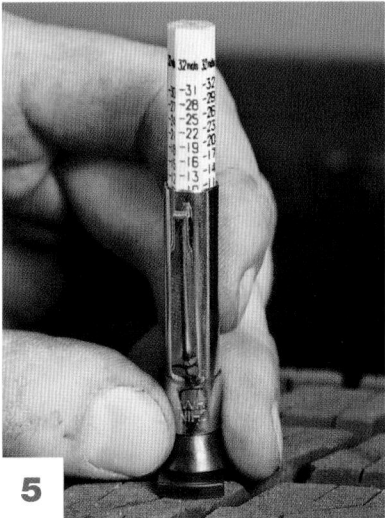

5

The good tire has about $\frac{10}{32}$ inch.

Chapter 6
Braking Systems

Up to this point we've discussed how to get your car moving (engine, transmission, and drivetrain). Now how do we stop it? There are two types of braking systems: disc brakes and drum brakes. How do they work? Why do they fail? What should you do to maintain them?

THE COMPONENTS OF DISC BRAKES

Master cylinder: The master cylinder is nothing more than a simple pump that forces brake fluid through the braking system to energize the various parts of the system to stop your car. The master cylinder is mechanically connected to the brake pedal through a system of steel rods called linkage. These rods operate at different angles using bushings that are typically made of nylon, rubber, or Teflon. When you step on the brake pedal, the linkage pushes on a steel rod that pushes into the back of the master cylinder. This creates the pumping action required to actuate the braking system.

Power brake booster: Located directly behind the master cylinder and bolted to it, the power brake booster provides power-assist during the braking process. When you press on the brake pedal, it only requires a light touch because of the additional power provided by this unit. Its name says it all; it boosts the braking power. Power assist units are usually vacuum-operated devices that pull vacuum directly from the engine. Some heavy-duty and custom vehicles use a hydraulic-assist system known as hydra-boost, which uses hydraulic pressure from the power steering pump to boost power when applying the brake pedal.

Typical hydra-boost system: Notice that the large vacuum canister behind the master cylinder is gone and a small hydraulic fluid block has replaced it. Power steering fluid under pressure is pumped to this fluid block, and when the brake is applied, hydraulic power-assist is applied to the master cylinder, thus reducing the amount of pedal pressure required to apply the brakes.

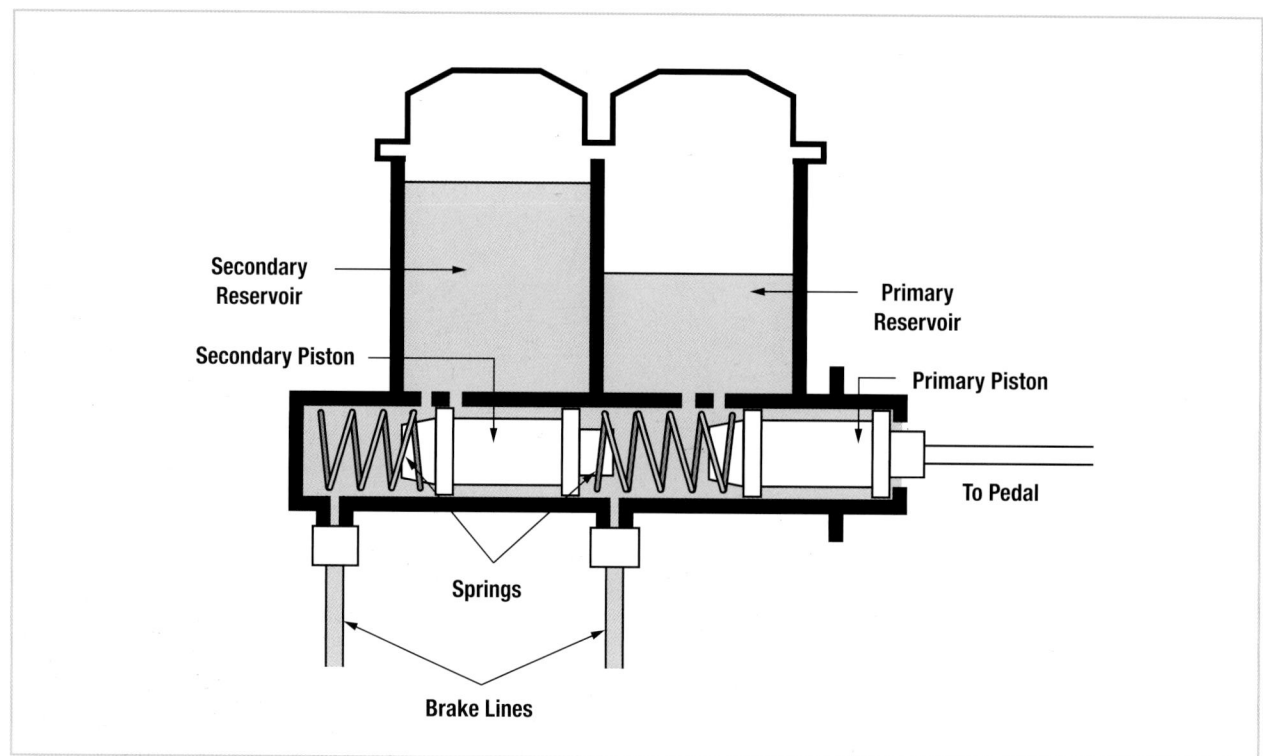

In the illustration above we see a typical brake master cylinder setup. Note that the reservoir has caps on it. This is where the unit is filled with brake fluid. In the cutaway view we see the inner workings of the master cylinder. We have a primary and secondary piston, the primary providing hydraulic pressure to the front brakes and the secondary the rear.

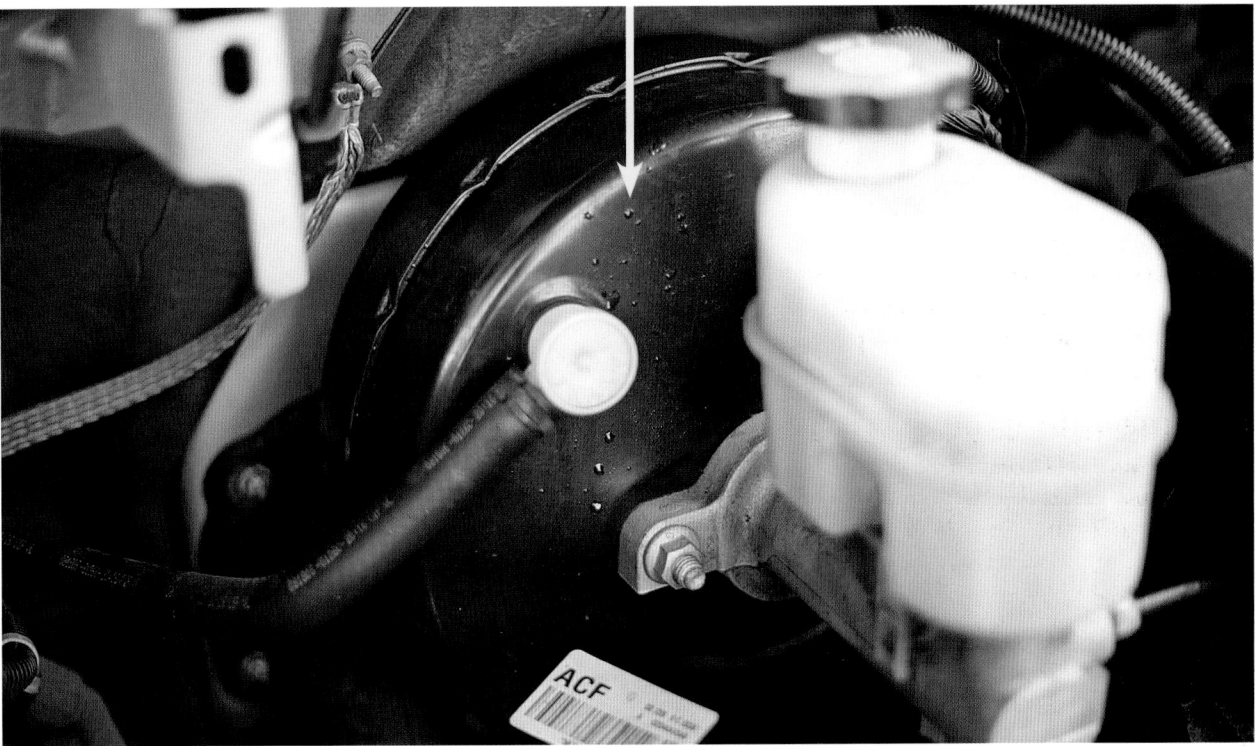

The power brake booster, which is a vacuum-assist unit, is large round black shape in this photo. Engine vacuum is drawn through the hose that connects to the booster unit. Inside the booster there is a vacuum diaphragm. When vacuum is applied to the diaphragm it provides power assist to the brake pedal, making braking easy, as opposed to manual brakes where much more pedal pressure has to be exerted to stop the vehicle.

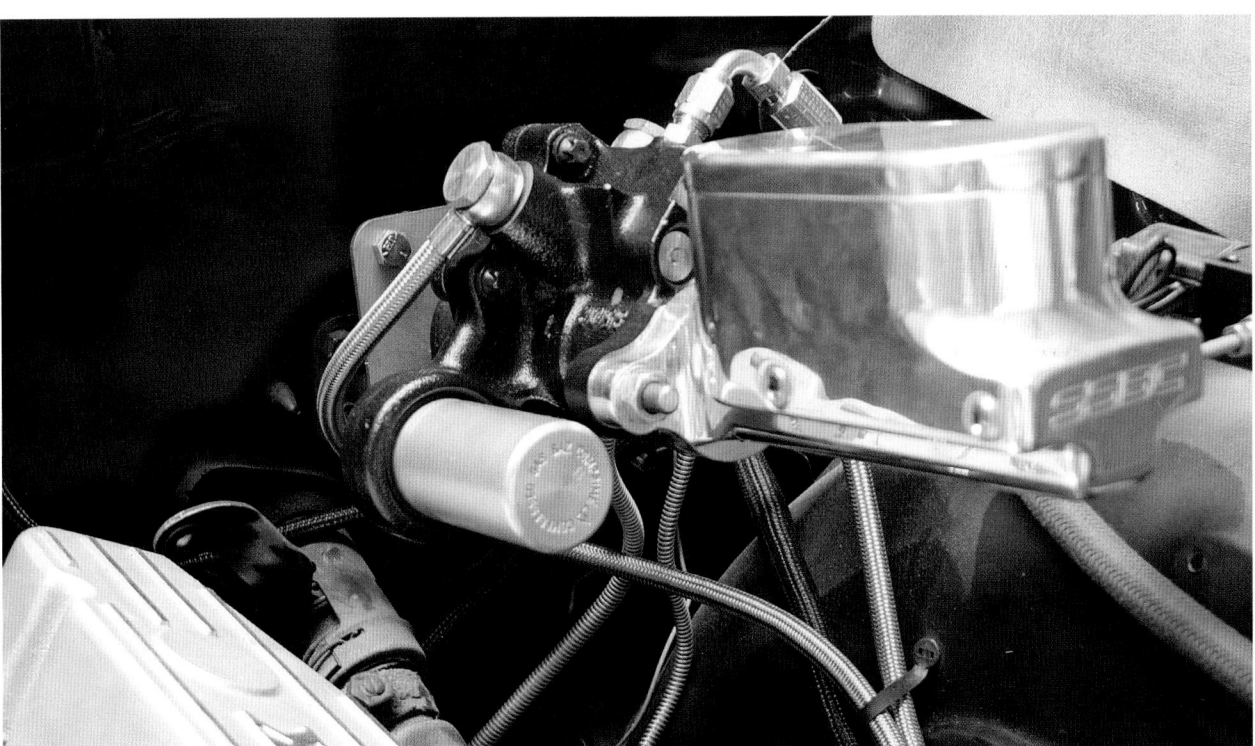

This is a typical hydra-boost setup. Note the large vacuum canister behind the master cylinder is gone and a small hydraulic fluid block replaces it. Power steering fluid under pressure is pumped to this fluid block. When the brake is applied, hydraulic power assist is applied to the master cylinder, thus reducing the amount of pedal pressure required to apply the brakes. *Photo by Jefferson Bryant*

Steel brake lines: The brake fluid travels through the braking system by means of an infrastructure made up of the steel brake lines.

Proportioning valve: This valve regulates and adjusts the amount of fluid that goes to the front brakes and to the back brakes. It is a necessary function because each set of brakes requires different volumes and pressures in order to apply equal braking power and stop the vehicle.

Brake calipers: The brake calipers are nothing more than powerful "C" clamps that are activated by hydraulic pressure produced when you depress the brake pedal. They slide on a mechanism (usually pins) that positions them so that they straddle the rotors. The calipers contain large pistons that act directly on the brake pads. The hydraulic pressure created in the master cylinder by pressing the brake pedal forces the pistons out of their bores and squeezes the brake rotor between the pads, slowing the vehicle.

Brake rotors (discs): Brake rotors or discs are flat round steel discs found behind the car's wheels. The calipers straddle them, and when you depress the brake pedal, the calipers clamp down on these rotors. The result is that the brake pads (which are attached to the calipers) make contact with the rotors, creating friction and stopping the car.

Brake pads: The brake pads are attached to the calipers. These pads are the friction material that's needed to stop the forward motion of the wheels. They are made of steel backing with friction material affixed to it (either by the use of industrial grade glue or steel rivets). Spring-steel clips are attached to the brake pads to keep them in place on the brake caliper. Without this anti-rattle hardware, the pads would make clicking and squealing noises when the wheels move.

A SUMMARY OF HOW DISC BRAKES WORK

When you press on the brake pedal, the master cylinder pumps hydraulic brake fluid through the system under high pressure. The fluid courses through the steel line infrastructure to the brake calipers. The pressure of the fluid pushes on the back of the pistons that are within the calipers. This forces the pistons outward, causing the calipers to clamp down on rotors (discs). The friction caused by the brake pads (which are attached to the calipers) when they come in contact with the rotors causes the vehicle to stop.

COMMON PROBLEMS WITH DISC BRAKES AND HOW TO AVOID THEM

When brake pads are left to wear down to the metal backing, rotors are damaged to the point where they can't be resurfaced. Have the pads replaced before the rotors are destroyed. Rotor replacement is expensive.

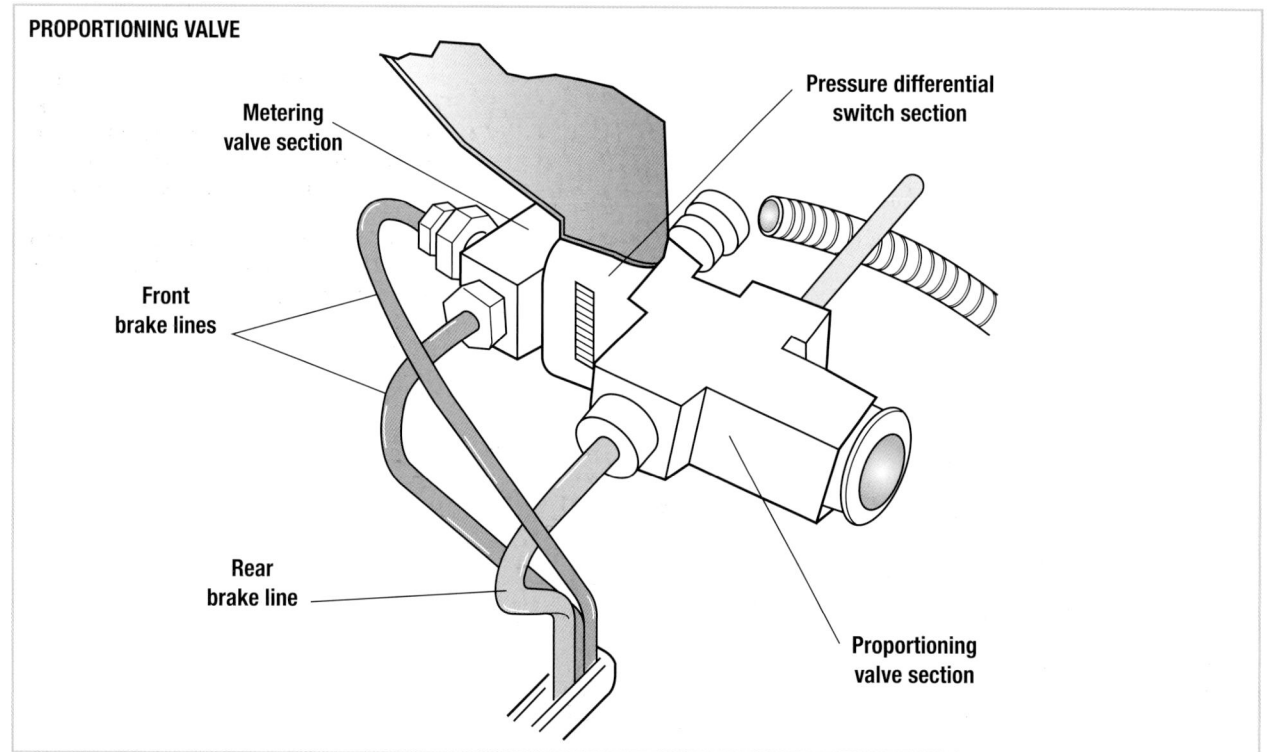

PROPORTIONING VALVE

Metering valve section

Pressure differential switch section

Front brake lines

Rear brake line

Proportioning valve section

The proportioning valve is a metering valve designed to differentiate hydraulic fluid pressure between the front and rear brakes. Typically, front brakes need more stopping power than rear brakes because there's a lot more weight in the front of the vehicle with the engine, transmission, axles, and so on than in the back. Therefore there has to be more braking power in the front to stop forward motion than in the rear.

This photo illustrates a brake caliper and how it is mounted on a vehicle. Note how it straddles the disc (or rotor) with the pads sitting on either side of the disc. When hydraulic pressure is applied to the caliper, it squeezes the pads tightly together, creating friction against the disc and thus stopping the rotation of the disc, which is attached to the wheels.

The brake rotor (or disc) is the smooth surface that the pads ride against. When brake pedal pressure is applied, the pads clamp down on the rotors, creating friction and stopping the wheels from spinning. When the friction material on the brake pads wear down from use, the rotors become scored and thus ineffective in stopping the vehicle. If too much metal has worn off, the rotor must be discarded for safety's sake. If only mild scoring is present and enough metal is present, then resurfacing rather than replacing is an option.

DISC BRAKE

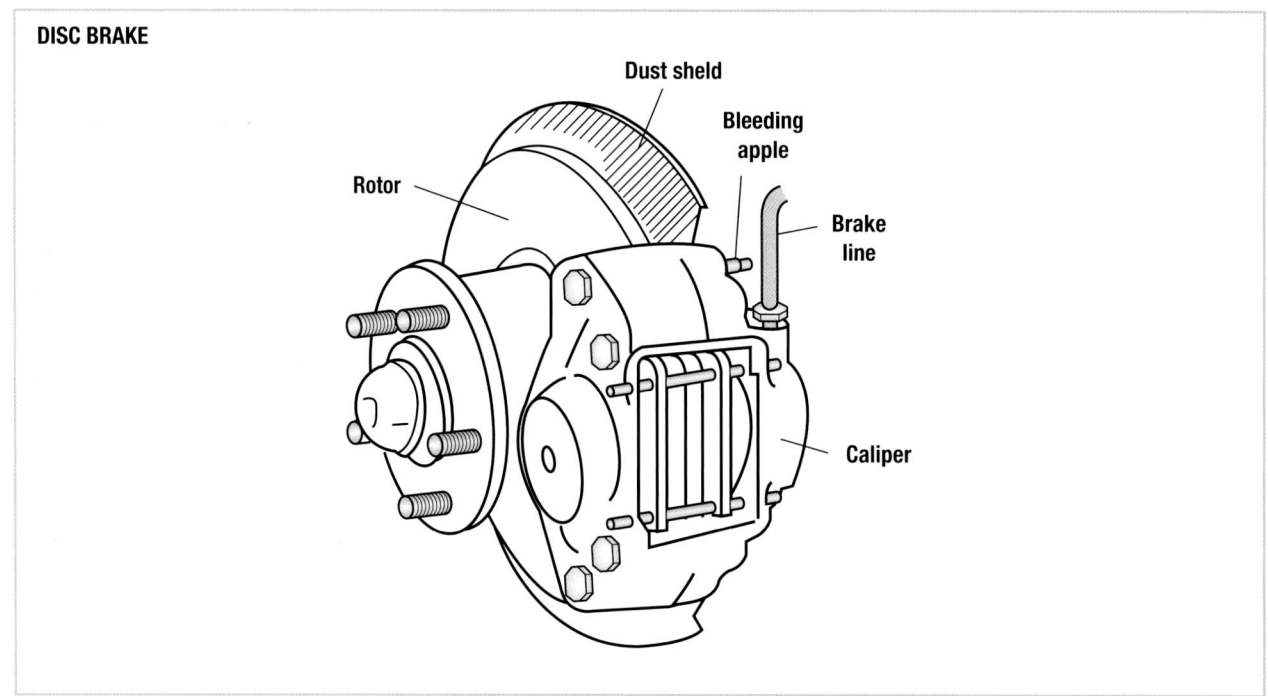

Here we have a cutaway drawing of a complete disc brake unit. Note how the caliper sits over the rotor, and the pads are seated on each side of the rotor face. The caliper is bolted directly to the steering knuckle, securing it and allowing it to follow the rotor wherever the wheels are turned.

DRUM BRAKE

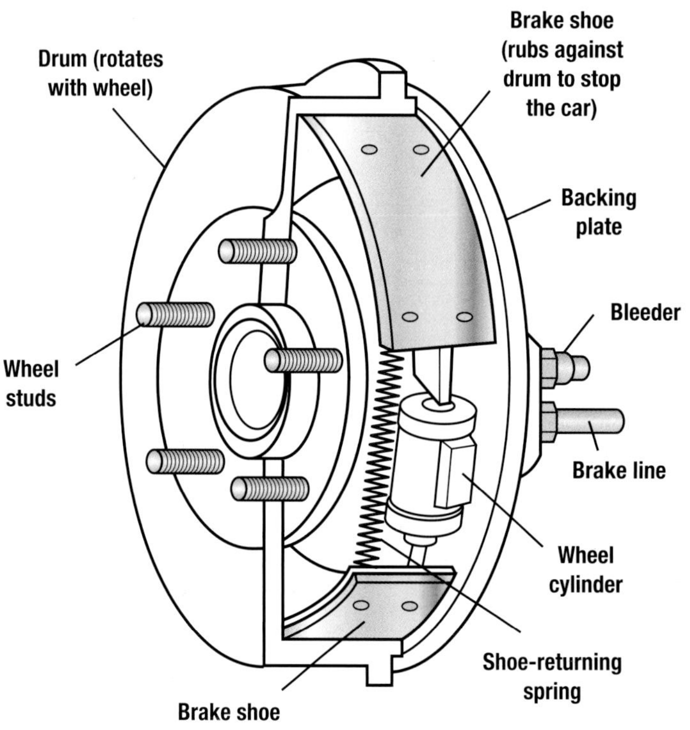

Here's how the brake drum fits over the brake assembly. It fits over wheel lugs and firmly against the hub assembly. Then it is firmly tightened against the whole assembly when the wheels are bolted into place. Then as the wheels spin, the drum spins around the brake assembly. When the brakes are applied, the shoes push out against the drum. This creates friction and thus stops the rotation of the wheels.

Another common problem that crops up with disc brakes is rusting caliper slides and pins. Rust prevents the calipers from sliding back and forth when the brakes are applied. When a caliper sticks in the applied position, the pads wear out prematurely. Keep the slides and pins cleaned and lubricated.

A rubber dust boot protects the pistons within the brake caliper from road dirt and grime, as well as weather elements. If the boot tears, then grime can accumulate and cause the piston to become stuck. This causes the brake to stay applied after releasing the brake pedal, resulting in premature brake pad failure. Have your brakes checked when you have your tires rotated every 6,000 miles or every other oil change. The technician will be able to see if a boot is broken.

On cars equipped with four-wheel disc brakes, the emergency brake cables must be kept free and moving. Why? Because it is the emergency brake cable that activates the e-brake. If the cable freezes up due to rust or fraying, when you apply the emergency brake it will not release. A frozen e-brake causes the brake pads to heat up and wear out. It will also cause the rotors to warp from the intense heat generated from friction.

THE COMPONENTS OF DRUM BRAKES

The drum brakes, like disc brakes, have a master cylinder, steel brake lines, and proportioning valve. Where drum brakes part from disc brakes in design is in the secondary hydraulic system and friction medium.

Here's how the parts list for drum brake systems differ from disc brakes:

- **Wheel cylinders** are attached to the backing plate to actuate the friction medium called brake shoes.
- **Brake shoes** are used instead of brake pads. These shoes are affixed to the backing plate via anchoring springs.

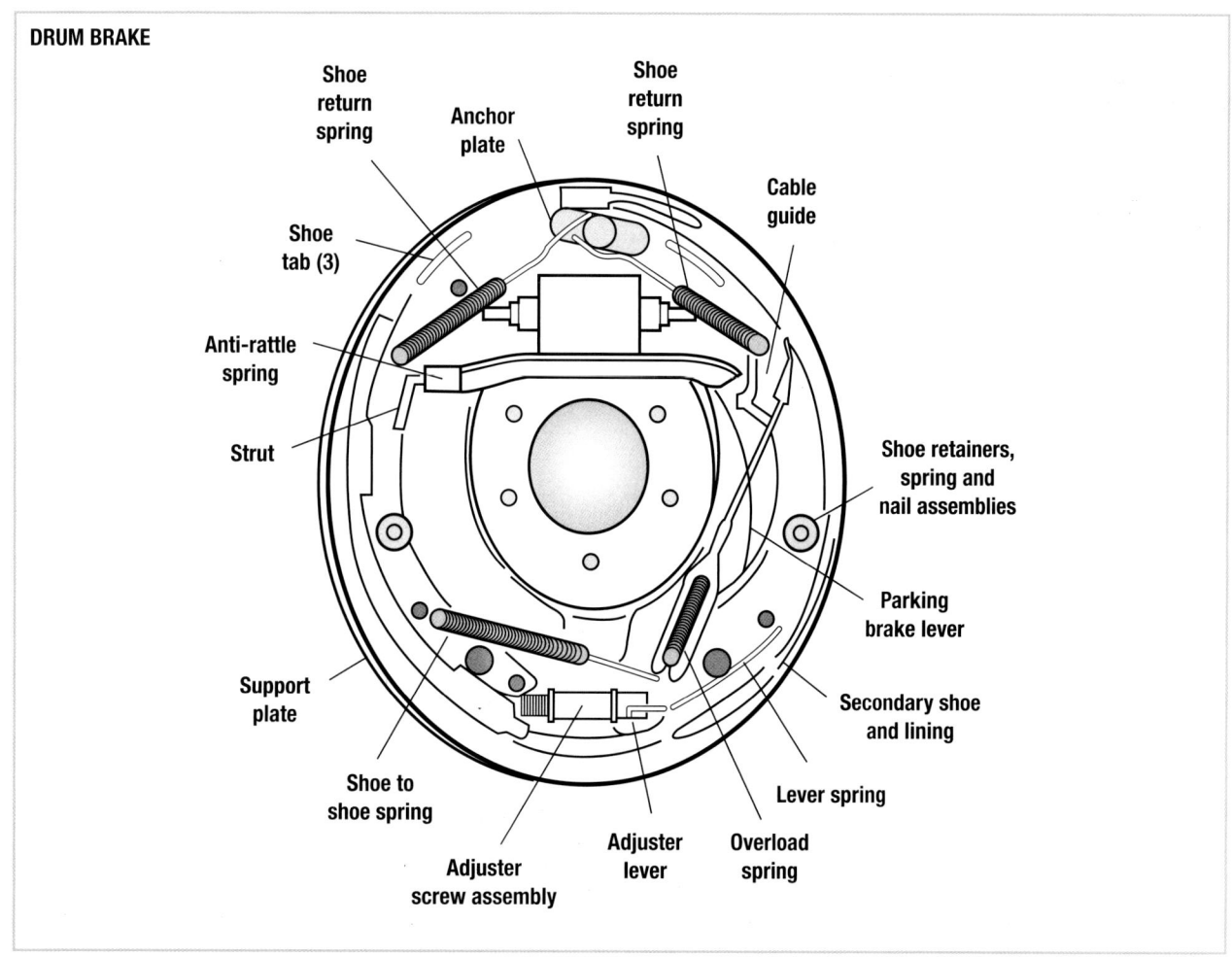

DRUM BRAKE

Here is a frontal view of a typical drum brake setup. The friction material is the long brake shoes, which run down each side of the setup. At the top are wheel cylinders. These are hydraulic actuators that push the brake shoes out against the drum when the brake is applied. The shoes are anchored to the backing plate by anchor springs. Return springs at the top of the setup ensure the shoes return to their respective seats when the brake is released. When the brake is applied, the shoes are pushed out against the smooth surface of the drum, which rides over the entire setup.

Return springs are located at the top and bottom of the shoes to ensure that when the brake pedal is released, the shoes return to their resting position. Also, drum brakes use an elaborate self-adjusting system comprised of cables, cable tracks, self-adjusting star wheels, and a lever to actuate the star adjuster unlike disc brakes, which simply rely on hydraulic pressure to keep the pads tight to the rotors. Some four-wheel disc systems do use a mechanical actuator for the emergency brake.

Drums cover the entire brake shoe assembly and provide the surface on which the brake shoes rub against to stop the

DRIVERS ASK, TOM ANSWERS: BRAKE PROBLEMS SOLVED

Q Dear Tom,
I have an '89 Corsica. The back wheels are locking up (especially on ice). I was wondering if the emergency brake could cause both wheels to lock up (or is the e-brake only on one wheel?). If it's not the e-brake, what else could it be?
Rob—Buffalo, New York

A Rob,
Parking brakes operate on both rear wheels. Some of the more common causes of the problem you describe are
- Incorrectly adjusted rear service brake
- Incorrectly adjusted rear parking brake
- Frozen or binding parking brake cables
- Leaking or seized rear wheel cylinders
- Incorrectly installed rear brake shoes or hardware

Through the trial-and-error method, experts have found that different brands of rear brake shoes can cause the problem you describe. If the first five potential causes I outlined above check out OK, I suggest replacing the rear brake shoes, even if they appear to be in perfect condition. Use a good brand brake shoe such as NAPA Safety Stop (SS prefix) or AC Delco. These have been found to solve the problem. There may be other brands, but experts tell me that the formulation of the friction material on these two brands will, in most cases, cure the problem.
Tom

Q Dear Tom,
I own an '07 Lexus GS350. The brakes make a metal-to-metal contact producing a black brake dust on the rims. The dealer changed the pads at 14,000 miles, and the symptoms are still the same at 22,000 miles. Any suggestions?
Tim—Anchorage, Alaska

A Tim,
The best course of action? Change to ceramic brake pads, put a light cut to the rotors, and check the calipers for sticking. When brake calipers stick, the brakes stay applied even when the brake pedal is not applied. This causes grinding away of the brake pads and thus the production of brake dust and premature replacement. Ceramic replacement pads will stop the black dust, dissipate the heat better, and cause less wear on the rotors. Success to you.
Tom

Q Tom,
I just replaced the drum brakes on my '85 Jeep CJ-7. I've been hearing a cyclical sliding noise (not squealing or grinding, but something is touching) when I drive at all speeds, and the driver side drum overheats excessively. I tried adjusting the brakes significantly to see if the shoes were too close to the drum, but that didn't help the problem. Do you have any idea what might be contacting the drum and what I can do about it?
Josh—Toledo, Ohio

A Josh,
The brake shoes on the side that gets hot are touching the drum. Check the emergency brake cable on the side that's overheating. I suspect it might be seized, causing the brake shoe to stay applied to the drum. If the cable is okay, then check for worn return springs, loose anchor springs, or a leaking wheel cylinder, because these conditions could cause the brake to hang up as well. Good luck.
Tom

Q Hi Tom,
I own a 2001 Toyota Avalon with 81,000 miles. I had the brakes changed to long-lasting heavy-duty brakes about 20,000 miles ago. When I step on the brakes the car stops fine; however, the front end shimmies. What could cause this shimmy?
Mark—Lancaster, Pennsylvania

A Mark,
Check the brake calipers to see if they are sticking. Also check for a blocked rubber brake hose, as this would prevent the brake from releasing after the pedal is released. Both of these conditions could cause the brakes to stay applied after releasing your foot from the brake pedal resulting in heating up of the rotors and warping, which ultimately causes the pedal pulsation or shimmy when braking as you call it.
Tom

Q Tom,
I own a Grand AM GT 2002. The ABS light, the "Trac Off" light, and the "Service Vehicle Soon" lights are on. The brakes seem fine. I am the only driver of the car and have kept up with services until these lights. I mentioned it to a fellow who said that if I don't fill up the gas tank until the low fuel warning light comes on (this is my pattern), then the sensor goes bad and that may be what is causing the three warning lights to come on. What do you think? I am now filling up at the gas pump when the gauge reads a quarter tank.
Joyce—Nashville, Tennessee

A Joyce,
Filling the gas tank or leaving it low has nothing to do with the lights that are on. These are related to the ABS brakes and Traction Control systems, so manipulation of the gas tank level isn't going to shut them off. The ABS braking and Traction Control systems operate through the brakes. There's a problem with one of these systems, probably the ABS system. Commonly, when an ABS wheel speed sensor goes bad it will cause both lights to illuminate. The ABS system will need to be scanned and the defective wheel speed sensor identified and replaced. Until the problem is repaired, the light will stay on and these systems will not operate properly.
Tom

wheels from spinning or rolling. Look at the illustrations below to see the differences in the systems:

A SUMMARY OF HOW DRUM BRAKES WORK

Compared to disc brakes, drum brakes are dramatically different in design and function as illustrated above. The friction media are the brake shoes and drums (not pads and rotors). Brake shoes are mounted on a backing plate over which the drum fits. When you apply the brake pedal, brake fluid courses through the system to the wheel cylinders. These cylinders are small hydraulic actuators that are bolted to the backing plate, usually at the top of the setup. Small pushrods are inserted into the ends of the wheel cylinders. When hydraulic fluid is forced into the cylinders, small pistons within the wheel cylinder press the pushrods outward against the top of the brake shoes. The brake shoes push out and make contact with the spinning drum.

This contact creates the friction needed to stop the wheels. When you release the pedal, the shoes are returned to their rest position by the pressure of the return springs. Drum brakes have a mechanism that automatically adjusts the brake shoes every time the brake pedal is depressed with the vehicle in reverse. This self-adjuster often sticks due to light corrosion or malfunction of the self-adjusting system and requires periodic manual adjustment of the brakes. It's a good idea to have periodic cleaning and adjusting of drum brakes to ensure dependable and durable operation.

Q Tom,
I own a 2006 Hyundai Sonata with 73,500 miles. I had the front brakes replaced last November. The other day while I was driving down the highway, the car started to ride rough as if it had a flat tire. I smelled smoke so I pulled over to the side of the road. Smoke was coming from the left rear wheel. I had the car towed to the nearest Hyundai dealer, and he said I needed rear brakes. What happened?

Abe—Kenosha, Wisconsin

A Abe,
Have the emergency brake cable checked on the left side to see if it's sticking in the applied position. Quite often the cables freeze up due to rust; this leaves the rear brakes in the applied position and wears them out prematurely. The other possible cause is that the left rear brake caliper is stuck, causing the brake pads to wear prematurely.

Tom

Q Dear Tom,
I have a new Jetta (2009). In questioning about my brakes, several repair shops have told me that the rotors on many of today's new cars (mine included) cannot be resurfaced because they are too thin. I was told this at a Volkswagen dealer as well as a couple of repair shops. Is this true?

Earl—Reno, Nevada

A Earl,
Unfortunately, in most cases with today's passenger cars, this is true and the rotors are often replaced when performing a brake job. It all depends on how much metal has been worn off the rotors; a measurement of rotor thickness should be part of the brake repair. If the rotors are too close to safety specs, the rotors should be replaced with new ones. Most passenger car rotors have enough metal for one, possibly two cuts.

Tom

Q Tom,
I own an '87 Ford Tempo with 75,000 miles. The e-brake light comes on during acceleration (25 to 35 miles per hour) and may turn off after a while, but usually it remains on until deceleration (at which time it turns off about 20 miles per hour).

Thomas—Bellingham, Washington

A Thomas,
Have the e-brake light switch checked. Sounds like it has come loose from its bracket and is making and breaking connection during driving, causing the light to intermittently come on and off.

Tom

COMMON PROBLEMS WITH DRUM BRAKES AND HOW TO AVOID THEM

When brake shoes are left to wear down to the metal backing, the drum is damaged to the point that it can't be resurfaced. Have the shoes replaced before the drums are destroyed. Drum replacement will eat a hole in your pocketbook.

When the rubber dust boot of the wheel cylinder tears, rust and dirt sets up inside the wheel cylinder bore. When this happens, the pistons seize and the seals leak. The brakes won't work as well because of the loss of brake fluid. Have your brakes checked when you have your tires rotated every 6,000 miles or every other oil change. The technician will be able to see if a dust boot is torn.

Finally, keep an eye on the emergency brake cables. They can cause problems when rust sets in and the cables freeze up in the applied position.

COMMON PROBLEMS WITH BRAKE SYSTEMS AND HOW TO AVOID THEM

Rusted brake lines: Steel brake lines are exposed to the environment and subject to oxidation (rust). If you live in one of the salt belt states, apply rust protection. Complete brake line replacement can cost several hundred dollars.

Bad master cylinders: The master cylinder pumps the brake fluid. When you apply the brakes, the master cylinder forces the fluid through the system, actuating all of the hydraulic components (brake calipers, wheel cylinders, and so on). The seals within the master cylinder can go bad. When this happens, brake fluid leaks (either internally or externally) and diminishes the brake operation.

SYMPTOMS OF BRAKE SYSTEM PROBLEMS

Brake pedal fades to the floor when the brake is applied at a stop: This symptom usually points to a bad master cylinder. Sometimes a brake fluid leak in a line or component will be the culprit.

Brake pedal pulsates up and down when the brake is applied: Brake pedal pulsation usually can be tracked to a warped brake rotor or drum. Warping occurs when a brake doesn't completely disengage when it's released. The excess heat produced from friction when the pads or shoes rub against the rotor or drum heats them up and causes the rotor or drum to warp. Excessively loose steering or suspension parts or a very loose wheel bearing can also cause pedal pulsation.

Car pulls to one side or another when braking: This symptom is usually a sign that a brake is dragging or not disengaging when the brake pedal is released.

Hot, smoking wheel: If you see smoke or smell a burnt odor coming from a wheel, then probably the brake is stuck on that wheel. Get the vehicle on a lift and check it out immediately.

PARKING BRAKE CABLE

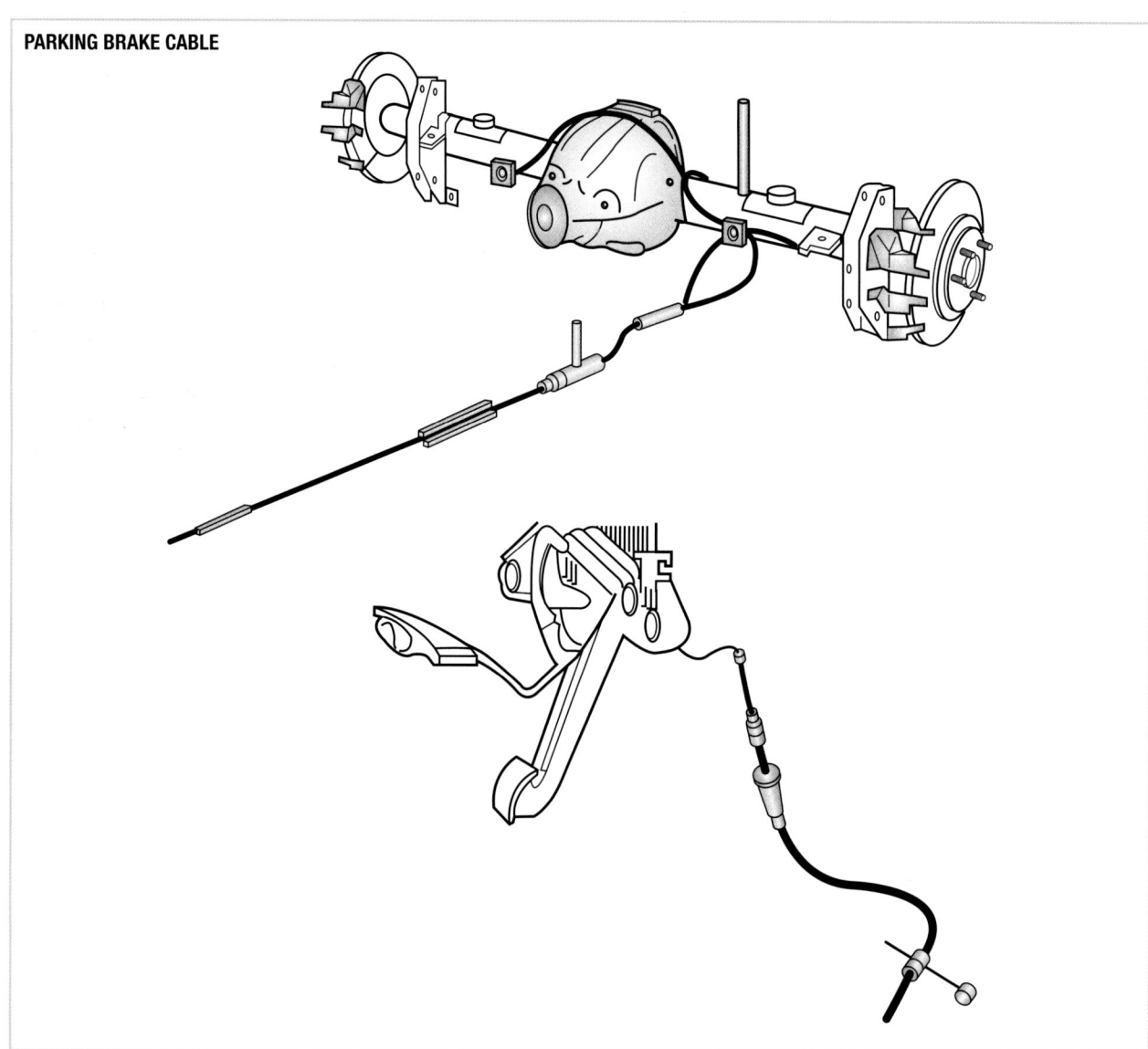

For an emergency brake to be an emergency brake, its application and operation has to be separate from the base hydraulic braking system, an alternative braking system in the event of failure of the hydraulic system. This is why emergency brakes for the most part are mechanical in nature. Emergency brakes may take different forms of design, but in the end, a series of cables and levers are the medium by which they are applied. Note the multiple cables and levers in this system.

When a braking system's hydraulic integrity is restored, a common problem occurs. The car comes back to the shop a few weeks later with a sinking brake pedal; this condition is called "brake fade." What's happened? The master cylinder, like the rest of the braking system, has experienced the same wear factors. When the rest of the system is restored, the master cylinder (which is not showing signs of an external leak, but is worn out internally) can no longer pump the fluid through the system. Hence, the fluid reverses flow back past the internal seals, resulting in "brake fade." The only way to fix this condition is to replace the master cylinder.

Rusted emergency brake cables: Emergency brake cables have a two-piece design. The outside housing is composed of a band of steel that wraps around a braided inner steel cable. When rust forms, the inner cable tends to seize inside the outer housing. This condition causes the emergency brakes to stay applied when released, leading to premature brake failure. Replace any seized cables.

ABS BRAKES

Today, most vehicles come from the factory with an antilock braking system, or ABS. Let's take a look at its design and function.

ABS uses wheel speed sensors, a hydraulic control unit, and a computerized electronic control module (the "brain" of the system). When you depress the brake pedal, the electronic control module monitors the speed of the wheels through the wheel speed sensors. If the control module detects that one or more wheels are about to lock up, the module signals the hydraulic unit to control hydraulic pressure to that wheel or wheels. This varying of pressure is much like "pumping" the brake. However, the wheel that is locking up (causing a

potential loss of control) is the only one being controlled; the rest of the wheels are free to roll. This individualized control of the brakes maximizes vehicle steer-ability in a braking situation.

Aside from the addition of these ABS components, the braking system pretty much remains the same in design and operation. Replacement of friction materials, such as brake shoes and pads, is the same. When the ABS light is lit on the dash, the system must be scanned with a hand-held computer. The computer uses ABS software that interfaces with the ABS data stream to track down the cause.

A few things you may notice the first time you use antilock brakes:
- When the pedal is applied and ABS is activated, the pedal may feel harder than usual.
- The pedal may seem to ratchet or pulsate (vibrate), or there could be a combination of these sensations.
- You may hear a noise that sounds like a motorboat engine. This is the hydraulic control unit operating.

All these traits are normal; no need to worry.

Two important things to remember when driving a car with ABS brakes:
- Maintain the same safe stopping distance as you do with conventional brakes. ABS will not make the vehicle "stop on a dime;" they simply improve steering when stopping.
- Do not pump the brake. Apply firm, constant pressure and let ABS do the work for you. You may feel a vibration or hear noise as the hydraulic control unit functions, this is all normal and there's no need to worry.

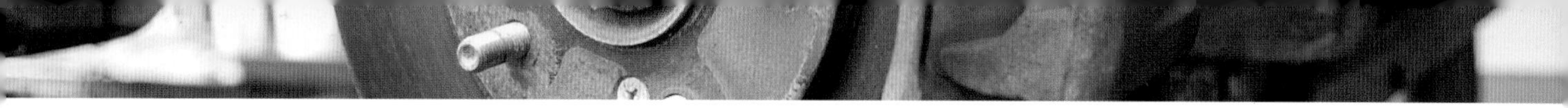

PROJECT 7
Check Brake Fluid Level

 Time Required: 15-45 minutes

Tools Required: None

 **Skill Level:**

 Cost Estimate: $0

Tip: Keep brake fluid off paint finish.

The brake fluid reservoir lies on top of the brake master cylinder, which is typically bolted to the firewall on the driver's side above the brake pedal.

TIP

If your brake fluid is low, it may indicate a system leak in need of attention.

Sometimes it's easier to see the fluid level if you remove the cap (see photo on opposite page). The fluid shows through this reservoir nicely. It is marked for minimum and full levels.

Remember, the fluid level in this reservoir will drop a bit in normal operation as the friction material on the brake pads and shoes wears away. More fluid will be drawn into the system to take up the slack as caliper and wheel cylinder pistons extend farther to apply brake pressure.

2

To top up the fluid level, pour in brake fluid of the proper specification as noted in your owner's manual. Most brake fluid attracts water and should be changed periodically to avoid corrosion in the system.

3

PROJECT 8
How to Jack Up Your Car

 Time Required: 15 minutes

 Tools Required: Floor jack, jack stands

Skill Level:

 Cost Estimate: $0 to $250

Tip: Always jack a car on a solid, level surface.

1

The jack that comes with your car is for changing tires only. Never work on your vehicle while any part of it is supported by this jack—it is absolutely not safe. The vehicle should be level and safely supported on jack stands, or with the front tires driven up and parked on metal ramps.

Most, if not all, of today's cars do not have a separate chassis or frame. Instead, the body and chassis are combined in a unibody construction. You must take care in jacking a new vehicle to avoid damaging it. The owner's or shop manual will identify the places underneath the vehicle where it is safe to place a jack. If you are not sure, ask a qualified mechanic for your make and model vehicle.

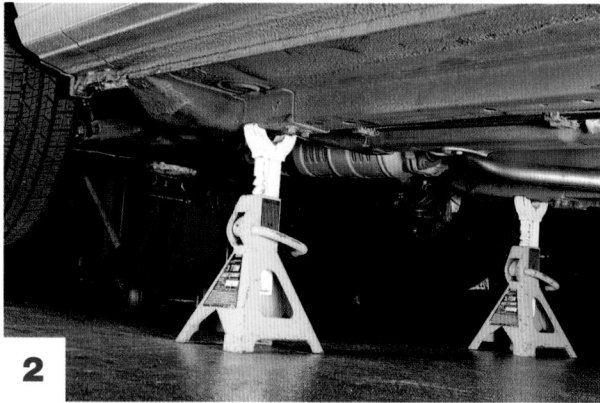

2

This Honda has a front crossmember that is strong enough to support the front end's weight. We placed a floor jack in the center of this crossmember and raised the vehicle high enough to place jack stands on either side. The jack stands are placed on frame-like members close to the engine compartment in front. Be absolutely sure you place the jack and the jack stands in a spot capable of taking the weight.

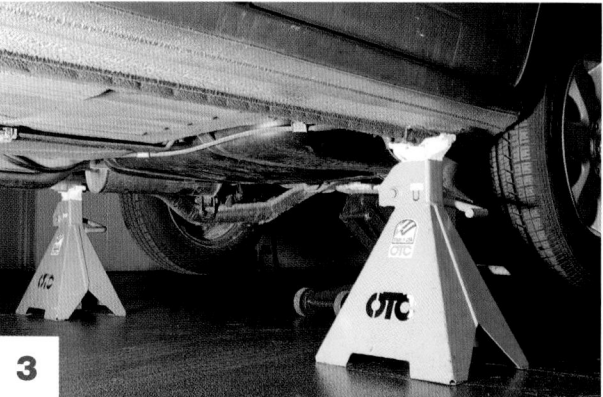

3

We placed the rear axle stands in the same spot designated to jack up the vehicle for a tire change. This is the spot designated by the manufacturer. With the car properly placed on jack stands, there is plenty of room to work underneath in comfort and safety.

Chapter 7
Ignition and Fuel Delivery Systems

In order to run, an engine must have the precise amount of fuel and ignition supplied to the combustion chamber at exactly the right time. Years ago, engines' ignition and fuel delivery systems were quite different than they are today. Primitive ignition systems used ignition points, condensers, and distributors. Fuel delivery systems included mechanical fuel pumps and carburetors. With the advent of computerized cars, things have changed a lot. Electronic fuel injection replaced the carburetor, and computerized ignition systems replaced distributors and point ignition systems. It's been an interesting evolution and one that's worth taking a closer look at.

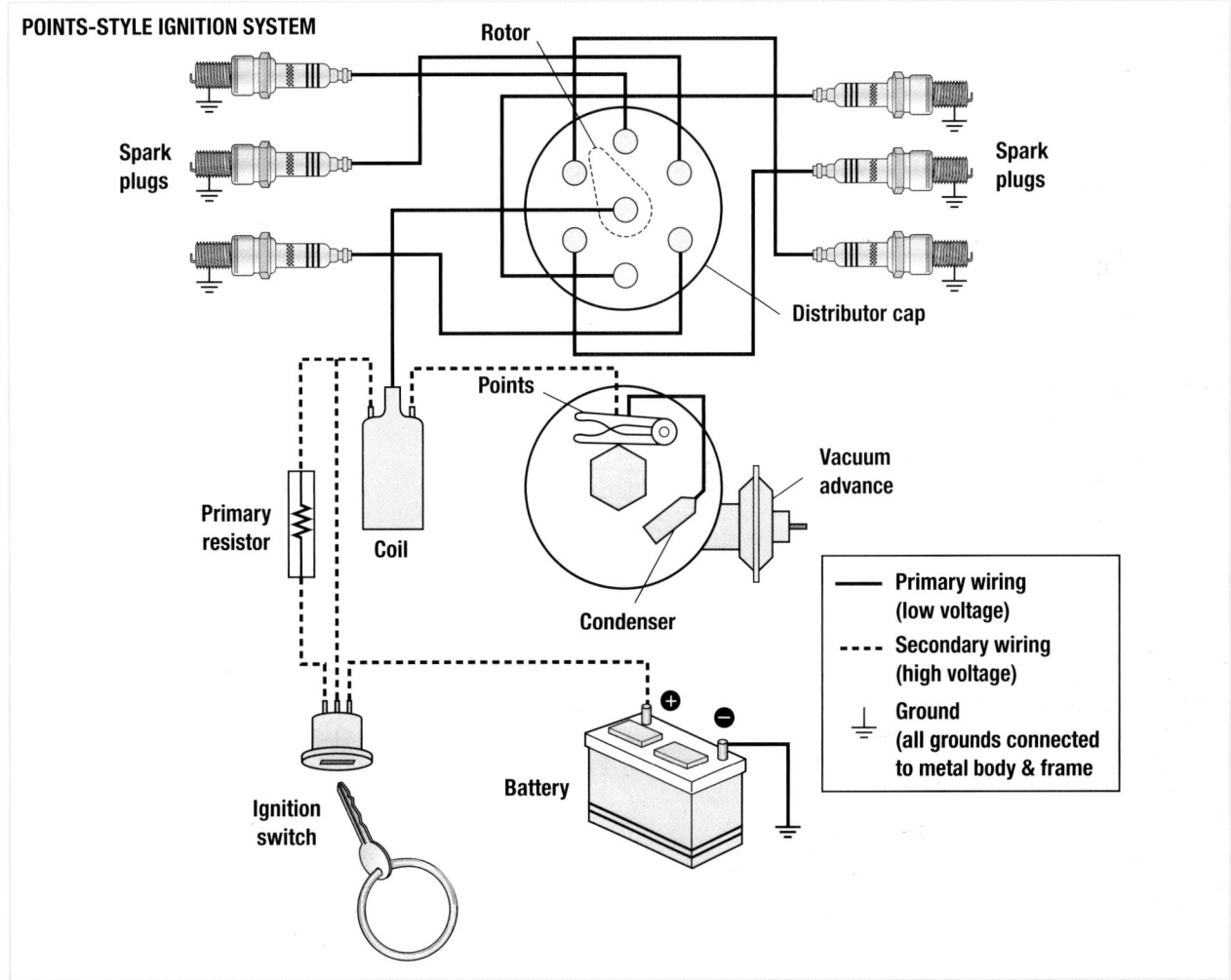

POINTS-STYLE IGNITION SYSTEM

Rotor

Spark plugs

Spark plugs

Distributor cap

Points

Vacuum advance

Primary resistor

Coil

Condenser

Ignition switch

Battery

— Primary wiring (low voltage)

--- Secondary wiring (high voltage)

⏚ Ground (all grounds connected to metal body & frame

Here we have a typical point ignition system. Note the parts in the distributor: points, condenser, and vacuum advance unit. In this setup, the weakness was the points mechanically wearing out from riding on the four-,six-, or eight-sided (depending on whether you had a four-,six-, or eight-cylinder engine) cam or the condenser electrically shorting out to the distributor body, resulting in drivability or starting problems. Also, the vacuum advance unit—which is connected to the point breaker plate inside the distributor to provide spark advance under acceleration in accordance with engine load—tended to go bad and create hesitation problems. Overall, it is a problematic system compared to advanced computer technology.

DRIVERS ASK, TOM ANSWERS: FUEL SYSTEM PROBLEMS SOLVED

Q Tom,
I own a 1988 S-10 blazer (4.3L). When I start the vehicle (after it has run and the engine is still hot) it stumbles and barely runs. If I give it gas, the engine stalls or just continues to rough idle. The vehicle does this for a minute or two, and then finally recovers and idles normally. In my opinion it seems to be re-learning the idle speed, so I think the ECU is bad. Aside from this problem, the vehicle runs fine (except for bogging down somewhat when stepping on the gas). Not too long ago I replaced the ECU, as well as just about everything else related to engine management. To no avail!! This problem really boggles me. Please help!

    Allan—Medford, Ohio

A Allan,
I think you are suffering from the application of an old adage: "A little knowledge is a dangerous thing." Symptoms of this malady usually manifest themselves in assumptions that result in self-destructive behaviors. For example, spending exorbitant amounts of money on parts you assume are bad, and ultimately ending up where you started—with an unrepaired vehicle. At this point, many do-it-yourselfers go to a service garage in frustration. When they are presented with a repair bill, they cry, "Rip off!!!" I hope you are not "one of those." So save yourself time, aggravation, and money by identifying the *real* problem (you cannot repair your computer-controlled vehicle for lack of expertise or tools), let go of your compulsion to repair it yourself, and—just a suggestion here—*get a computer diagnostic by a professional automotive diagnostician!* Good luck.

    Tom

Q Tom,
I bought a '96 Grand Marquis with only 36,000 miles in mint condition. While driving at night in Colorado more than 10,000 feet above sea level, it stalled and would not restart until it sat for ten minutes. The fuel pump was running, and a new fuel filter was in place. When the car was put on a lift I noticed that the fuel line ran only a couple of inches from the exhaust. Is there any connection between heat from exhaust, slow driving speed, and lower air pressure at high altitude? Or does the computer have to be reset for high altitude?

    Dave—Katy, Texas

A Dave,
Sounds like you either work for, or want to work for, NASA. I think you are barking up the wrong tree. Unlike carburetors, the fuel system doesn't rely exclusively on atmospheric pressure to move fuel to the cylinders. On your fuel-injected engine, the fuel pressure regulator is sensitive to changes in air pressure and will actually increase system pressure automatically. Increasing fluid pressure increases the boiling point. That's why we pressurize cooling systems. By increasing the pressure in the fuel lines, we decrease the likelihood that a vapor lock would occur.

    Many times, problems like the one you describe become apparent because not all of the maintenance was performed on the vehicle at the appropriate times. Air filter, breather filter, PCV valve, plugs, wires, and so on should be replaced routinely. It may be the result of simple neglect by the previous owner and all your car needs is a good old-fashioned tune-up.

    Tom

Q Tom,
I am having problems with my 1999 Mitsubishi Galant. The car idles poorly and the service engine light is on. My service technician said it was a problem with the throttle sensor. So I changed the throttle sensor and put a new distributor cap and wires on the car. It still runs poorly. What could be wrong?

    Adriana—Goldonna, Louisiana

YESTERDAY'S IGNITION SYSTEMS

As a young auto mechanic in the 1970s, I frequently heard the phrase, "My car needs a tune-up." The common complaint? The customer felt the engine was running poorly, usually meaning the ignition system needed to be refurbished. In the old days, ignition systems consisted of a set of electrical breaker points that were driven by the distributor (the part that governed the firing of the spark from the ignition coil), a condenser (the part that stored electricity when the points were open to prevent misfiring), a mechanical spark distributor, distributor cap and rotor, sparkplug wires, and sparkplugs. This system had many bugs that demanded constant attention.

The way the system worked was really quite simple. The distributor was mechanically driven (spun) off the camshaft or some other gear-driven engine part. This spinning action caused the points to open and to close, making and breaking the electrical circuit between the ignition coil and the distributor. This making and breaking of electrical flow caused voltage to buildup within the coil and a high-intensity

spark was dispersed through the distributor cap to the rotor at precisely the correct time. The rotor delivered the spark to each tower on the distributor cap. The spark traveled through a sparkplug wire that was connected to the tower and eventually arrived at the spark plug. At this point it jumped an air gap and ignited the compressed, highly volatile air-fuel mixture in the combustion chamber. This process created the energy needed for the downward power stroke to power the engine.

This design is simple in theory. But, as with any mechanical or electrical system, there's always a weak link that causes failure or poor performance. In this case, there were several weak links: the electrical points, condenser, distributor cap, and rotor. Points wore out, condensers grounded internally, and distributor caps and rotors developed cracks and dirty contacts, which resulted in misfire, backfiring, stalling, hesitation, and a myriad of other complications. The insulation on sparkplug wires broke down frequently from extreme changes in temperature that caused voltage leakage. This leakage caused cross firing and "breakdown under load."

Adriana,

Changing parts without proper diagnosis is a hit-and-miss scenario. It costs you money and rarely solves your problem. Your car has a minimum airflow and a throttle position specification that has to be set according to the manufacturer's specifications. If either of these parameters is out of adjustment, the computer will have a difficult time controlling engine idle. Before replacing any more parts, have your technician perform a throttle plate cleaning, and set the minimum airflow rate and the T.P.S. (throttle position sensor) to the proper specs. This should correct your problem. If not, further diagnostics are required. Good luck!

Tom

Dear Tom,

Some time ago I was having trouble starting my van. I thought it was from the change in weather and would straighten itself out. The other day when I went to start the van, the muffler blew out at the seam from a backfire. We had the muffler and catalytic converter replaced. The shop suggested that we have a diagnostic test done on the vehicle to see why it is getting too much gas. What do you suggest?

Laurie Jo—Minnesota

Laurie Jo,

Yes, your problem could be electronically based. For instance, if the coolant sensor were shorted, it would dump fuel in the system (not just on cold startup, but all the time). This could cause an excessive amount of unburned fuel and vapors to accumulate in the converter and muffler. Upon ignition from hot exhaust gases, this would result in an explosion (or backfire). I would have the system scanned as soon as possible and then perform the needed repairs. Letting a problem of this nature go could result in further damage to related system components.

Tom

Tom,

I own a '98 Ford F-150 and the check engine light is on. AutoZone informed me that the code says there is a problem with the EGR valve. What does that mean? Do I need to replace the valve or can it be cleaned?

Steve—Los Alamos, New Mexico

Steve,

EGR stands for "exhaust gas recirculation" system. This system recirculates exhaust gas to cool the catalytic converters and re-burn unburned gases in the engine (thus lowering tailpipe emissions). Carbon buildup is common in Ford EGR systems. If there is buildup on the valve, then I can assure you that the EGR passages under the intake manifold and in the cylinder heads are also clogged and must be cleaned in addition to replacing the EGR valve, or the problem will continue to rear its ugly head.

Tom

Tom,

I own a 2005 GMC 1500 pickup that won't start in cold damp weather. When it's dry outside the truck runs fine; it only happens when it's rainy. Any suggestions?

Ed—Buffalo, New York

Ed,

Repairs of this nature are difficult because you have to replicate the condition. Try wetting down the engine compartment with a spray bottle of water while the engine running. With any luck, you will duplicate the condition you describe. Electrical maladies of this nature are usually tracked to a poor electrical connection in the ignition system or bad sparkplug wires leaking voltage. Raise the hood in the dark after wetting down the engine compartment. If the sparkplug wires are leaking voltage, you will see a light show under the hood.

Tom

Under heavy load conditions, such as hauling a heavy trailer, the engine would miss, hesitate, and backfire. Sometimes this even happened when tooling around town, up and down hills, with a full passenger load. Yes, early ignition systems certainly had their idiosyncrasies.

The mid-1970s brought electronic systems with their solid-state design. Characteristically, these systems offered better performance overall. However, they had their own special set of problems. They were affected by engine heat and failed prematurely without any warning, leaving you stranded. By the early 1980s electronic ignition systems were more complex; carmakers were able to monitor the engine environment and make necessary adjustments, rendering the systems more reliable. Meeting EPA standards for tailpipe emissions began to look easier to the engineers.

There was still one hurdle to overcome, however: The ability to make "on-the-fly" engine performance adjustments while driving. Computer-controlled ignition systems were the solution. With such systems, engine commands could be monitored and adjusted during operation by gathering real

time information from various sensors located throughout the engine. These sensors measure such things as coolant temperature, exhaust oxygen, airflow, and air temperature. They provide pertinent information to the computer at any given time so that it can make the adjustments necessary to realize optimum engine performance under any operating condition or demand. Systems started with controlling a few engine- and transmission-related operations. Today, computers control most electronic operations of the vehicle, including engine management (fuel delivery-ignition-emissions), transmission shifting, climate control, vehicle lighting, braking, and on some vehicles equipped with electro-hydraulic suspensions the suspension. This is a far cry from small beginnings.

With the evolution of engine management, the need for highly trained technicians, sophisticated diagnostic and test equipment, computerized information systems, and advanced diagnostic strategies have become paramount. Carmakers have full-time technical people in the field collecting data on technical problems stemming from design flaws. A few years

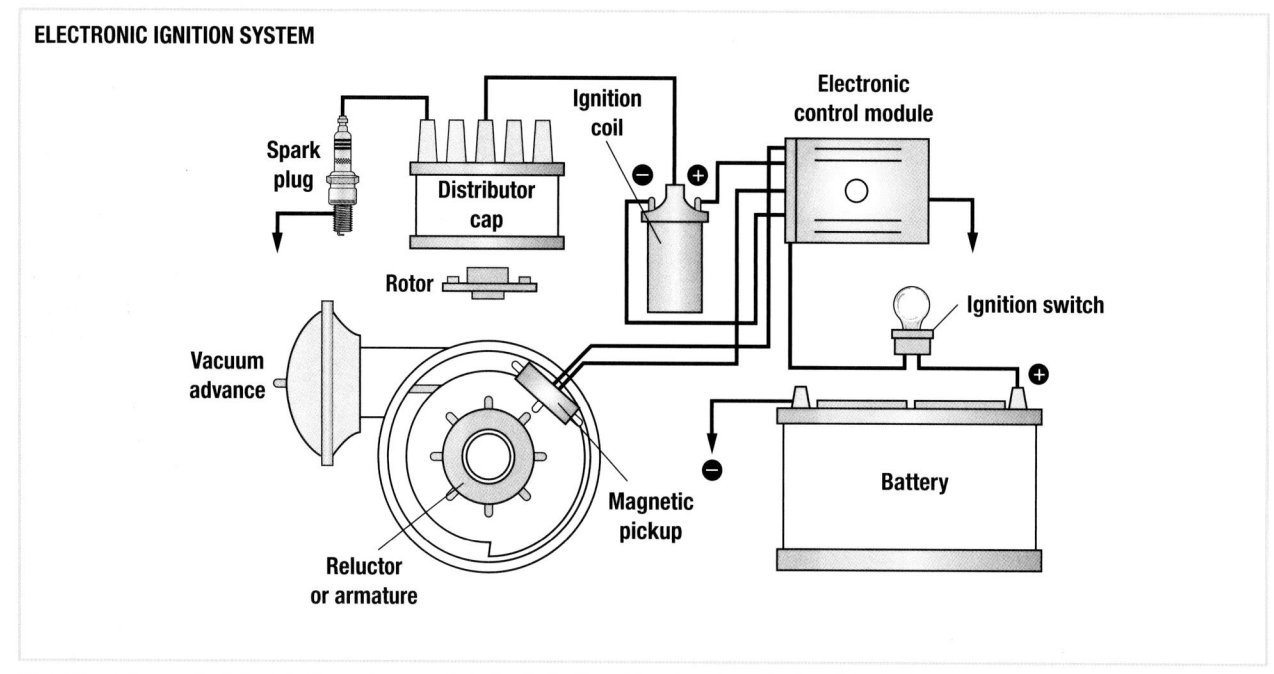

ELECTRONIC IGNITION SYSTEM

The positive major move in electronic ignition systems was eliminating the ignition points and condenser. In place of the mechanical ignition points to trigger the spark to the sparkplug was a magnetic pickup and reluctor. Now the spark was triggered by a magnetic impulse rather than the turn of a camshaft against small ignition points, which wore out every 10,000 miles. It was better but not the ultimate. The ultimate is automatically adjusting, long-lasting ignition systems.

back I spoke with the technical rep for the Eastern Seaboard for Chrysler. He travels from dealer to dealer, collecting data on specific repairs and malfunctions. From his input, the carmaker creates a database for dealerships and technicians across the country to use in their efforts to repair any maladies that pop up during vehicle operation.

Today, the average automobile has more computing power than Apollo 13. How does the drivability system work in an average computer-controlled car? For argument's sake, let's say that we have components A, B, C, D, and E. Component A is the computer; B and C are sensors gathering information from sources within the engine (specifically, water temperature and the amount of oxygen in the exhaust). These sensors send the information in the form of electrical impulses to the computer. The computer "reads" these impulses and then makes the necessary adjustments based on pre-set parameters from the factory (taking into consideration performance, emissions, shift points, and so on). These adjustments are translated into commands to the engine controls, which in this example are D and E (electronic fuel injection and ignition timing). These work in concert with one another on the fly to make sure that your car delivers optimum performance.

Problems start when there's a glitch in the system such as a broken wire or a bad component. That's when the Domino Theory takes flight. Since the computer works in a certain parameter, and it can only read what is fed to it by the sensors, it will "tax" itself and any component within the system in order to operate within factory set parameters—even if it means over-compensating or under-compensating the adjustments of other systems and components. As a result, more often than not, systems and components suffer. For this reason, keeping your car's performance system maintained according to factory specifications is *so important*! In a properly maintained vehicle, the computer can achieve automotive synergy, harmony, peace, and balance within.

FUEL DELIVERY

To fully appreciate the electronic fuel delivery systems of today, one has only to look back at previous technology. For starters, let's look at the basic carburetor, intake manifold, and mechanical fuel pump of old.

The carburetor: In its day, the carburetor did a great job of delivering fuel to a car's engine. It mixed, metered, and atomized the fuel as it entered the engine through the intake manifold by feeding raw fuel into a stream of high-velocity air created by a "venturi" system. A venturi is a device that increases the velocity of air by creating a restriction in the air stream.

An overview of the process: Air is drawn into the engine through the action of the pistons. A venturi increases the velocity of this moving air. Then the accelerator pump within the carburetor (responding to the depression of the accelerator pedal by the driver) pumps raw fuel into the high-speed air stream. The fuel is atomized (separated into tiny droplets) when it hits the air stream, creating a highly volatile air-fuel mixture necessary for combustion. When ignited, this air-fuel mixture powers the engine.

Problems with the carburetor: This wonderful device called a carburetor wasn't without problems. It had many moving parts that were affected by dirt, rust, wear, and varnish buildup. Linkages, internal parts such as needle valves and seats, floats, and jets wore out or clogged up with dirt. This resulted in either too much fuel (flooding) or too little fuel in the system.

The fuel filter was usually located at the front of the carburetor. It fit into a housing made of brass, which threaded into the carburetor. The carburetor was made of a softer white metal (less corrosive than brass and dissipated heat more effectively). If you weren't careful, it was easy to strip the softer threads on the carburetor when replacing the fuel filter. If this happened, then the carburetor had to be replaced.

Finally, there was a problem with the design of the automatic choke system. This system consisted of large butterfly valves connected to bimetallic springs through a series of tiny steel rods called "mechanical linkage." These butterfly valves, located at the mouth of the carburetor, controlled the airflow into the carburetor. The bimetallic springs connected to these valves were designed to respond to temperature changes. When it was cold, the spring would contract, pulling the butterfly valve closed, which restricted airflow and forced the carburetor to suck larger amounts of fuel needed for cold startup. When the engine got hot, the spring expanded, opening the valve and leaning the fuel mixture for normal operating temperatures. The linkages and springs would wear out and the valves would not open and close as needed. These dinosaurs had their idiosyncrasies.

This is a four-barrel carburetor. Typically used on larger vehicles with large cubic inch engines, large carbs such as this have upward of 100 small parts inside to achieve fuel delivery to the engine under a wide array of driving conditions. An exploded view of this device would reveal to the trained eye a series of "circuits" through which fuel passed to achieve power, cold start, idle, passing gear, and virtually any other driving demand. The problem with these dinosaurs was that with so many parts immersed in gasoline that either left varnish deposits or carried dirt from the gas tank, operational problems were common along with constant adjustment, cleaning, and repairs to keep them running dependably.

Here we have a typical Chevrolet V-8 intake manifold. The carburetor is installed to the manifold to do its job of delivering an air-fuel mixture to the engine to be combusted. Air and fuel are dumped into the manifold and fed to each cylinder as needed. Problems arise when intake gaskets leak, causing drivability problems and engine coolant leaks.

Intake manifold: For lack of a better analogy, the manifold sat on top of the engine and acted like a distribution center for air and fuel. The carburetor was mounted atop the intake manifold, which acted like a funnel into which all the fuel was poured into the engine. The manifold was usually cast out of iron or aluminum. It had chambers through which the air-fuel mixture flowed to each cylinder for combustion.

Mechanical fuel pump: The mechanical fuel pump was located somewhere on the engine; it was driven by either the camshaft or by a separate drive-mechanism. The fuel pump was connected in series in the fuel system with the fuel tank and the carburetor (and sometimes a fuel pressure regulator). This pump generated fuel flow to the carburetor. Problems cropped up when either the mechanical arm (or driver) of the fuel pump wore out, or the diaphragm within the pump wore out, resulting in loss of fuel pressure and contamination of the crankcase with wayward fuel.

TBI injection: When computers started coming on the scene in the early 1980s, carmakers decided to modify the fuel delivery systems, along with the ignition systems. First, they tried electronic feedback carburetors, but they still had to deal with the pitfalls of carburetors (despite the fact that they were electronically controlled). In addition, they still had manifolds, which diminished effective fuel delivery. These were the forerunners of a primitive fuel injection system called TBI (throttle body injection). TBI took the place of a carburetor. Still sitting atop a manifold (but now called a plenum), TBI consisted of a single fuel injector that delivered fuel to the engine based on electronic commands from the engine control module.

Multi-port fuel injection: As technology raced forward so did fuel systems, with the emergence of multi-port fuel injection. Engineers decided to eliminate the plenum and deliver the fuel directly into each cylinder via the cylinder head. Now the fuel was injected directly into the combustion chamber at the precise time it was needed, controlled by

This is a mechanical fuel pump. With this design, the fuel pump was driven mechanically off the engine. Problems cropped up when the diaphragm tore and raw gasoline fed into the crankcase, diluting the oil and causing lower end problems. The other problem with this design was the mechanical arm, which after long mechanical service broke or bent, resulting in engine shutdown from loss of fuel.

FUEL INJECTOR

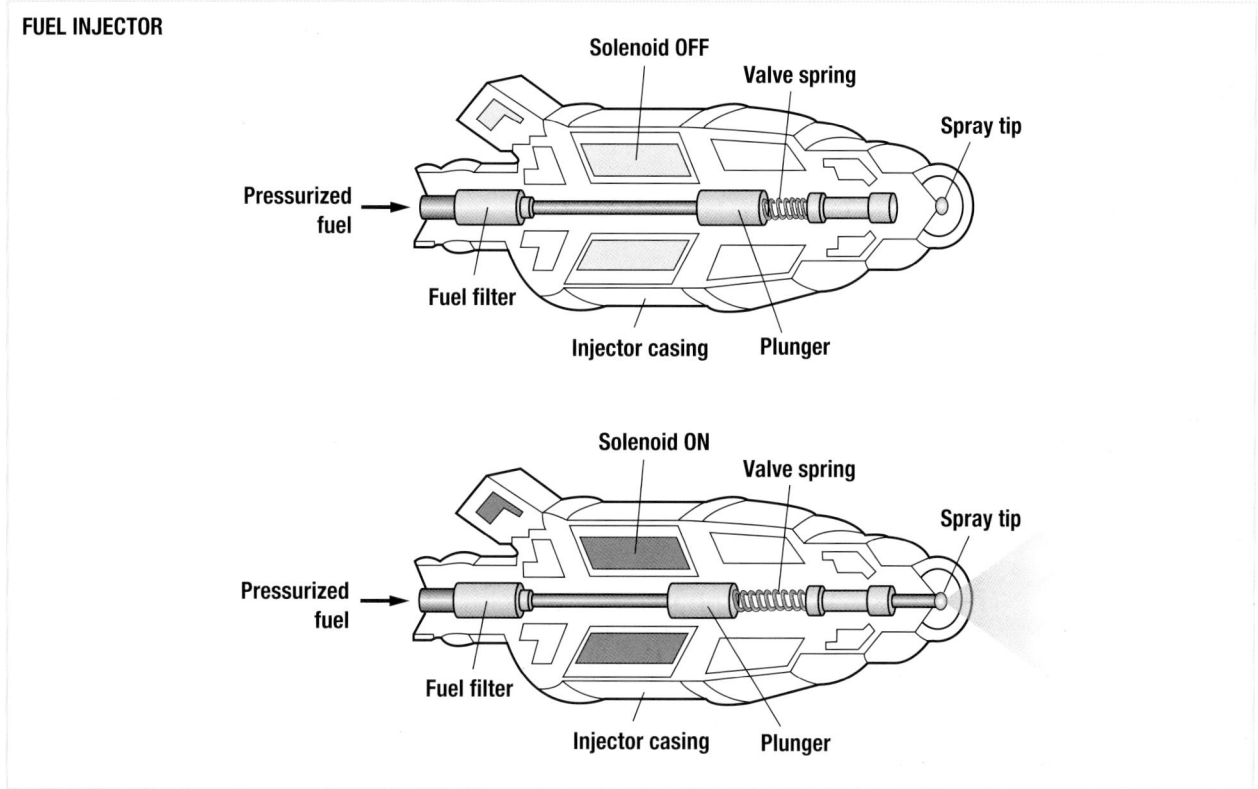

This is a cutaway view of a typical electronic fuel injector in a multi-port system. An injector is an electronically controlled and timed fuel sprayer. In a multi-port fuel-injection setup each cylinder has its own fuel injector. The engine control module (ECM) electronically times when each injector sprays fuel into each cylinder. This way the air-fuel mixture is timed and metered perfectly for each cylinder. Injector output is adjusted by the ECM based on electrical inputs from various sensors located throughout the engine to maximize fuel and combustion efficiency.

Here we have a picture of an electric in-the-fuel-tank fuel pump. Typically the fuel pump, pickup, and fuel gauge sending unit are incorporated into one unit making it easy to package and install in the system. Being located inside the fuel tank makes fuel pickup and system delivery easy. Also, when mounted inside the fuel tank, the pump is protected from the outside elements and cooled by being immersed in the fuel. This is not the case with externally mounted electric fuel pumps.

EFI FUEL SYSTEM

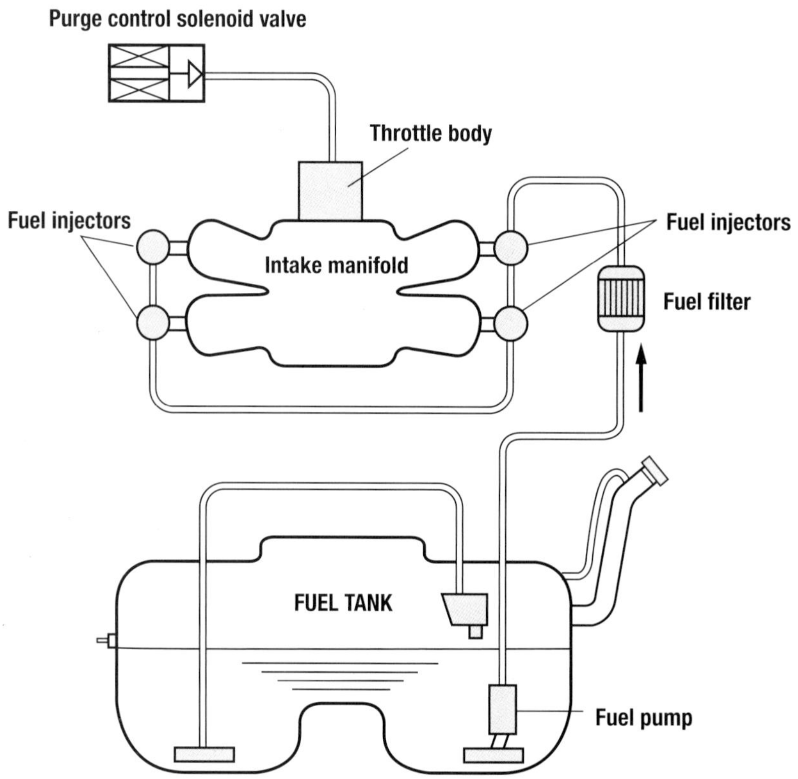

Purge control solenoid valve

Throttle body

Fuel injectors

Intake manifold

Fuel injectors

Fuel filter

FUEL TANK

Fuel pump

This illustration depicts a complete fuel injection system. Note the location of each injector at number 4, feeding directly into each cylinder. The rest of the fuel delivery system is outlined as well. At the bottom of page 81 is a cutaway view of a single fuel injector in a multi-port setup.

the computer. Today's computers are able to adjust fuel delivery based on environmental and engine conditions by reading data from various sensors located throughout the engine, measuring such things as coolant temperature, air temperature, and velocity.

Electric fuel pumps: The fuel injection design requires that the fuel be delivered at high pressures in order to atomize the fuel into a fine mist. Engineers designed the electric fuel pump, capable of much higher pressures than their mechanical predecessors. Once again in a cost-cutting move, they combined the fuel pump, fuel gauge sending unit, and fuel pickup into one unit and placed it in the fuel tank saving money, space, and mechanical energy from the engine.

THE IMPORTANCE OF MAINTAINING A CLEAN FUEL INJECTION SYSTEM IN TODAY'S CARS

Fuel filters must be changed regularly, and injection systems must be kept clean. Fuel injection and system cleaning ensures that your engine operates efficiently. Gasoline leaves varnish deposits throughout the fuel system. They build up as gas flows through the system, and they form a restriction within the injector nozzles. This restriction causes the injector to dribble (rather than spray) fuel into the combustion chamber, decreasing gas mileage as well as performance. In addition, it becomes harder to start the vehicle when it's cold.

Finally, when gas is not burned completely within the combustion chamber, the unburned gas forms a solid, hard carbon residue that soaks up fuel from the air-fuel mixture as it enters the combustion chamber, thus causing a lean burn condition. The O_2 sensor sends a "lean fuel" message to the computer; the computer responds by dumping more fuel into the engine, the carbon residue soaks up more fuel, and a vicious cycle is established.

Next, the O_2 sensor gets "coked up" from carbon contamination; the catalytic converter gets overloaded with gas because it can't process the gas fast enough, so a rock of carbon forms in the converter. This carbon buildup restricts exhaust flow and dramatically reduces power. The dominos fall on and on until the car fails to start because you did not maintain the fuel system according to factory standards.

This should illustrate clearly why maintenance is so important to the life of your vehicle.

This machine is an example of an upper carbon cleaning and fuel injector–cleaning machine. During the process, the air intake is cleaned with a carbon cleaner and then the machine pumps a high-strength carbon and fuel system cleaner into the injection system via the fuel injection rail. The vehicle is run with this cleaner being fed into the engine for long enough to thoroughly soak into the varnish and carbon deposits built up in the fuel system and engine. After running for a while, the engine is shut off, allowing the cleaner to further penetrate and liquefy the varnish and carbon. Then the engine is started up again after another cleaner is added to the gas tank. This service is necessary every 35,000 miles or so to ensure proper fuel delivery, efficient combustion, and maximum fuel mileage. Check your owner's manual for exact mileage recommendations. *Photo courtesy of Snap-On*

PROJECT 9
Change Fuel Filter

 Time Required: 15-30 minutes

 Tools Required: Screwdriver or spring-clip remover

 Skill Level: to

 Cost Estimate: $10–$50

 Tip: Use a rag over the fuel line fittings as you remove them to minimize spilled gas.

1

Garages have tools to depressurize a fuel injection system. You can accomplish this at home by removing the fuel pump relay, then turning the key repeatedly. The vehicle will not start, or will start only momentarily and stall. Either way, you reduce the fuel system pressure.

 This will not completely depressurize the fuel system or completely eliminate fuel leakage when fuel lines are loosened or disconnected. Wrap a rag or shop towel around the connection to catch and soak up any spilled fuel.

2

Fuel filters are often on the chassis rail underneath the vehicle, as on this Ford Ranger truck. (The arrow points from the fuel tank toward the engine to show proper mounting orientation.)

 Never use incandescent light sources or smoke when working on fuel systems. Use a sealed-beam flashlight instead.

3

Remove the filter from its bracket, which may be a clip or screw-down type or like this one from which the filter simply pulls free.

4

Remove the clip or clamp securing the hose.

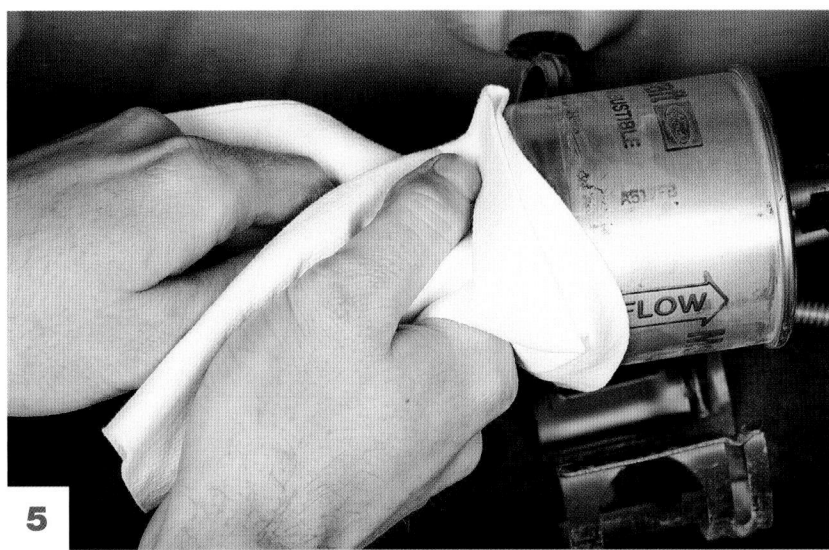

Place a towel over the fitting to avoid spraying gas and pull the fuel line off the filter.

5

Remove the front clip.

6

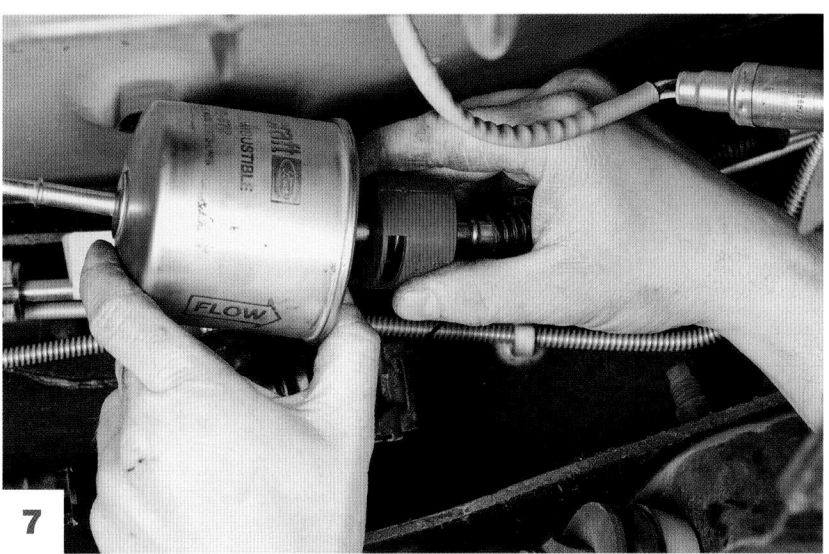

The front fitting uses a round spring clip that resides inside the fuel line where it connects to the filter. This type of fitting requires a special, inexpensive tool. Open the tool, fit it around the fuel line, and then press a collar inside the tool up into the fitting holding the spring clip. This releases the clip and allows you to pull the filter free. Note: Some fuel filters reside in inconvenient places and may require a lot more work, such as disconnecting and lowering the fuel tank. If you buy the filter and find you are in over your head, stop before you disconnect any fittings. Any garage can change the filter for you. Your manual will tell you the service interval for filter replacement. Typically, it's 15,000–30,000 miles. To install the new filter, reverse the removal procedure.

7

Chapter 8
Charging, Electrical, and Starting Systems

It's the first major snowfall of the year. As you head out for work, you open the front door with anticipation, inhale the fresh and invigorating smell of new snow, and hesitate for a few moments on the steps, lost in the beauty of the glistening branches of the mountain ash in the front yard. Then you look toward the driveway and wonder, "Where's my car?"

You head for a heap of snow that vaguely resembles the shape of your chariot. After finding an entrance, you put the key in the ignition, turn it, and nothing happens. You check the headlights, the horn, and the radio—nothing. Talk about a bad start to your day. Now you have to call a tow truck and you're late for work. How could this have been avoided? By maintaining the starting and charging system.

The charging and starting system consists of the battery, battery cables, alternator, starter motor, and ignition switch.

THE BATTERY

The cold weather is a huge factor in battery failure. A battery in marginal (weak) condition will fail the first time a cold snap hits, so make sure you start the winter season with a strong battery.

What other factors can contribute to battery failure? What tests can be done to reveal potential problems with the charging and starting system and avoid costly and inconvenient episodes? Let's take a close look at the answer to these questions.

Vibration: Another factor that can contribute to battery failure is excessive vibration. When a battery is allowed to vibrate and jiggle around under the hood, the plates within it can come loose, causing internal electrical shorts and battery failure. The vibrating motion can even wear a hole into the

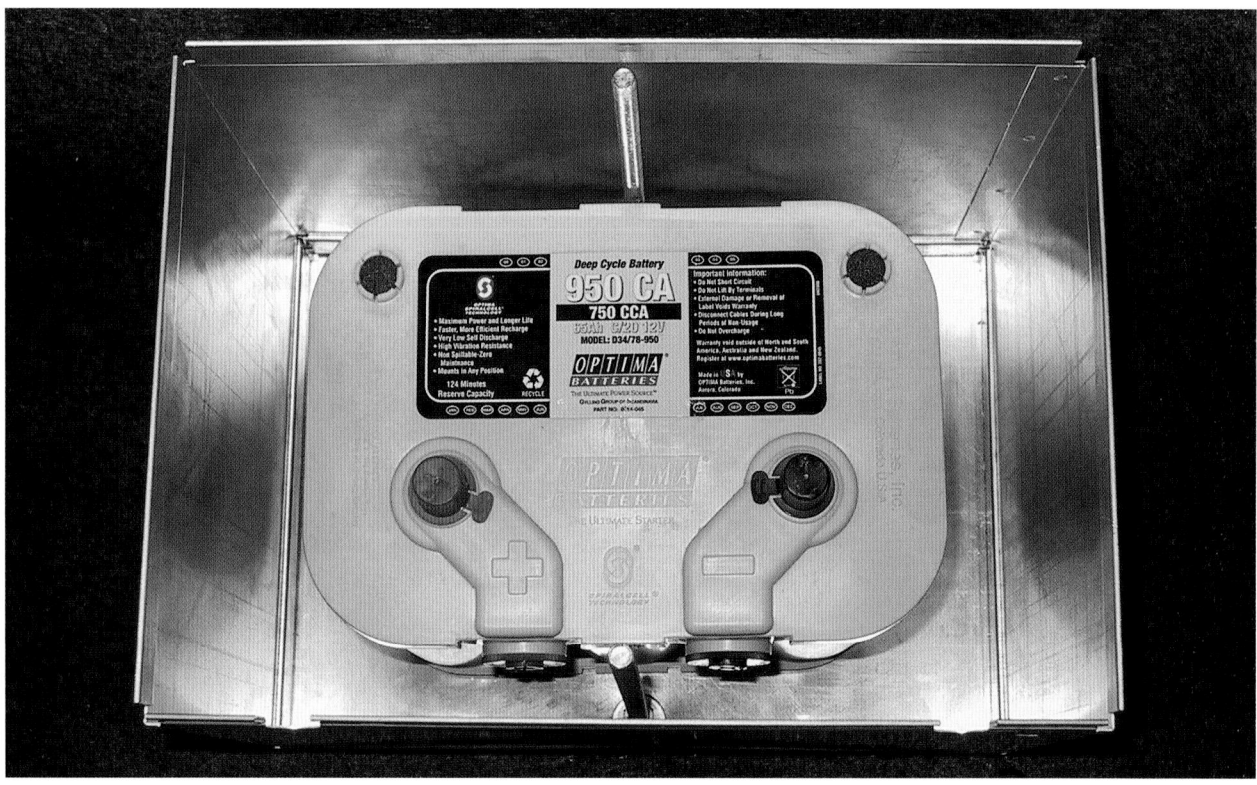

Pictured is a typical automotive battery. Note the red-and-black terminal caps. This denotes positive and negative or polarity, which in this case is a negative ground (common on most vehicles). It is important when installing a battery that you follow this polarity designation. If you get the terminals hooked up backward, electrical damage will occur to the vehicle's electrical system. If you're not sure, consult an expert before hooking up the terminals to the vehicle.

battery case, which results in the loss of acid from the cells. To avoid these problems, make sure your car's battery is secure within its case, using the proper securing brackets.

Sulfating: A condition called "sulfating" kills batteries. Dried battery acid forms a crust in the internal plates that inhibit the flow of electrons. Sulfating is caused by acid leakage or by overcharging of the battery. If the condition is due to acid leakage, it's probably because vibration has worn a hole in the case (either the battery is loose within its case or there's a loose body or frame part rubbing up against the battery). If the battery is being overcharged, it could be due to a bad alternator, a bad voltage regulator, or an electrical short in the system.

Electrical shorts: A dead electrical short can kill a battery as well. A wire, an electrical junction block, an electrical component, an electrical relay, or a switch can go bad, closing an electrical circuit directly to the battery. This is called a short circuit. It goes undetected while the vehicle is running. However, when you shut the vehicle off, electricity is drawn directly from the battery. This phenomenon is referred to as a "parasitic electrical draw." If an electrical draw is evident, each circuit within the vehicle must be tested to determine the source of the draw. Once the offending circuit is identified it must be painstakingly traced down to the root cause of the voltage loss and repaired.

Bad alternator or belt: A faulty alternator or a loose drive belt can kill your battery, so make sure the alternator and drive belt are up to snuff.

> ### MAINTENANCE TIP
>
> A simple way to avoid battery trouble when the cold weather hits is to have a battery load/hydrometer test performed. During this procedure, the battery is put under an extreme electrical load for a predetermined amount of time. Then the technician releases the load and observes how it returns to a complete state of charge. The hydrometer test reveals the state of charge between each cell. If more than a 20 percent variance is found between cells, then the battery is junk and should be replaced.

BATTERY CABLES

The battery cables carry high amperage to the starter motor to spin the engine and start the car. These cables can come loose at the starter or at the battery from vibration. They can oxidize when exposed to battery acid, or they can get pinched between metal parts of the vehicle. Any one of these conditions could result in a dead vehicle.

> ### MAINTENANCE TIP
>
> Check battery cables when doing an oil change on the car. This check includes making sure the battery terminals and cable ends are tight and clean of green crust from oxidation that sets up over time. Also, check the starter connections to make sure they are tight. This will ensure a crisp start every time.

Battery terminal connections are either at the top post (shown) or side post type. Always make sure the connection is tight because a loose battery terminal connection will result in corrosion buildup and hard starting or no starting at all. I like to insulate the terminals with an anti-corrosive coating. This can be bought if the parts store in aerosol cans.

DRIVERS ASK, TOM ANSWERS: ELECTRICAL PROBLEMS SOLVED

Q Tom,
My 1992 Buick Park Avenue keeps blowing the instrument panel fuse whenever the doors lock. Sometimes the park light fuse will blow also. Please help me. My husband needs to know how to fix this problem.

Thank you very much.
Karen—Kansas

A Karen,
Tracing shorts can be an exercise in frustration for someone who has little inkling as to how electrical circuits operate. Basically, a fuse blows because of too much electrical current flowing through the circuit it protects.

The best method of finding the short is to eliminate the components in the circuit one at a time until the fuse no longer blows. Your husband will need a good wiring diagram and a component locator to find those parts.

I often recommend taking a problem of this nature to a professional repairman, as electrical problems can be very complicated for novices to identify and repair. However, if your husband must proceed, he needs to get his hands on a good wiring diagram and the proper test equipment, i.e., digital volt ohmmeter and a logic probe to trace circuits. Tell him to be careful where he probes wires, as he could damage fragile electrical components that operate on milli-volts and meg-ohms when (and if) they take a direct 12-volt and high amperage hit.

Tom

Q Tom,
We have a 1993 Tempo that just developed a problem with one headlight. It keeps blowing the low-beam element on the driver's side. It uses a 9004 halogen plug-in element, and I have replaced it twice. It works for a day, then blows. Do I have a moisture problem, wiring problem, or what? Is there an easy way to test a circuit? Please let me know if you have seen this before. Thank you.

John—Columbia, South Carolina

A John,
Check the headlight lens for fogging. If moisture is present on the inside of the lens, then it could be cracked, allowing the moisture in, thus blowing the bulb. I would also check the wiring harness to the bulb and the plug. These could be shorting, resulting in a blown bulb. Finally, if no moisture is present and the wiring checks out, then check the headlight bucket assembly. It could be loose and vibrating from road jarring, which in turn is blowing the bulb. Good luck.

Tom

Q Tom,
I have a 2000 Pontiac Grand Am. The gas gauge registers one-quarter when the tank is empty. When I fill it up, the gauge goes to the full position, but still registers one-quarter when the tank is emptied. This is frustrating because I run out of gas, thinking I still have a quarter of a tank of gas! What could be wrong?

Ed—Sydney, Australia

A Ed,
Get the car into a shop and check the fuel tank sending unit and the wiring to the sending unit. The problem could be due to a bad power or ground connection or a bad rheostat within the tank unit. If the sending unit and wiring are found to be good, then check the wiring to the gauge and the gauge itself. Good luck mate.

Tom

Q Tom,
I own a 1997 Mercury Sable GS 3.0 liter. The parking lights and dashboard lights are not working at all. I was driving down the road and the lights just went out. All the warning lights still work, as well as the headlights and signals; however, the headlights will not turn off by the headlight switch. They will only turn off when I use my keyless entry control. Can you please tell me what fuse or relay switch needs to be replaced? Or could it be caused by something else? I tried checking the fuses; however, the box was not marked. If I have to pay to have it fixed, how much should I expect to pay?

Roger—Pittsburgh, Pennsylvania

A Roger,
It sounds like you may have two separate problems going on at the same time:

1. The problem with the parking lights and dash lights is most likely the fuse. They share the same fuse. It is located in the fuse block below the headlamp switch. You will have to use your owner's manual to determine the fuse location within the fuse block. Unfortunately, Ford does not label the fuse box itself (Ford usually uses a number system). The owner's manual outlines what number fuse protects which circuit.

2. The problem with the headlamps not responding to the headlamp switch could be related to a part called the headlamp module or GEM (generic electronic module). To diagnose a problem relating to your headlamps, you can expect to pay anywhere from $45 to $75 (depending on the shop rate in your area). Based on the findings, you may incur additional charges for parts or wire and materials.

Unless you have automotive electronic experience and proper wiring diagrams, the problem you are experiencing with the headlamps is one that you will want a professional to track down and repair. I wish you success.

Tom

MAINTENANCE TIP

Inspect the drive belt for the alternator. If it's worn or glazed, replace it. On cars equipped with a serpentine belt (one belt drives everything), check the automatic tensioner to make sure it's maintaining the proper belt tension. If it's too loose, then replace it because a loose belt will slip on the alternator pulley, meaning it cannot properly charge the battery. Finally, have a charging system analysis performed annually, preferably just before winter sets in. This test measures the alternator's ability to generate voltage and amperage. If its performance is below factory specifications, then it's ready for the trash heap.

Q Tom,
I own a 1990 Olds Cutlass Supreme. The left turn signal doesn't work, so I bought the flasher, but I can't find where to put it.

Chris—Bangor, Maine

A Chris,
Check the bulbs first. When one side doesn't work it's usually due to a burned-out bulb, a bad ground in the socket, or a poor power connection to the socket. Living in Maine you get a lot of snow. The salt and liquid brine used by the road crews get up under the car, mix with water, and cause corrosion of the light sockets that are exposed to the elements. As for the flasher location? It's hard to say where it is, because carmakers hide them everywhere under the dash. Consult an electrical component locator in a professional grade service manual for your car. It will give you the approximate location. I wish you the best.

Tom

Q Tom,
I own a 2004 Chevy Silverado extended cab pickup. The battery is new and it won't keep a charge. I had it charged twice this week and, although it started the following day, the clock goes back to 12:00. When I turn the ignition on, sometimes it starts and sometimes it doesn't. I am selling the truck so I don't want to buy another expensive battery. I'm wondering if it would be all right to put in a rebuilt battery and let the person who buys it deal with the problem.

Charles—Texas

A Charles,
At this point I would suspect a rogue parasitic electrical draw sapping the life energy out of the battery when the key is off (not a battery problem). In order to track this down, a technician will have to monitor the battery voltage while eliminating each electrical circuit until the draw is eliminated. When the offending circuit is identified, then it must be traced to find the problem and repair it. Otherwise, you will have to keep a full stock of batteries on hand. Or, you can just pass the problem on to the next owner. I guess it all depends on whatever you can sleep with.

Tom

ALTERNATOR

The alternator keeps the battery charged and ready to meet the electrical needs of the vehicle. It is designed to maintain smooth, stable electrical voltage and amperage when the vehicle is running regardless of what electrical load is placed upon it. The alternator is driven by a belt, which is driven by the engine.

The alternator keeps the battery charged and provides enough electrical stream to power the vehicle's electrical accessories. For the alternator to do its job it must have a strong and steady electrical stream of voltage and amperage from the battery. Also, the drive belt must be properly adjusted to turn the alternator pulley when an electrical load such as headlights is placed upon it. A loose belt will result in the battery being drained and you getting stranded with a car that will not start due to a dead battery.

STARTER MOTOR

The starter motor is a small high-output electrical motor powered by your car's battery. Its job is to spin the engine and start it up. Starters usually give you notice when they are ready to give up the ghost. Indicators include grinding, groaning, clicking, and pure unadulterated silence when you turn the key to start the vehicle. What's the noise all about?

Starter is grinding. Grinding could be due to a bad starter drive (the small gear that meshes with the flywheel on the back of the engine). Or it could be due to ground up teeth on the flywheel. The flywheel is a large ring gear. The starter meshes with this gear and spins the engine to start it. When the flywheel teeth get worn, broken, or chipped, you will hear grinding when you turn the key. Flywheel tooth damage usually occurs when a starter drive goes bad and is not replaced. The starter drive tries to mesh with the flywheel and grinds the flywheel teeth. Starting your vehicle with a bad starter drive results in irreversible flywheel damage, and that means more money out of your pocket.

Starter is groaning. If the starter groans or drags when you turn the key, it means that high resistance may have built up in the armature windings. Worn armature bushings will also cause this condition. A simple starter electrical draw test will confirm this; a high-amperage draw means that the starter needs to be replaced. So replace it or it could leave you stranded the next time you go to start the car after it sits for a while. Another clue that a starter has high resistance: When you start the car after it's warmed up, the starter groans and drags. Replace it.

Starter is clicking. A clicking sound when you turn the key could indicate a faulty starter solenoid (the electromagnetic switch that actuates the starter). A few simple tests will confirm whether this is the case or not. Clicking can also be an indication of loose starter solenoid connections, because the solenoid is subject to engine vibration and often the nuts at the starter connections come loose and cause the clicking sound.

Starter is silent. Silence when you turn the key could mean a dead spot inside the starter. This happens when an area of the starter develops an open circuit. The starter motor spins when starting the engine; it then coasts to a stop. If the armature rests on a dead spot, the next time you try to start the vehicle you will get silence. Usually a tap on the side of the starter motor with a hammer will confirm this condition. What happens when you tap on the body of the starter? The armature inside is dislodged from the dead spot to a live portion of the armature and electrical power to the starter is restored. Replace the starter if this is the case.

IGNITION SWITCH

The ignition switch is found on the steering column. When the key is turned, a small gear turns and actuates a lever that is attached to the linkage rod that goes to the ignition switch. The linkage rod pushes on the ignition switch and activates it. Voltage is routed to the starter circuit, and the vehicle starts. The ignition switch goes bad from age and wear. Electrical contacts within the switch wear out, so the starter circuit doesn't engage and the car is dead. A few tests will confirm a bad switch. If so, replace it and you're off to the races.

A starter motor is a small high-output electrical motor powered by the battery when you turn the key to start the engine. Starters vary in configuration. Some are small bodied to make for engine compartment room, and the way in which they bolt to the engine can vary too. Most times they are located below the engine in the engine compartment. Sometimes they are located on top of the engine. You will always find the starter in close proximity to the flywheel because the flywheel is what the starter motor meshes with to crank the engine to start.

PROJECT 10
Clean Battery Posts

 Time Required: 15 minutes

 Tools Required: Battery post cleaner or wire brush, commercial cleaner or baking soda

Skill Level:

 Cost Estimate: $0–$10

 Tip: Wear old clothes and gloves whenever working with a car battery, as acid readily makes holes in clothing.

1

Battery posts, terminals, and cables can—and usually do—corrode over time, leaving a white crusty substance. This substance interferes with current flow and should be removed. Wear safety glasses and gloves when working with your battery. Wash your hands and your clothes as soon as you finish the job.

2

Detach the battery cables, negative connection first.

3

Using a wire brush, clean the corrosion from the battery cable and terminal.

4

An inexpensive battery post cleaner has both a regular brush and post brush.

5

Clean the posts by placing this over each one and rotating it back and forth to remove corrosion.

6

Once the posts are well cleaned, use a solution of baking soda and water with a bucket and sponge, or a splash of diet soft drink to cleanse and neutralize the acid and corrosion. Don't forget to remove corrosion from the battery support and battery tray.

7

Auto stores also sell aerosol sprays and felt O-rings treated with an anti-corrosive agent that you can place underneath the battery leads to inhibit future corrosion.

8

Reinstall the battery cables. Positive first, then negative.

PROJECT 11
Test and Replace Fuses

 Time Required: 15-30 minutes

 Tools Required: Fuse(s), tester

 Skill Level:

 Cost Estimate: $25–$40

 Tip: Your owner's manual should explain which fuse goes where and controls what. Relays, which are boxes or cylinders plugged into the fuse box, can also fail, rendering a component (such as the fuel pump, turn signal, or air conditioner) inoperable.

1

See your owner's manual for fuse locations and functions. An inexpensive test light is the easiest way to check a fuse's condition. Clip the test light's negative lead to the battery's negative cable, then touch the tip to each leg, or end of the fuse, in turn. On plastic blade-style fuses, there's a little slot or opening at the top of each leg; that's where to touch with the probe. If power is available at the fuse and the fuse is good, the test light will glow on both sides. If the fuse is bad, it will only glow on the power or battery side of the fuse. Another way is to remove the fuse and check it visually. The wire in a bad fuse will be broken.

2

To remove a blade-style fuse, grip it on each side, and pull it free. An inexpensive plastic fuse puller, available at parts stores, makes this job a bit easier. To remove the older style glass BUSS fuse, use an inexpensive fuse puller to grasp the glass tube near one end, pull it loose, and then pull the fuse free.

3

Replace a fuse by pressing it back into the proper slots in the fuse box If a fuse is blown, there's a reason. It could be either a momentary short circuit or the circuit is drawing too much current. Never try to fix a blown fuse by installing a higher amperage fuse. Doing so is an invitation to overheated wiring and a potential electrical fire.

4

If the fuse is good, the metal connection (S-shaped on this fuse) between the two contacts will be visibly intact. If the fuse is blown, this connection would be burnt through and open. Sometimes a fuse that looks good will not work correctly because it isn't properly seated in the fuse box. For this reason, a test light is a better indicator of a fuse's behavior than a visual inspection.

PROJECT 12
Replace Battery

 Time Required: 15-30 minutes

 Tools Required: Small wrench for cables; socket wrench with extender may be necessary for bracket bolt

 Cost Estimate: $50–$150

 Tip: If you store a vehicle, periodically charge the battery, or use a trickle charger to keep it alive.

 Skill Level:

1

Again, make sure you're wearing safety glasses and gloves. Disconnect and pull aside the negative battery cable. Do the same with the positive battery cable.

2

Disconnect and remove any battery mounting brackets or hardware, which may be attached at the bottom (lower left), as it is here, or may run across the top of the battery.

3

Lift the battery free, keeping it level to avoid possibility of spilling acid. Any inexpensive battery lifting strap (available at auto parts stores) makes removing a top terminal battery much easier. If your battery has top terminals but you use the side ones, as shown here, keep the top terminals capped to eliminate the risk that a metal tool or part could short across them and create a fire hazard.

Chapter 9
Cooling Systems

Nothing kills a car engine faster than overheating it. Today's engines are predominantly made of aluminum, which is unforgiving at excessive temperatures. Also, engine operating temperatures are higher than they were years ago in order to achieve lower tailpipe emissions. Finally, throw in the possibility of a bad thermostat, and you have a recipe for engine meltdown. That's why proper cooling system maintenance is paramount.

The engine's cooling system is made up of a radiator, water pump, thermostat, hoses, water jackets (in the engine block and cylinder head[s]), and cooling fan. What do they do? What can go wrong with them? What should you do to prevent problems with the cooling system?

RADIATOR

Coolant absorbs heat from the cylinder walls as it courses through the engine's water jackets. The coolant then goes to the radiator where it travels through small tubes that are surrounded by air foils. These foils direct outside air over the tubes so that engine heat is released from the coolant. The radiator is made up of a core and two tanks.

WATER PUMP

The job of the water pump is to move the coolant through the system. It is driven by a belt (the timing belt, serpentine belt, or V-style belt). Inside the pump is an impeller that spins at high speeds, creating coolant flow.

Automotive radiators vary in shapes, sizes, and what they are made of. Radiators of old were made of tin; today's radiators are made of aluminum and plastic to save weight. The shape and size depends on cooling system capacity necessary to cool the engine and body design. You can get special radiators that provide greater cooling ability for special applications like towing, racing, or off-road applications.

Water pumps also vary in shape and size, depending on engine design and cooling system specifications. While they vary in shapes and design, the basic principal of pumping water is fundamental to water pumps. Every water pump has a shaft that drives a vane of some sort. This vane combined with a sealed system and channeling of the coolant into the engine is what creates coolant flow. Water pump drives are mostly mechanical by the engine either via the timing belt or a drive belt. Some engines have an electric drive, but that is usually found on high-performance engines where the builder doesn't want power drawn from the engine by the water pump.

The impeller is attached to a shaft that rides on bearings inside the pump. When the bearings go bad, the shaft starts to wobble and the water pump fails. The water pump can also fail as a result of a worn impeller or the poor performance of a bad belt or a belt that needs adjusting.

THERMOSTAT

The thermostat is a temperature-sensitive valve in the cooling system that opens and closes according to internal engine temperature to regulate the flow of engine coolant through the cooling system, radiator, and back to the engine. This allows the engine to be controlled and run at factory-specified temperature parameters, ensuring that the engine runs at optimum performance and efficiency.

As illustrated below, the thermostat is a valve. The opening and closing of the valve is controlled by a bi-metallic spring that is sensitive to temperature changes. When the cooling system is cold the spring contracts, shutting off coolant flow and accelerating engine warmup. Once the coolant temperature reaches a predetermined operational temperature (usually 212° F) the spring contracts (valve opens), and coolant flows freely through the system. When the valve shaft of the thermostat wears out (or the spring breaks, bind, or wears out), this causes the thermostat to stick closed, then over-heating occurs.

HOSES

Coolant hoses make up the infrastructure through which the coolant flows to and from the engine, radiator, and heater core. These hoses are designed to withstand 14 to 17 psi, high temperatures, continual expansion and contraction, and exposure to coolant chemicals. They are made of tough rubber with fiber reinforcement. Because of tight engine compartments and thus tight clearances, they are usually pre-formed from the factory.

Because of the rigorous operating environment, coolant hoses are subject to degradation. They become either extremely soft or extremely hard and brittle. Hose failure is often the cause of breakdowns on highways, leaving you stranded. The best way to prevent a breakdown is to check the condition of your hoses regularly. Ask your tech to check them at every oil change. Hoses should be resilient to the touch. If they are either too soft or too hard, replace them.

WATER JACKETS

Water jackets are channels that line each cylinder; they are cast into the engine block and cylinder head(s) when they are made. Engine coolant flows through these channels, absorbing the heat of the combustion chambers (cylinders). Keep fresh coolant in your engine to keep these channels clean and free of rust and scale. The drain and refill interval should be two years or 25,000 miles, unless otherwise stated by the carmaker.

COOLING FAN

The cooling fan is designed to draw air across the face of the radiator core, decreasing the temperature of the coolant as it flows through the radiator. Cooling fans are either electrical or mechanical in nature. If electrical, their operation is governed by a coolant temperature sensor. When the coolant temperature reaches a certain level (usually 212 degrees Fahrenheit), voltage is directed to the fan, causing it to kick on. When the coolant temperature drops below the trigger level, the fan shuts off. A mechanical fan is belt driven by either a serpentine or V-style belt that is powered by the engine's pulley system.

Cooling system maintenance includes regular visual inspection of the radiator, hoses, and water pump pulley for wear. It also includes checking thermostat operation and coolant protection and condition. Have your car's cooling

Automotive thermostats come in different temperature ranges to accommodate different operating temperature ranges as specified by the carmaker. Thermostats are also critical in engine management. The computer is constantly monitoring engine coolant temperature and making adjustments to the performance system to ensure maximum efficiency. When the thermostat goes bad or is removed, the computer goes crazy trying to compensate for the deviation from factory set parameters. The thermostat must operate properly for the engine to run efficiently.

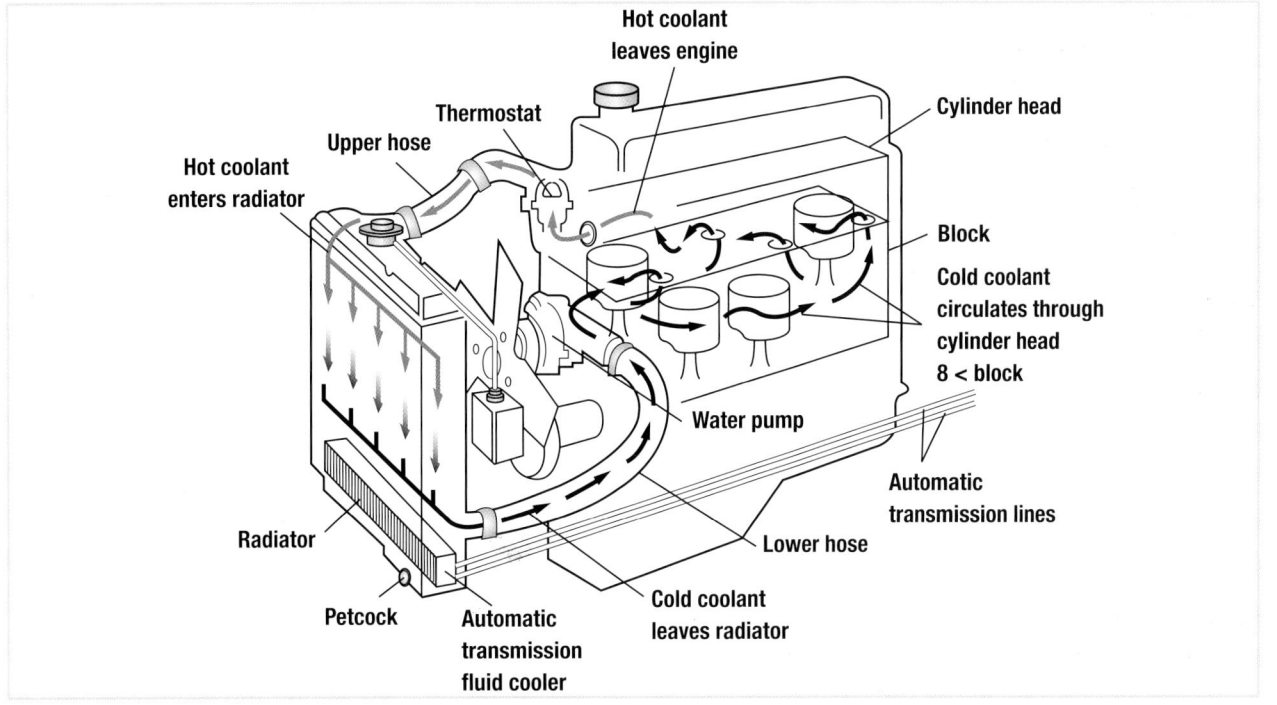

Hot coolant
leaves engine

Thermostat

Upper hose

Hot coolant
enters radiator

Cylinder head

Block

Cold coolant
circulates through
cylinder head
8 < block

Water pump

Automatic
transmission lines

Radiator

Lower hose

Petcock

Automatic
transmission
fluid cooler

Cold coolant
leaves radiator

Water jackets line each cylinder in the engine, which carry cooling water to absorb the heat caused by engine combustion. The water then flows away from the cylinders via the water jackets to the radiator, where it is cooled. Water jackets also run through the cylinder heads and intake manifold to cool these engine parts and provide a crossover to each side of the engine.

The fan for the cooling system is located in front of the radiator to draw fresh cool air over the face of the radiator core and thus cool the water and coolant mix within. Cooling fans are either driven by an electric motor or mechanically driven by a pulley connected to the crankshaft of the engine. A shroud to direct the air to the fan is used; this creates a venturi (rushing of air) action maximizing fan operation.

system checked every six months. A proper cooling system analysis includes the following procedures:

- A cooling system pressure test (including the radiator cap) to uncover any leaks.
- An antifreeze protection to tell you if the antifreeze protection level is acceptable (-34° F is safe).

- Check the condition of the hoses and belts. Replace any soft or brittle hoses and cracked belts. Tighten all loose hose connections.
- A flow test tells you if the coolant is flowing properly and if the engine is operating at optimum temperature levels. Address poor flow issues with a cooling system flush and refill and thermostat replacement.

DRIVERS ASK, TOM ANSWERS: COOLING PROBLEMS SOLVED

COOLING SYSTEMS

Q Tom,
I own a 1995 Pontiac Grand Prix. It has no water leaks and no problem with overheating, and yet the engine coolant light flashes on and off. I recently replaced the coolant thinking that might solve the problem, but it did not. Could the sensor be bad?

Cecil—Valdosta, California

A Cecil,
Yes, it is possible that the coolant level sensor is bad. If the system has been checked, levels are good, and the system holds pressure when pressure tested, then you might want to replace the switch (providing you are sure the wiring and electrical plug are okay). The low coolant module (switch) is located on the left side of the radiator and can be changed in about a half hour of "shop time." I express replacement in terms of "shop time" because, if you're going to replace the sensor yourself, tools and equipment and experience can affect installation time. Good luck!

Tom

Q Tom,
I have a 1988 Chevy C/K1500 pickup, 5.7-liter automatic. Recently the truck has been overheating. The air temperature was about -5° F this morning when I went to work (four miles away). Two miles into the trip, the truck overheated and the temperature gauge pegged close to "hot." I recently had the water pump and thermostat replaced; I am not losing any antifreeze. What problems could possibly cause the vehicle to overheat?

Thanks, Peter—Appleton, Maine

A Peter,
Have the cooling system pressure tested to make sure there are no leaks in the system. If none are found, then have a cylinder leak tested to determine if the engine has a blown head gasket or a cracked or warped cylinder head. For further verification, have a block check performed to see if there are hydrocarbons in the cooling system when the engine is running. During a block check test, the technician will take a sample of engine coolant and mix it with a special chemical that identifies if there are unburned gases in the coolant. Good luck!

Tom

Q Tom,
I have a 1990 Ford Ranger with a 2.3 engine. My heater blows lukewarm air. I installed a new thermostat, a new water pump, and a new radiator, and I am still getting lukewarm air!! Any help you can give me will be greatly appreciated.

Thanks, Dan—Madison, Wisconsin

A Dan,
Based on what you have done on the vehicle to this point, it would appear the problem might be traced to a plugged or restricted heater core. The heater core is a mini-radiator located in the passenger compartment that heats the air forced over it by the blower motor. The heater core could be compared to the steam radiators in an old house. Without a good flow of hot water through the core, there isn't enough heat to transfer to the air. Testing the core is as easy as feeling the heater hoses. If both hoses are good and hot (provided the cooling system is full), the core is probably OK. If one is hot and the other one is significantly cooler, it's likely the core is either restricted or plugged. Sometimes back flushing the core will remove the accumulated sediment, restoring proper flow. However, more often than not on the Ranger and Explorer models, the core will need to be replaced. Success to you.

Tom

Q Tom,
I am changing the water pump on my '99 Dodge Ram 1500 pickup (odometer: 95,000 miles). The hoses are fine. Should I change them anyway? One of them is tough to get to (must remove the AC compressor).

Chris—Phoenix, Arizona

A Chris,
I would change the hoses mainly because you can't see the degradation of the rubber compound. Also, you might as well change them since you are right there, rather than having to tear it down a second time when a hose does burst (this advice is based on personal experience).

Tom

Q Tom,
It is my understanding that coolant (anti-freeze) will corrode an aluminum block engine by an acid that is either in the coolant or becomes present over time in the cooling system. If I mixed baking soda with the coolant, would the soda reduce the acidic content of the coolant and slowdown the corrosion action?

Ray—Orchard Park, New York

A Ray,
You did not tell me the year, make, or model of the vehicle. Based on my vast knowledge of vehicles, I will assume you are referring to a GM vehicle using Dexcool coolant. Yes, when the system is allowed to go low over time and is left in too long, acid will build up. This results in corrosion of the aluminum or head gaskets.

The best way to thwart this action is to flush and refill the cooling system every two years or 24,000 miles (whichever comes first). Baking soda will have no effect on this condition. I would relegate the baking soda to your refrigerator to eliminate offensive odors or use it in the culinary baking arts.

Tom

Q Dear Tom,
I have a problem of my own making. I was trying to change the thermostat on my '97 Dodge Caravan, and I snapped the first bolt while trying to loosen it. About a half-inch of the bolt came off, but the other inch remained in the engine. I am a novice home mechanic and have never drilled out and re-tapped a threaded hole. I called a local shop for a price and they told me it would cost $78 an hour to do the job. He said it could take 15 minutes or 2 hours, which would be $156 in labor costs for a $1 bolt! I know the alternator will need to be loosened and moved (to get clearance to the right housing bolt hole). Can you give me some advice?

John—Springfield, Ohio

A John,
Make sure the area you are working on is clear of obstruction. *Any* component that is in the way should be cleared of the work area, alternators included. Next, make sure you center punch the broken bolt so you can drill in the center of the broken bolt. Use a drill that has variable speed control, and drill slowly and deliberately holding even, steady downward pressure on the drill. I suggest you get a titanium drill bit set and start with a small bit, working up one size at a time until you are one size away from drilling out the threads. Once you have gotten to this point, take a tap that fits the hole and thread size and start running the tap into the bolt hole. *Slowly* and *deliberately* turn a half turn, then back out and turn a little deeper, then back out, and so on. The tap will cut the old bolt out and find the original threads. Use lubricant and air (if available) to clear the hole of metal as you work. This job can be done if you take it slowly and meticulously.

Tom

PROJECT 13
Check Fluid Concentration

 Time Required: 5 minutes

 Tools Required: Tester

 Skill Level:

Cost Estimate: $10

Tip: Some coolant comes pre-mixed; read the label carefully.

1

When the engine is cold, remove the radiator cap. Squeeze the rubber bulb on the antifreeze tester. Insert the tube into the radiator filler neck and release the bulb.

2

Draw coolant out until it fills the plastic reservoir and read the indicator. It will show the freezing point of your coolant mixture. This point must be below the lowest temperatures experienced in your area. If the strength is too weak, add pure antifreeze coolant; if it's too strong, add distilled water. Then retest.

TIP

Recommended coolant replacement interval varies with manufacturer. The rule of thumb is two years or 25,000 miles (whichever comes first). Some vehicles use Dexcool coolant that allows for longer drain intervals. Keep a regular eye on Dexcool because it can go bad before its recommended drain interval (150,000 miles). In this case, open the system every two years or 25,000 miles just to make sure there's no rust and scale buildup. Other problems that crop up include worn water pumps, coolant leaks, and blown hoses. A regular cooling system inspection will head off these problems at the pass and save you money in the long run.

SECTION 2
RULES TO FOLLOW TO MAKE THAT CAR LAST FOREVER

INTRODUCTION TO CHAPTERS 10–14

Chapters 10–14 discuss certain maintenance practices in more detail, giving you the tools you need on your quest to make your car last forever. These expanded topics include a close look at lubrication, filtration, and healthy fluid characteristics. Also discussed is the importance of maintaining your car's body, both the interior and exterior. This section ends with a look at the most common summer and winter-related vehicle woes and what you can do to avoid them.

Chapter 10
Lubrication and Filtration — Another Key to Longevity

Lubrication is a major key to extending the life of your car. It's so important that you often hear it referred to as "cheap insurance." People have a lot of questions on this topic. What systems and parts of a car need lubricating? Car manuals outline normal service and severe service schedules. What is the difference between these two? How reliable are oil life monitor (OLM) systems and how do they work? What is oil viscosity? What do all the letters and symbols on an oil can mean? Why buy expensive oil filters? What's the best oil for a car, synthetic oil or conventional oil? These are great questions. Here are the answers.

The parts of your car that need lubricating are the engine, the transmission, transfer cases, differentials, the power steering system, and the cooling system (yes, really!).

SERVICE SCHEDULES
Manufacturers offer three service schedules for engine oil and filter changes, as well as for the maintenance of other systems in your vehicle: severe, normal, and OLM. How do they compare?

Severe Service Schedule as per GM
Follow the *severe* schedule if any one of the following are true:

* Most trips are less than 5 to 10 miles (8 to 16 kilometers). This is particularly important when outside temperatures are below freezing.
* Most trips include extensive idling (such as frequent driving in stop-and-go traffic).
* The vehicle is operated in dusty areas frequently.
* The vehicle tows a trailer or uses a car-top carrier frequently.
* The vehicle is used for delivery service, police, taxi, or other commercial applications.

Many GM vehicles have an "Engine Oil Life Monitor" lamp that can illuminate any time between intervals depending on driving conditions. The oil should be replaced at that time, regardless of mileage, and the oil life monitor" reset.

Normal Service Schedule as per GM
Follow the *normal* schedule only if none of the conditions from the *severe* schedule apply.

Again, many GM vehicles have the Engine Oil Life Monitor. It can illuminate anytime between intervals depending on driving conditions. When it does, replace the oil, regardless of mileage, and reset the monitor.

Other carmakers vary on their recommendations for severe or normal service schedules. Ford, for instance, suggests that you change the oil more frequently if the vehicle operates in dusty environments, tows a trailer, or uses E-85 fuel more than 50 percent of the time. Overall, the burden is on you to check your owner's manual for suggested service intervals based on your driving experience.

OIL LIFE MONITOR
OLM systems monitor crankcase temperature, combustion chamber events (the work the engine does), and the time since the last oil change in order to come up with an approximate percentage of usable life left in the engine oil. Computer algorithm specifics for these systems vary from carmaker to carmaker. However, overall they are accurate in determining the amount of serviceable life left in the engine oil. The key is to make sure you use the recommended oil the carmaker specifies and to reset the monitor every time you have an oil change. Otherwise the system will be thrown off because it's not intuitive.

GM's Oil Life Monitor (OLM) is a very accurate system. The caveat is to make sure every time you change the oil you reset the system, or it will inaccurately report oil condition. There are other oil life monitoring systems out there, and they need to be reset after each oil change too. Make sure you use the oil the carmaker recommends or the system will be inaccurate as well.

Opposite page photo credit: Shutterstock

OIL VISCOSITY

Viscosity is defined as the rate of flow of the oil or lubricant. Most carmakers use multi-viscosity oil, which adjusts its rate of flow based on outside temps and internal engine temperatures. Always use the recommended viscosity oil for your vehicle. For instance, on many of their engines Ford recommends the use of 5W-20 semi-synthetic motor oil. Why? Because of tight internal engine tolerances and elevated combustion chamber temperatures designed to achieve lower tailpipe emissions. If you use anything else in the engine and it fails, then Ford will deny warranty claims. I have seen this happen time and again. Follow recommendations so your warranty stays intact.

Carmakers specify types and viscosities of oil for their engines. For example, GM uses Mobil One Synthetic in its Corvette engines. Whatever the carmaker suggests, use it! Both the carmakers and the oil companies have done significant lab testing to determine exactly what type of oil to use in their powerplants.

TIP

When you buy oil (or have it changed), make sure you pick the right API rating for your engine. Also ask for the SAE viscosity recommended in your owner's manual. Car manufacturers recommend multi-viscosity grades, which are suitable for use over a wide temperature range. Automobile manufacturers specify the proper SAE viscosity rating in your owner's manual. Multi-viscosity oils provide excellent protection in virtually all parts of the United States. SAE viscosity rating becomes especially important when you take into consideration the vehicle's warranty. You don't want to use the wrong oil and void the warranty.

ENGINE OIL FILTRATION

Don't be skimpy when it comes to buying an oil filter. Always use a high-quality oil filter when changing your oil. Cheap filters are made of poor quality filter media that doesn't screen out harmful and abrasive dirt from the oil. This dirt courses through your engine and causes damage. Cheap filters usually omit critical aspects of OEM filter design like check valves, which are used to prevent oil from draining out of the filter when the engine is not running. When the oil is allowed to drain out of the filter, the engine loses its prime, which results in dry startup. This condition damages bearings and metal mating surfaces, causing engine failure over time. Always select a high-quality OEM comparable oil filter when you change the oil.

COMPARISON OF SYNTHETIC OILS AND CONVENTIONAL PETROLEUM OILS

Many people want to know what type of oil they should use in their cars, synthetic or conventional. The information in this book about the differences between the two types of oil and their applications was gleaned from Dan Watson, a friend and colleague. Watson is a certified lubrication specialist (STLE) and a retired lieutenant commander in the U.S. Navy, as well as a nuclear propulsion specialist. In addition, he is a lubrication consultant and the owner of D&J Diversified, LLC, a lubrication sales and consulting firm. Watson is also the owner and publisher of *maxxTorque* magazine www.maxxtorque.com. His website on lubricants is www.thelubepage.com.

Watson's article "Synthetic Versus Petroleum" discusses the differences between synthetic and conventional diesel lubricants (this information also applies to gas engine lubricants). The article appears in the maxxtorque.com E-zine, winter 2009 issue, volume II, number 1, page 15. His evaluation of the topic is thorough. Here are some excerpts from this article for you to consider when deciding whether or not to use synthetic oil. The argument for synthetic-based lubricants is compelling to say the least. If you're considering the switch over, consult your owner's manual to make sure your carmaker does not recommend against the use of synthetic oil, then consult a professional to make sure it's the best choice for you.

A note here regarding turbocharged engines: Engines equipped with turbochargers benefit greatly from using synthetic motor oil because turbos, being driven by exhaust, tend to heat up dramatically and tend to burn engine oil resulting in viscosity breakdown. Synthetic motor oil is highly resistant to heat and friction, thus maintains lubrication and protection to the turbocharger.

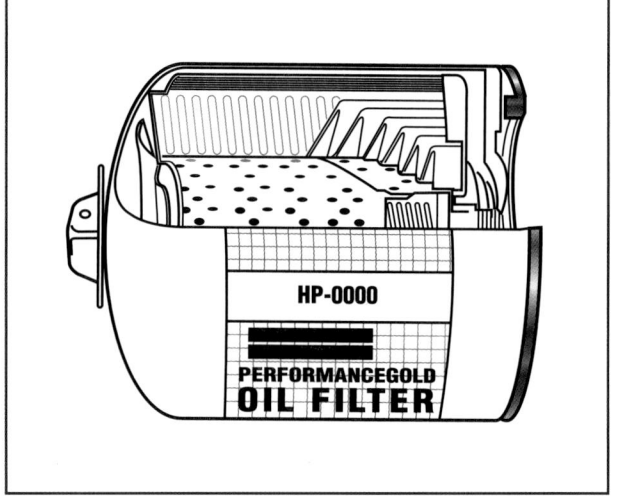

A cheap oil filter on an engine can result in engine damage. Today, carmakers build into their oil filters check valves to ensure the oil stays in the engine overnight and doesn't drain out, leaving the engine dry during cold starts. In addition, high-grade filter media is used to make sure the tiniest speck of dirt is filtered out, thus protecting the engine. Installing a cheap knockoff filter puts your powerplant in danger.

Reading the encryption on an oil can can be like deciphering Egyptian hieroglyphs if you don't know what you're reading. Its best to go to your owner's manual. If you don't have one, call your dealer service department. It's especially important to use the correct oil in today's engines because of tight internal tolerances and high operating temperatures. Using the wrong engine oil can result in engine failure.

UNDERSTANDING THE DESCRIPTION ON AN OIL CAN

Q *What do the letters and symbols mean on the bottle, such as API, SJ, CF, CG-4? Or SAE 5W30?*

A **API** stands for the American Petroleum Institute, which provides the standards that high quality oils must meet.

SL means it's for all automotive engines currently in production. SL oils are designed to provide better "high-temperature deposit control" and lower oil consumption.

SJ means it's for 2001 and older automotive engines.

SM oils are designed to provide improved oxidation resistance, improved deposit protection, better wear protection, and better low-temperature performance over the life of the oil.

CF was adopted in 1994 for use in indirect injected off-road diesel engines that use a broad range of fuels, including those with high sulfur content. It offers effective control of piston deposits, wear, and corrosion of the copper-coated bearings used in this type of engine.

CF-2 is formulated for use in two-stroke diesel engines requiring highly effective control over cylinder and ring-face scuffing and deposits.

CF-4 covers oils for use in high-speed, four-stroke diesel engines. They are designed for use in on-highway heavy-duty truck applications.

CG-4 describes oils for use in high-speed, four-stroke diesel engines, and is suitable for both highway and off-road applications. They provide effective control of high-temperature piston deposits, wear, corrosion, foaming, and oxidation stability and soot accumulation.

These oils are especially effective in engines required to meet 1994 emission standards.

CH-4 is for use in high-speed four-stroke engines designed to meet 1998 exhaust emission standards. CH-4 oils are specifically compounded for use with diesel fuels ranging in sulfur content up to 0.5 percent weight. It can be used in place of CD, CE, CF-4, and CG-4 oils.

CJ-4 is for 2007 and newer diesel engines. It was developed to address special concerns regarding emission control engines and their operation on ultra-low-sulfur diesel fuel (ULSD).

SAE stands for Society of Automotive Engineers. Motor oils have SAE grades, or numbers, that indicate viscosity. In other words, the SAE numbers tell you the thickness of the oil. The higher the number, the thicker the oil.

Q *What does a viscosity rating of 5W30 mean?*

A **W** signifies its winter rating, showing that it will perform well in cold weather. The number and letter designation signifies the winter flow weight of the oil. Colder temperatures tend to thicken oil so that it flows more slowly, which can be disastrous to your car's engine. Therefore, in mixing the oil, the refinery adds a chemical (or package) that adjusts and stabilizes the oil at the lighter weight when it gets cold outside. Consequently, it will flow more easily and freely at subzero temperatures. The higher number at the end of the viscosity rating represents the weight the oil adjusts to at higher temperatures. High temperature tends to break oil down and affects its lubricating ability. Therefore, the refinery adds a chemical package that toughens the oil to stand up and maintain enough body in order to perform its job at high operating temperatures.

SYNTHETIC VERSUS PETROLEUM

Any oil properly rated for use in a high-performance turbo-charged engine is a remarkable lubricant regardless of the base oil used in the finished oil. In this article, I will compare synthetic engine oil to petroleum engine oil, draw some conclusions, and make some recommendations. To start, we should compare several performance criteria for synthetic versus petroleum oils.

Thermal stability: How well does the oil hold viscosity as temperature increases? This is reflected in the Viscosity Index (VI) rating illustrated in chart one. Oils that maintain rated viscosity instead of thinning out at higher temperatures are better oils. Thin oil will reduce film strength and result in higher wear rates of critical engine parts.

Advantage: Strong for synthetics

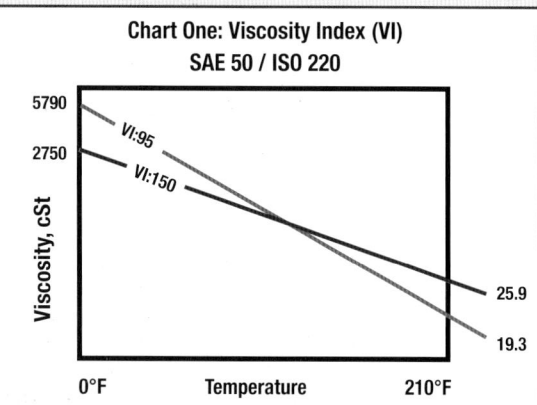

Chart One: Viscosity Index (VI)
SAE 50 / ISO 220

Higher viscosity index (VI) liquids are less responsive to temperature extremes. At 0°F, the VI 95 petroleum oil is thicker (measured in centistokes, a dynamic measure of resistance-to-flow) than the synthetic oil with a VI of 150. On the hot side at 210°F, the VI 150 synthetic maintains viscosity better than the VI 95 petroleum oil that thins out more easily.

Temperature range: What are the highest and lowest temperatures the oil can tolerate and provide proper lubrication, for both continuous and intermittent duty? This range is established by measuring the pour point (lowest temperature the oil will pour) and the highest temp the oil can hold sufficient viscosity to lubricate. Chart Two demonstrates the superior performance of synthetic oils over petroleum oils. A strong temperature range is paramount to providing proper lubrication, especially in severe duty or extreme temperatures.

Advantage: Very strong for synthetics

Oxidation stability: How well does the oil resist oxidation and sludge formation? As oil oxidizes, it thickens and deposits sludge in the engine. Sludge may eventually clog critical oil passageways preventing necessary oil reaching vital engine parts. This causes excessive wear and eventually failure of various engine parts. Synthetics simply do not react with oxygen. Petroleum oils readily react with oxygen. To counter this reactivity petroleum oils are treated with anti-oxidation additives. When oils are operating in the intermittent temperature range (higher than normal) they are susceptible to higher rates of oxidation and thus, sludge buildup. Unfortunately, today's engines are forcing oils to operate at 230 to 250 ° F routinely. This puts petroleum oils in a range of temperatures that causes increased use of the anti-oxidants in the additive package and shortens the life of the oil. Synthetic oils are in the normal operating band for temperatures in excess of 330 ° F and

suffer little or no oxidation at all. This is one of the reasons you hear of technicians reporting how clean engines that use synthetics are even with high mileage.

Advantage: Very strong for synthetics

Volatility: How easily does the oil vaporize or boil off? When oils are hot, vaporization can result in significant oil consumption and thickening of the oil. Not only is this a problem for oil consumption, but also results in increased tailpipe emissions. Because of the chemical makeup of synthetic motor oils, they are much sturdier and more durable than petroleum oil in the hot engine environment; consequently, they resist vaporization or boil-off from high operating temperatures much better than petroleum oils.

Advantage: Strong for synthetics

Seals: How are seals affected? Will the oil cause them to shrink or to swell? And is the oil chemically compatible with them? Seals are made of a variety of compounds to provide rigid but flexible surfaces that promote good sealing in order to keep liquids in and dirt out. Petroleum oils are fully compatible with the seal materials used in modern engines and will slightly swell the seals. Some synthetic oils tend to shrink seals, therefore causing minor oil leakage. Historically, seal compatibility issues have caused real and imaginary problems for synthetic oils in the market place. Currently, seal issues for properly blended synthetic oils are no longer an issue.

Advantage: Slight for petroleum

Lubrication/wear protection: How well does the oil lubricate and prevent wear? The chemical makeup of synthetics results in a superior lubricating film. Additionally, the thermal stability of synthetic oils maintains a protective oil film in much more severe conditions and at higher temperatures than petroleum. In standard anti-wear testing such as the Shell four-ball wear test, some synthetics achieve up to four times the wear protection when compared to petroleum oils. When higher temperatures and pressures are used in such tests, the results significantly favor synthetic oils.

Under Normal Conditions
Advantage: Slight for synthetics

Under Severe Conditions
Advantage: Very strongly synthetics

Oil life/endurance: How long can the oil provide proper lubrication and perform all required functions? Oil life is a function of time and severity of service and can vary from vehicle to vehicle. Oil is said to be *condemned*, that is, not fit for continued service, when one or more of the following conditions exist:

* Viscosity has decreased by one grade or increased by *more* than one grade
* Fuel contamination is greater than 3 percent
* Soot level exceeds 4 percent

- Total dissolved solids are greater than 4 percent
- Total base number is less than two
- Critical additives are depleted
- Oxidation number greater than 50 (30 for petroleum)
- Nitration number less than 50 (30 for petroleum)

As explained above, synthetic oils are less likely to thicken as the result of vaporization or oxidation and stay in proper viscosity grade for significantly longer periods of service. Several of the other factors for condemnation are the same for either synthetic or petroleum oils and are more dependent on the quality and concentration of chemical additives to continue to provide service. Soot and total dissolved solids are products of engine combustion and are proportional to fuel air management; turbo-charged engines tend to burn cleaner than naturally aspirated engines. Filtration will have direct effects on soot and dissolved particles and can be effective at increasing oil life. Since lubricating oils are products of base oils mixed with chemical additives it becomes painfully obvious that the failure of the base oil or the depletion of additives will result in condemnation of the oil. Simply put, oils are unique when compared to each other; even if two synthetics are compared, the choice of synthetic base oil and the quality and amount of the additives can produce widely varying finished products.

Oil life is best determined utilizing *used oil analysis* and then evaluating the remaining oil life based upon the results of a given analysis. Some oil companies, like *Mobil* and *AMSOIL* have amassed significant data through oil analysis that enables them to make categorical recommendations for longer drain intervals. It is improper to assume that because you are using synthetic oil it automatically has an extended drain interval. Some major oil companies (*Valvoline* is one) are on record as saying that their synthetic oil has the same additive package as their petroleum; so, the additives in their synthetic oils deplete just as quickly as their petroleum oils.

Advantage: Synthetics (varies between synthetic manufacturers)

Cost: What is the real cost to use synthetic oil compared to petroleum? To correctly assess cost it is necessary to differentiate between *price* and *cost*. What you pay for an item is the price; how the price is distributed with respect to product utilization over time is cost. For example, if you pay $160 for an 80,000-mile radial tire, then that is how much you pay to purchase the tire. To determine the cost, you have to distribute the $160 over the 80,000 miles; this determines the *cost per mile* to use the tire. This method allows the direct comparison of products that are priced differently, but that have variable life expectancy. Calculating cost is a mixed bag when comparing synthetic and petroleum oils. Not all synthetic oils are designed for extended oil drains and some petroleum oils will perform much better than others. Comparisons are best done on a case-by-case basis. In general, most any synthetic will run longer between oil drains; however, only a select few are designed for very long drain intervals. For the synthetic oil to be equal or less costly, it must have approximately three times the drain interval of a given petroleum oil. There are other, indirect cost benefits to synthetic oils, including improved fuel economy and superior lubrication that results in less maintenance. One unheralded feature of synthetic oil is *insurance*: by that I mean protection from unexpected calamities. The blowing of a radiator hose, the loss of oil or water pump failure, in most cases, may result in engine damage from excessively high temperatures. When good quality synthetics are used, engine damage is highly unlikely. This *insurance* can mean saving thousands of dollars on costly engine repairs.

ADVANTAGE: SYNTHETIC

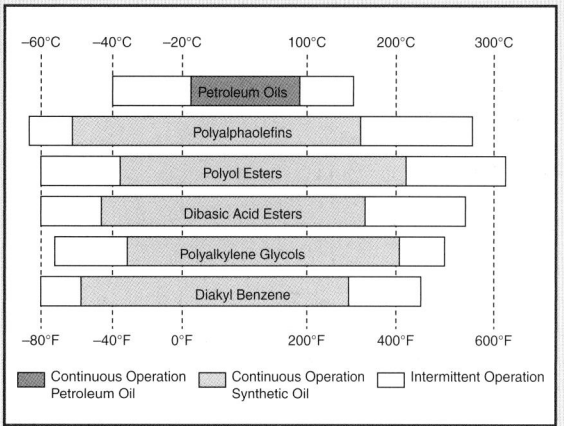

In summary, comparing the features of synthetic oils versus petroleum oils is an exercise that all lubrication professionals enjoy, but what is the bottom line for the consumer and what action should you take? Clearly, synthetics win in head-to-head features and benefits and they also provide intangibles such as *insurance*, but should every owner switch? The answer is "no." If you own an older vehicle with more than 100,000 miles, you should *not* switch unless you have an experienced professional to guide you through the process. If you have a vehicle with leaks that you cannot fix, then it makes no sense to pour the higher priced synthetic oil on the ground. If for some reason, your engine is consuming oil at an alarming rate, again, it is not cost-effective to use synthetic oil. On the other hand, synthetic oils are superior in performance; the right synthetic is more cost effective than petroleum so there is little reason not to switch. The high temperatures (600°F) possible in the turbo-charger make good quality synthetic oils clearly the best choice; one failed turbo buys a lot of synthetic oil. If you are towing or otherwise involved in severe duty operations, then synthetics offers so many superior benefits and enhanced protection, it is the only right choice. Using petroleum rather than synthetic oil is an option analogous to using bias ply tires instead of radial tires. Of course the bias ply tire can get you from point A to point B. The difference is in the load-carrying capacities, heat range, traction, handling, and tread life. For simple casual driving with no severe conditions the bias ply tire is fine, but in the event of something outside normal conditions, the radial is superior; it is simply a matter of the quality of each tire's construction.

The decision, whether to use synthetic oil or petroleum oil, is dependent on your unique situation; each of us has his own set of circumstances to assess in order to make a decision based on facts. Understanding the benefits and limitations of engine oil will help you make an informed choice. Making sense of the relationships between oil properties and how those properties protect and preserve an engine is the only real way to analyze true cost effectiveness. Sometimes the decision is obvious; severe duty situations call for synthetic oils. Critical components subject to high temperatures like the turbo-charger are best protected by synthetics. I recommend synthetic engine oils in order to provide the most cost effective method to achieve the best lubrication possible for your engine.

Thanks Dan.

You can contact Dan Watson with any lubrication questions you have at dan@maxxtorque.com or danwatson@thelubepage.com

TRANSMISSION LUBRICATION
Automatic Transmissions

Just like the oil in your car's engine, the transmission oil (or fluid as it is known) is subject to degradation from heat, friction, and dirt. Over time, degraded transmission fluid can cause the transmission to fail. According to the Automatic Transmission Rebuilder's Association (ATRA), close to nine out of ten transmission failures are caused by overheating and fluid contamination.

Automatic transmissions require regular maintenance according to the Transmission Rebuilder's Network International. The rule of thumb is to replace the fluid and filter every 30,000 miles or once annually, whichever comes first. A complete transmission transfusion is usually recommended.

This procedure exchanges all of the old fluid for new. There is one caveat here. On vehicles with a poor transmission service history, seek the advice of a professional before doing a complete fluid exchange. There are many documented cases where a complete transfusion on transmissions with a poor service history caused the transmissions to fail.

A poor transmission history means that the fluid is burnt (evident of overheating) or that the fluid has been in the unit over 80,000 miles. Why do they fail? If the unit has overheated, the glue on the back of internal clutches is probably crystallized. When the unit is soaked in a bath of fresh high-detergency transmission fluid, the crystallized glue is scrubbed clean, rendering the clutches (and thus the transmission) useless. On units with high mileage,

---

DRIVERS ASK, TOM ANSWERS: LUBRICATION PROBLEMS SOLVED

Q Dear Tom,
I own an '05 Honda Pilot. The manufacturer recently recommended changing the oil at 7,500 miles. What do you think? I did not follow this recommendation because I thought the manual said to change the oil at 15,000 miles. However, at about 13,000 miles the vehicle started making a heavy groaning sound (coming from the rear). It only happened when I try to move out of a parking spot at an angle. I took it to the dealer, and they changed the differential oil and the problem is now gone! It's hard to believe! What do you think?

Sydney—New York City

A Sydney,
I believe it. Gear oil is critical to the proper operation of lock up and limited slip differentials. When it wears out (gets contaminated with wear material or gets overheated and breaks down), differential operation will be hampered. Quite often carmakers will go to petroleum companies to engineer a fix in their fluid for a drivability problem with transmissions, gearboxes, transfer cases, or differentials.

Tom

Q Dear Tom,
I own a 2001 Toyota Camry, and I change the oil every 3,000 miles. If I use synthetic oil, do I need to replace the oil filter every change or every other change?

Dave—District Heights, Ohio

A Dave,
I'll never understand why people ask this question. Are you trying to save money? If this is the case, then consider the following information, and then answer the question yourself. The oil filter is the storehouse for dirt in the engine. Dirt, sludge, soot, and the likes produced in the crankcase environment are filtered out of the oil and trapped in the filter. This dirt stays in the filter until it is replaced. Why leave a dirty filter for another 3,000 miles? Why not remove it and restore a clean operating environment for the engine? This will ensure longevity, proper oil pressure, reduced internal wear, and reduced friction and heat, and thus increase the function and life of the engine.

So, in case you did not get what I am saying here: *Change the oil filter every time you change the oil. It's cheap engine insurance!*

Tom

Q Tom,
I have used synthetic oil in my '05 Silverado from my third oil change until my last oil change recently. I want to switch back to conventional oil at this time. Will I have any problems with this move? The truck has about 83,000 miles.

Jim—Dallas

A Jim,
No, there will be no problem with switching back to conventional oil (same viscosity as you are using). Just go to regular oil change intervals every 3,000 to 5,000 miles, depending on how hard you work the truck. Check your owner's manual for severe and normal service recommendations and follow that as a guide for oil change intervals because it is based on using conventional oil.

Tom

Q Hello Tom,
My wife purchased a BMW 335i in November of 2009. She pays close attention to the monitor, and it called for an oil change after 17,000 miles. There is no oil dipstick. What are your thoughts on a 17,000-mile drain interval? Thanks.

Leon—Phoenix, Arizona

A Leon,
High-performance 5W20 synthetic motor oil as specified by BMW is used in this engine. The oil life monitor measures engine operating environment with a computer algorithm to accurately calculate serviceable engine oil life. So, in answer to your question, since you're using synthetic oil specified by BMW and following the oil life monitor dictates, I have no problem with this drain interval

Tom

Q Dear Tom,
I own a 2000 Lexus ES 300 Platinum Series. I purchased the auto three and a half years ago, and it had only 4,400 miles on it. An elderly man who owned the car was the original owner. I now have nearly 39,000 miles on the car and it appears to be running fine (the Lexus dealership has never indicated any problem). However, I wonder if there might have been sludge buildup when the car sat idle during its previous ownership and, if so, could this cause trouble later on? Would it be evident by now?

Sandra—Hollywood, California

it's probably best to change just the filter and the fluid in the pan.

What fluid should you use? Because of the many specified fluid offerings for the numerous applications out there, the best advice here is to either consult your dealership service department or a qualified shop that has access to manufacturer's fluid specifications before adding transmission fluid. The same goes for any component in your car. Often carmakers will address a specific mechanical problem or performance idiosyncrasy of a component by coming up with a new fluid or lubricant to solve the problem, so it's better to be safe than sorry before adding fluid. Always consult your owner's manual, service department, or service professional before topping off of filling a fluid.

A Sandra,
Sludge buildup is not a result of a car "sitting." Sludge will build up when oil is left in the crankcase for extended periods of time and the vehicle is operated without changing the oil according to manufacturer's specs. Excessive heat from friction (which is caused by oil that has lost its lubricating property) causes oxidation; the combination of oxidation and excessive heat causes sludge, an oily cake-like substance that soaks up oil and causes lack of lubrication. Keep the oil changed according to manufacturer's specs and you should not have a problem.

On a side note, Toyota did have a sludging issue with its engines due to restricted cooling system passages on these cars, and so did many other models from this time frame. The use of restricted cooling system passages was in response to meet stringent EPA tailpipe emissions standards. Restricted cooling system passages increased engine-operating temperatures and resulted in engine oil sludging. Toyota extended the warranty on these engines.

So keep a watchful eye on the engine oil. If you observe excessive oil consumption, then contact your dealer. They will replace the engine under the extended warranty action from Toyota. I wish you success.

Tom

Q Dear Tom,
I own a '98 Honda Accord V-6. Every time I get the oil changed, I'm told that an oversized drain plug is needed (and that's okay, because it's relatively inexpensive). However, I'm also told that a new oil pan would be a good idea, and they are really expensive (about $300 to $400)! Seems to me that there ought to be an easier fix than a new oil pan. Got any ideas?
Samantha—Long Beach, California

A Samantha,
The reason for the oversized drain plug is because the OEM threads in your oil pan have been stripped. This happened as a result of someone cross threading the drain plug back into the pan and forcing it against the resistance of the threads. Oh well, that's water over the dam; however, I suggest you go to a different place for oil changes. There is no way around this problem except to replace the oil pan or use an over-sized self-tapping drain plug. If a good quality plug is used, this is an acceptable solution to the problem. Best to you.

Tom

COST COMPARISON: PETROLEUM VERSUS SYNTHETIC CHEVY/GMC DURAMAX (24,000 MILES)

Petroleum Oil

4,000-Mile Changes		(6x)
Ten quarts @ $3.75 each	$37.50	$225
Pleated paper oil filter	$15	$90
TOTAL FOR MATERIALS:	$52.50	$315
TOTAL FOR LABOR:	$20	$120
ANNUAL TOTAL FOR OIL CHANGES:		$435

Synthetic Oil

24,000-Mile Changes (Extended Drain)		
Twelve quarts @ $8.75 each	$105	$225
Pleated paper oil filter	$19	$90
TOTAL FOR MATERIALS:	$124	$315
TOTAL FOR LABOR:	$20	$120
ANNUAL TOTAL FOR OIL CHANGES:	$144	$435

*Two quarts added for make-up oil

FUEL ECONOMY COMPARISON (24,000 MILES)

Petroleum Oil

1,600 Gallons @ $3 per gallon - $4,800 in annual fuel charges
Based on Fuel Economy of 15 mpg

Synthetic Oil

1,520 Gallons @ $3 per gallon - $4,560 in annual fuel charges
Based on Fuel Economy of 15.79 mpg
(five percent average improvement)

AVERAGE ANNUAL FUEL SAVINGS USING SYNTHETIC OIL: $240

Standard Transmissions

Standard transmissions are not quite as touchy as the automatics. However, it's a good idea to have them checked every oil change. Standard transmissions use one of three lubricants: ATF (automatic transmission fluid), 30W motor oil, or gear oil.

When you do a fluid check, you are not only checking the fluid level, but you are examining the fluid for the presence of moisture (which turns the fluid milky) and the presence of wear particles. A small amount of wear material is acceptable, but excessive wear material can indicate a problem. The maintenance interval for transmissions that use ATF and 30W motor oil is every 50,000 miles. For gear oil the recommended interval is 80,000 miles. Once again, follow the carmaker's maintenance schedule because some can and do vary.

TRANSFER CASES ON 4 × 4s

All 4 × 4s have a transfer case. The maintenance of the transfer case is the same as the standard transmission, unless otherwise specified by the carmaker. Determine what fluid is in the transfer case and service it according to factory recommendations. Transfer case maintenance is critical to its long and reliable life. This maintenance involves changing the fluid at regular intervals unlike the units of old, which could go for years upon years with the same gear lube in them. Carmakers use specially formulated synthetic fluids to ensure optimum performance, longevity and reliable operation of these units.

DIFFERENTIALS

Besides 4 × 4s, cars with rear-wheel drive and all-wheel drive have differentials as part of the drivetrain system. There's not a whole lot to do to these except check the fluid level at every oil change. The technician should check the gear lubricant for proper level, color, and consistency. Low lubricant level indicates a leak, a milky color indicates moisture in the lubricant, and the presence of metal in the lubricant indicates mechanical wear. Check your owner's manual for the recommended fluid change intervals.

POWER STEERING SYSTEMS

Power steering uses hydraulic power-assist to ease the effort of steering the car. A power steering pump that uses hydraulic fluid pushes the fluid under pressure through the system to the steering gear, making it easier to steer your vehicle. The fluid in this system is a lot like transmission fluid. It's a hydraulic fluid that is subject to heat, friction, heat expansion, and cold contraction. Over time it loses its viscosity (ability to flow). You must perform periodic checks to determine its health. If the fluid smells burnt, or appears to be brown or black in color, or has metal flakes in it, it must be replaced. These fluid conditions will destroy the power steering system in short order.

COOLING SYSTEMS

The coolants used in cooling systems contain lubricants. Engine coolant (in addition to absorbing heat from the engine and offering cold weather protection) has a lubricating property to keep water pumps lubricated and to slow down the process of rust and scale buildup. Over time the lubrication property of the coolant is diminished, as are the rest of the chemical properties. As a result, friction increases heat, and more rust and scale forms. These wear factors cause water pump failure and degradation of the cooling system. That's why manufacturers recommend cooling system flushes and refills every two years or 24,000 miles. Intervals may vary depending on what type of coolant is used.

Remember to check the service schedule for your particular car to determine if you fall into the normal or the severe schedule for each system of your vehicle.

PROJECT 14
Change Air Filter

 Time Required: 5-15 minutes

 Tools Required: None, screwdriver or small wrench, depending on style

 Skill Level:

 Cost Estimate: $10–$15

 Tip: Check your air intake for obstructions such as leaves, particularly with the type that open to the grille.

1

Older air filters, as on this 1994 Dodge Dakota, typically reside in a round housing on top of the engine. Loosen the wing nut to open. Tip: Check your owner's manual for service intervals (period of replacement) for your air cleaner and other maintenance items. If you use your vehicle in dirty settings, such as dirt roads or off-roading, check and replace the filter more often.

2

Lift off the metal lid.

3

Remove the filter element. This one is plenty dirty. Dirty filters reduce engine efficiency. Carefully wipe any dirt or debris from the air cleaner housing before replacing the filter element.

4

Newer vehicles typically have an air box, like this one, off to one side of the engine bay. You access the filter element by loosening a screw on a hose clamp or undoing a series of clips. The air filter then lifts out. Again, make sure the housing is clean before installing the new filter element. Note the orientation of the old filter and insert the new in the same direction.

Chapter 11
Reading the "Tea Leaves" of Fluids

Nothing can tell you more about the health of the human body better than a fluid analysis. If there is a health problem, blood and urine samples will identify it. The body's fluids also indicate if there is an underlying ongoing condition that will eventually cause poor health. The same is true for vehicles. The analysis of engine oil, transmission fluid, power steering fluid, and other fluids reveals the condition of the various systems. So what should we look for in vehicular fluids to determine the health of your car?

The most common fluids in a vehicle include the following:

- Engine oil
- Engine coolant
- Automatic transmission fluid
- Power steering fluid
- Brake fluid
- Manual transmission fluid
- Differential lubricant
- Transfer case lubricant

What do these fluids tell us?

ENGINE OIL

The engine oil is the lifeblood of the engine; it must deal with harsh factors in its environment, including friction, intense heat, and contaminants.

Friction: Hundreds of moving metal parts rub against each other in your engine, causing friction. Friction produces intense heat and pressure, which would destroy the engine in a short time. Engine oil provides a lubricating film between the tight-tolerance moving parts of the engine to decrease friction and its negative effects.

Intense heat: In water-cooled or air-cooled engines, approximately 60 percent of the cooling is achieved by water or air; the oil performs the rest of the cooling function. As the oil circulates rapidly through the engine at 50 to 70 pounds per square inch of pressure, it carries heat away from the camshaft, rods, pistons, and valvetrain. The oil then circulates in the lower structure of the engine, where it is mixed with cooler oil. This oil is cooled by air passing over the crankcase (also known as the oil pan).

Contaminants: Contaminants can build up in your vehicle's engine in the form of soot, ash, acid, and moisture. These substances form sludge, varnish, and resins that become baked onto engine parts and interfere with performance and oil flow. A detergent is built into the motor oil in your vehicle's engine that disperses the dirt, keeping it suspended in the oil until it's filtered out (or drained away when you change the oil).

Besides dealing with harsh environmental conditions to maintain proper lubrication of the moving parts, the engine oil performs another vital function: the prevention of a condition called "blowby," which causes the engine to

 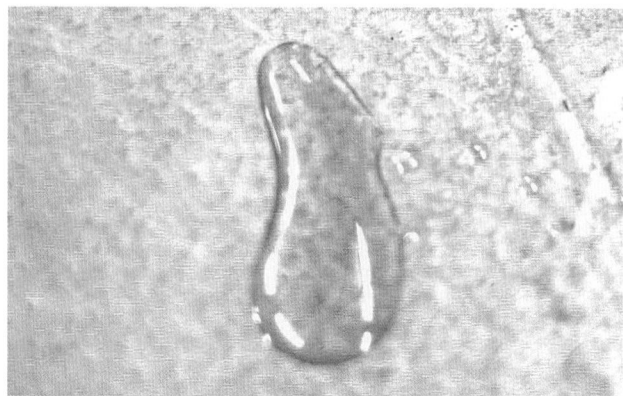

Note the color of the engine oil on the left is black and dirty. I guarantee if you smell it, it will smell burnt. This is what happens to oil when it is overheated. It becomes black and loses its ability to cool and lubricate the engine. The oil on the right indicates a healthy engine. The oil is caramel colored, clean, and translucent. If you were to smell it, it would give off fresh, petroleum-like smell.

lose power. To the naked eye, the piston rings and cylinder walls of the engine appear perfectly smooth, but they aren't. Under microscopic examination, a large number of "hills and valleys" appear. These impressions provide an escape route for vapor and gases during the compression and power stroke of the engine. When this occurs, it is called blowby. Engine oil seals these gaps and prevents this condition so that the engine can run at maximum power.

In summary, the demands made on the oil are draining (no pun intended). The oil eventually loses its ability to lubricate, clean, and flow freely. Each function is extremely important to the performance and life of the engine.

There are three characteristics to evaluate when checking automotive fluids: color, consistency, and smell.

Color

Healthy oil is caramel colored and translucent, indicating that there is little dirt in the oil and that it has not been overheated. A dark brown or black color indicates the presence of dirt or overheating of the engine. Intense heat actually boils the oil and destroys its chemical fortifiers. As a result, the oil loses its viscosity (ability to flow and adjust rate of flow to temperature change), its lubricity, its ability to protect against chemical contamination, its ability to absorb heat, and its rust-inhibiting quality. This puts the engine at risk for premature engine damage. Upon inspection, if the oil is a milky color it means there is moisture in the oil. It got into the oil through the cooling system or from the outside. In either case, you must find the source and do the required repair immediately before major engine damage occurs.

Consistency

The engine oil should be smooth and slippery to the touch. If it's gritty and doesn't feel slippery, change it because it's dirty or viscosity breakdown has occurred, rendering the oil ineffective in lubricating and protecting your engine. The presence of metal or plastic (some engine parts are made of plastic) in the oil means that there's internal engine wear that needs to be dealt with.

Smell

If the engine oil smells burnt, it should be changed. This indicates that the engine was overheated. Leaving burnt oil in the engine causes engine damage due to inadequate lubrication and heat transfer. A great way to determine internal engine condition is to have an oil analysis done; this is much like having a doctor analyze your body fluids. In such an analysis a vial of engine oil is taken from your engine during an oil change. It is then sent to an oil analysis lab for an evaluation of its contents. A lab can tell if there's excessive wear material, engine coolant, acid, or anything else that would be detrimental to your engine in the oil alerting you of potential problems. One oil analysis lab that comes to mind is Blackstone. There are others, just ask your car dealership or repair facility who they use.

ENGINE COOLANT

The engine coolant ensures that the engine operates at safe temperature levels. The 50-50 mix of coolant and water creates a fluid that protects against freezing in cold weather, lubricates the water pump, keeps rust and oxidation at bay, and absorbs heat from the engine. This heat is carried to the radiator where it is released. If coolant is left in the engine too long, it no longer performs these vital functions. What should you look for when checking your vehicle's engine coolant? Color, consistency, and smell.

Color

The color of healthy engine coolant is green (for ethylene glycol) or orange (for Dexcool). A rusty color indicates that the rust inhibitor in the coolant has broken down and it can no longer control rust and scale buildup. The system must be cleaned and flushed and a fresh 50-50 mix of coolant installed

This is a coolant reservoir containing Dexcool. Dexcool is orange. If the coolant is dark orange or rust, it needs to be replaced. A dark rust color indicates that the coolant has lost its ability to protect against rust, and oxidation and rust have taken over. This happens when the coolant loses its ability to lubricate and protect the cooling system. This color indicates that the system is now internally rusty and scale buildup is accelerating. The system should be tested for integrity, then flushed and filled with a fresh 50-50 mix of coolant. I recommend replacing the thermostat as well because the system probably overheated.

to restore integrity. A milky color indicates the presence of oil in the system. This is not good; it usually means that a head gasket, intake manifold, or transmission oil cooler is leaking oil or transmission fluid into the engine coolant. This is a deadly mix that will kill an engine or transmission in short order. Get it taken care of immediately.

Consistency

The engine coolant should feel slippery to the touch and smooth (like the engine oil). If it feels gritty, the coolant is dirty and should be flushed and replaced with a fresh 50-50 mix. If it's lost its lubricity (not slippery), then the lubricating and rust inhibitor agents are gone and the system is at risk for rust and scale buildup as well as water pump wear.

Smell

Change the coolant if it smells burnt. Also change the thermostat; it's probably gone bad because it was exposed to overheating (or it caused the overheating). Overheating damages the bi-metallic spring that opens and closes the thermostat valve. Most important, find out what caused the system to overheat and repair it, or face major engine damage.

TRANSMISSION FLUID

The transmission fluid lubricates, cools, and creates hydraulic pressure within the transmission. If the fluid is compromised from overheating or dirt, it can affect the operation of the unit.

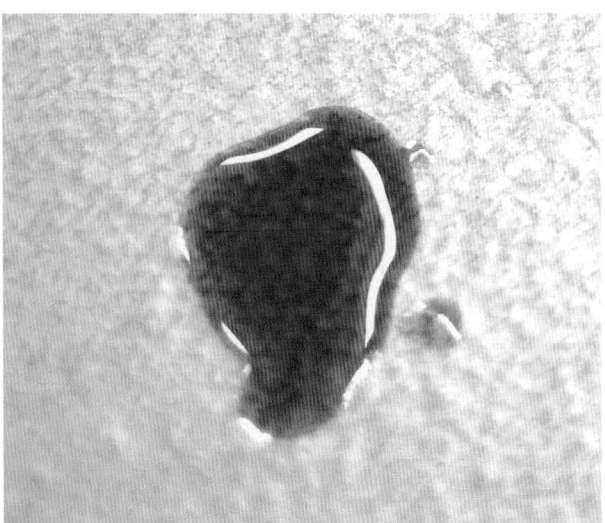

This picture shows new automatic transmission fluid. Clean, fresh automatic transmission fluid is usually red, smells like fresh oil, and is absent of gritty matter. Dark fluid that has been left in the transmission too long and thus has been burnt, is probably full of gritty wear material, and smells burnt. Leaving transmission fluid like this in the transmission too long will result in internal damage to the unit in the form of increased wear, scorched clutches, and bands, and worn bearings and bushings.

Color

Transmission fluid should be red. Dark brown or black indicates that the transmission was overheated at one point. There are dos and don'ts regarding changing the fluid on transmissions that have been overheated.

On vehicles with a neglected transmission and high mileage, changing the fluid after it's been burned is a crapshoot. If the transmission has overheated, a couple of things happen internally. The seals harden and allow fluid to pass by them. Less fluid in the system decreases hydraulic pressure. The drop in pressure causes additional overheating and friction buildup. In addition, the glue that affixes the clutches' friction material to their steel backing crystallizes, so that when new high-detergent fluid is introduced into the system, it scrubs away the crystallized glue. The friction material then falls away from the steel backing, rendering the transmission useless. At this point the transmission has to be rebuilt or replaced.

In summary, on transmissions where the fluid is dark brown or black, proceed with caution. Drop the pan and inspect for wear material. If wear material is evident inside the unit, just change the fluid in the pan, install a new filter, close it up, and drive it. If the fluid is a milky color (like a strawberry milkshake) then there's moisture in the unit usually due to a ruptured oil cooler in the radiator. This is not good. When engine coolant mixes with transmission fluid, the transmission usually fails in short order because the water and engine coolant compromise the rubber seals. If this happens, the transmission usually has to be rebuilt or replaced.

Consistency

The fluid should be slippery and smooth to the touch. A gritty feeling usually means that there's wear material in the pan and that the unit should be opened up and inspected.

Smell

The fluid should smell like oil. A burnt smell indicates transmission overheating. Usually when the fluid is burnt it's darker in color. Follow service procedures as outlined in the color section above for overheated transmissions.

POWER STEERING FLUID

Like the transmission fluid, the power steering fluid lubricates, cools, and creates hydraulic pressure (which produces the power-assisted steering). When checking it, take note of three things: color, consistency, and smell (do you see a pattern developing here?).

Color

The steering fluid should be red or clear. If its black or dark colored, this is an indication that it has been overheated. Also, look for metal flakes. If present, this means that the rack or power steering pump are worn and are grinding themselves to pieces. You will have to replace the pump or steering rack and

Here we have the power steering pump. If you could see inside, you'd note the color of the fluid: It's red, clear, and absent of any grit and dirt. I guarantee that this fluid would smell like fresh oil. Power steering fluid that has been overheated is black, smells burnt, and depending on how badly the system is worn, may have metal flakes floating in it.

When power steering fluid gets worn out, it loses its ability to lubricate, create hydraulic pressure, and cool the system. Power steering gears, whether they are rack-and-pinion or standard design, must have clean healthy fluid to operate properly and safely.

perform a power steering flush. Sometimes if you catch the problem early you can save one or the other component.

Consistency

Power steering fluid should be smooth and slippery to the touch. A gritty consistency indicates either dirt or wear material.

Smell

If the power steering fluid smells burnt, then the system has overheated and must be checked for wear. If no wear is evident yet, flush the system and refill with new power steering fluid.

BRAKE FLUID

Hydraulic braking systems rely on the master cylinder to create hydraulic pressure by pumping brake fluid through the system under high pressure when the brake pedal is applied. Brake fluid is hydroscopic in nature (meaning it absorbs water). Thus, when a hydraulic brake system is left open to environmental conditions, the brake fluid absorbs moisture, which finds its way to the lowest point of the system

Brake fluid is usually a clear or slightly amber-colored hydraulic fluid, as is obvious by this picture. Being hydroscopic (moisture absorbing) in nature, brake fluid must be sealed from the outside atmosphere. This is why the master cylinder has a rubber seal on the filler cap, and the brake hydraulic system is sealed.

(usually the brake calipers or wheel cylinders, as well as the steel lines). This water causes oxidation (rust) that eats away from the inside out, compromising system components and disabling the braking system. Evaluate three characteristics when examining brake fluid: color, consistency, and smell.

Color

Healthy brake fluid is a translucent clear color, not rusty or black. If it is rusty, then the system has moisture in it and rust has formed. Sometimes a simple brake fluid flush can avert further damage. However, the system should be closely inspected to make sure that rust has not damaged any parts before doing a brake fluid flush. If the brake fluid is black, the system has overheated. Brakes can overheat if they are abused when in use, or if a brake caliper sticks and does not release. The excessive heat causes the brake fluid to boil and burn, turning it black and causing it to lose its hydraulic properties. If this is the case, determine the cause of overheating and repair as needed. Then do a fluid flush and refill with fresh fluid.

DRIVERS ASK, TOM ANSWERS: FLUID PROBLEMS SOLVED

Q Dear Tom,
I own a 2001 Ford Ranger (4.0 engine) with 116,000 miles. When I start the truck after sitting over night, I hear what sounds like crankshaft bearing noise that lasts about two seconds after the engine starts. Do you think synthetic oil or "Motor Honey" will help prolong the engine life?
Darlene—Lubbock, Texas

A Darlene,
I think you need to find the cause of the engine knock. Oil changes or additives like Motor Honey, STP, or any one of the plethora of other such products out there do not correct metal wear and fatigue inside an engine. Engine knocks happen because metal has worn off the bearings and crankshaft journal(s). Have an oil pressure test done to confirm the low oil pressure that I suspect you have as a result of internal wear. If the pressure is low, then partial engine disassembly with removal of the oil pan will be necessary to determine the extent of the internal wear. If you find that the crank and bearings are worn, look into replacing the engine with either a factory rebuilt or Jasper remanufactured engine.

You might ask, why replace rather than rebuild? Because the labor, parts, and machine shop service involved in rebuilding your old powerplant will probably be more than replacement with a good quality rebuilt unit.
Tom

Q Tom,
I own a 2001 Buick Century Custom that I purchased used with 59,000 miles. I didn't notice any engine noises until after several oil changes. In the morning, or when cold, the engine knocks. Usually the knock goes away after the engine is warmed up. Is there an additive to quiet it down when it is cold? What are some symptoms to watch for that would indicate a more serious problem?
J.D.—Kirksville, Ohio

A J.D.,
Oil additives don't solve mechanical problems, such as worn main, rod, cam bearings, or oil pumps. Have an oil pressure test performed to verify the low oil pressure at cold startup. If it's low, start diagnostic procedures; that is, remove the valve covers to check for sludge buildup; remove the oil pan and check for worn main or rod bearings or an oil pump. I think you'll find worn internal engine parts. You may be asking, "Why on an engine with only 59,000 miles?" Three possible explanations come to mind: (1) The oil was never changed during the life of the vehicle before you owned it. (2) The engine was badly overheated and burned the oil and thus the bearings. (3) The odometer was rolled back before you bought it, and the engine has many more mileage than what reads on the clock.

Did you have a Carfax report done to check the vehicle's title history before buying it? If not, don't make that mistake again.
Tom

Q Dear Tom,
Help! When I parked my car yesterday and turned off the engine, all this green water came pouring out all over the driveway. My car is a 1997 Pontiac Grand Am with a V-6 engine. What's wrong?
Claudia—Lyerly, Washington

A Claudia,
The green water that you refer to is engine coolant. There is a coolant leak in your car. Have a cooling system pressure test performed. With this test, the technician forces air pressure into the car's cooling system in an effort to force a leak at the weakest point, exposing exactly where the coolant is leaking out of the engine. Sometimes coolant leaks are hard to find and only exhibit themselves under certain circumstances. If this is the case and the leak is hard to find, find a shop that has an ultraviolet leak-detection system.

The technician will install a fluorescent dye into the cooling system and then you will drive the car for a few days. Take it back to the shop, and they will shine an ultraviolet light on the engine. If there's a leak, it will show up under the light as a bright yellow color because of the dye.
Tom

Q Tom,
I have a 2001 Ford Explorer. The other day I checked the radiator fluid and it was rust colored. Should I just replace the antifreeze or flush the system?
Clyde—Tennessee

A Clyde,
The rusty color indicates that the antifreeze has stopped doing its job of inhibiting rust and scale buildup in the system. Emptying a portion of the cooling system just to add good antifreeze after bad is ineffective and will not stop rust. I suggest you completely flush the system and refill it with a new 50-50 antifreeze and water mix. Rust is relentless and will not be stopped unless system integrity is restored.
Tom

Consistency

The brake fluid should feel slippery and smooth to the touch. The presence of grit indicates that dirt is also present. Find the leak and repair it, then bleed the system to restore integrity.

Smell

If the brake fluid smells burnt, then a component of the system has overheated. Inspect the entire system, find the culprit, and repair or replace as needed.

Q Tom,
I have a 2006 Dodge Ram pickup. The brake fluid has a rusty sediment in the bottom of the master cylinder. What could this be, and what should I do about it?
　　　Joe—Chicago, Illinois

A Joe,
Rusty sediment in the brake fluid is an indication that moisture has gotten into the system. Check the filler cap to see if the gasket is torn. This will allow moisture to contaminate the system. When water gets into a braking system, it travels to the lowest points in the system, setting up oxidation and rust. My suggestion to you is to have the system power bled to flush the old contaminated fluid out. I hope that rust has not set up housekeeping too aggressively. Flushing the old fluid out can stop the progression of it.
　　　Tom

Q Tom,
I have a 2002 Chevy Cavalier with a 2.2-liter four-cylinder engine. Lately, it has been running rough. The other day I checked the oil to see if it was low, and it looked weird. Instead of that clear caramel color, it looked like light chocolate milk. Is this an indication of trouble? Please help!
　　　Candy—Cincinnati, Ohio

A Candy,
This would explain the engine running rough. Based on the color of the oil you describe, I would say that a head gasket has blown in your engine. When a head gasket blows, if it's close to a coolant passageway in the head, water is allowed to spill down into the crankcase (or oil pan). This contaminates the oil, causing it to take on a milky appearance. If run too long in this condition, the lower end of the engine will suffer. Rod and main bearings will be damaged because the oil has mixed with water, which causes heat and friction buildup. If let go too long, it causes engine failure. Get it into a shop to confirm my suspicions. I think you'll find this to be the case.
　　　Tom

The brake fluid in this reservoir has been overheated as is evident by its dark color. When overheated, brake fluid loses its hydraulic properties, and the brake system function suffers. The reason for overheating was probably due to a brake caliper sticking as a result of either corrosion on the brake caliper or a pitted piston. When checking brake fluid, also look for rust and sediment buildup in the master cylinder reservoir. If moisture has contaminated the system, it will find its way to the lowest points of the system and set up rust. Check your owner's manual for the suggested intervals to flush the brake fluid.

MANUAL TRANSMISSION LUBRICANT

Manual transmissions are sealed units that have gears, shafts, bearings, bushings, blocker rings, and synchronizer rings that house their own lubricant. They are less touchy than automatics, but they still must be inspected and maintained according to the manufacturer's specs. Fluid level, color, consistency, and smell are critical when inspecting manual transmissions. Manual transmissions use one of three fluid types: motor oil, automatic transmission fluid, or gear oil. Your owner's manual will outline exactly what type of lubricant is used.

Color

When inspecting manual transmission fluid, it should appear red if it's automatic transmission fluid, caramel if it's motor oil, or black if it's gear oil. It's important to look closely for metal flakes in the fluid. Metal flakes indicate that there is internal wear in the transmission. If this is the case, open the unit and inspect for wear before putting the transmission back into service. If you run a transmission that exhibits wear, it will fail in short order. A milky color indicates moisture contamination. In this case, replace the gear lube immediately or else heat and friction will buildup and the transmission will fail.

Consistency

Transmission fluid should be smooth and slippery to the touch. Grit indicates the presence of either dirt or wear material. Further inspection is warranted to prevent premature transmission failure.

Smell

A burnt smell indicates internal overheating due to friction or lack of lubrication. The unit should be opened up and inspected for bearing or gear wear or failure as well as for leaks.

DIFFERENTIAL LUBRICANT

The differentials transfer engine power to the drive wheels, enabling the vehicle to move forward or reverse. Differentials are sealed units that have gears, bearings, and axles that house their own lubricant. They must be inspected and maintained. Fluid level, color, consistency, and smell are critical when inspecting differentials. Differentials use one of three fluid types: motor oil, automatic transmission fluid, or gear oil. Your owner's manual will tell you exactly what type of lubricant is used.

Color

Healthy differential fluid is red (automatic transmission fluid), caramel (motor oil), or black (gear oil). Inspect closely for the presence of metal flakes because they indicate internal wear. If metal flakes are present, open the unit and inspect it thoroughly before putting it back into service. Left to operate with wear, the differential will eventually fail. A milky color means moisture is in the system, and the gear lube must be replaced immediately or heat and friction will buildup and the differential will fail.

Consistency

Differential lubricants should be smooth and slippery to the touch. Grit indicates the presence of dirt or wear material. Further inspection is warranted to prevent premature component failure.

Smell

A burnt smell indicates internal overheating caused by friction and lack of lubrication. Open the unit and inspect for ring and pinion, carrier, axle, or pinion bearing wear or failure as well as leaks.

Differential fluid is usually clear or slightly amber-colored, but can vary in color by carmaker. As always, the key to proper inspection is to identify what fluid type the unit is supposed to take, and then compare it to the original color. Also check for smell and wear material. If the vehicle goes off-road, watch for signs that the fluid has been contaminated with water, giving it a milky appearance. If this is the case, I would closely inspect the inside of this differential for wear, as water tends to thin out the lubricant and cause increased friction.

TRANSFER CASE LUBRICANT

Transfer cases provide high- and low-drive range selection for 4WD vehicles. They are sealed units that have gears, bearings, and shafts that house their own lubricant (much like manual transmissions and differentials). They must be inspected and maintained. Fluid level, color, consistency, and smell are critical when inspecting transfer cases. They use one of three fluid types: gear oil, automatic transmission fluid, or special synthetic lube designed specifically for transfer cases. Your owner's manual will define exactly what type of lubricant is used.

Color

When inspecting transfer case fluid, healthy fluid is red (automatic transmission fluid), clear, blue, green, or red (synthetic lube), or black (gear oil). Look closely for the presence of metal flakes, which indicate internal wear. If metal flakes are present, open the unit and inspect for wear before putting it back into service. Left to operate with wear, the transfer case will eventually fail. A milky color indicates moisture contamination. In such a case, the lube must be replaced immediately or heat and friction will buildup and the transfer case will fail.

Consistency

Transfer case lubricants should be smooth and slippery to the touch. Grit indicates the presence of either dirt or wear material. If this is the case, further inspection is warranted to prevent premature failure.

Smell

A burnt smell indicates internal overheating caused by friction and lack of lubrication. Open the unit and inspect for bearing, gear, or shaft wear or failure as well as leaks.

DO MAGIC ELIXIRS REALLY WORK?

The "Wonder Elixirs" are supposed to fix your car without any mechanical repairs. Is this possible?

ENGINE OIL ADDITIVES THAT PROTECT YOUR ENGINE IN THE ABSENCE OF OIL

Years ago I "slapped the gauntlet," so to speak, to the companies that produce lubricant enhancers. My challenge? Present to me solid, scientific proof that their elixirs really do lengthen the life of an internal-combustion engine. What do I get? Countless testimonial letters from people who claim they have run their engines dry of oil. Then, in response to an article I wrote for *PC World*, I get an e-mail from a reader who suggests I view a website that offers "scientific proof" that a particular oil additive works. The site presented more personal testimonies reminiscent of late-night programming.

It seems that everyone is looking for the magic elixir, the "Engine Extender," the "Fountain of Youth," the "Mechanic in a Can." Is this a reasonable quest? Companies that make these products claim that, by using their oil additive, the oil in your engine performs better and lasts longer. Unfortunately, the intense claims of these products give people a false sense of security. As a result, people put off oil and filter changes, and the consequence is often premature engine failure. For several years I have been entertaining questions on this topic. Here are a few sample questions and my responses:

Q: If I use XYZ Product, will it make my engine last longer?

A: I don't know. No hard evidence has been presented to substantiate the claims yet. (I call this statement "pleading the Fifth.")

Q: If I use this product, will it quiet the engine noise I'm hearing?

A: If your engine has a noise in it, it's because excessive wear or mechanical failure has occurred. Tapping and knocking is the result of gaps that have formed because of the absence of metal or the failure of a mechanical part.

Q: If I use this product, can I go double the mileage between oil changes?

A: Pleading the Fifth

Q: If I use this product, will it make my engine run cooler?

A: Pleading the Fifth

Q: If I use this product, will it give me better gas mileage?

A: Pleading the Fifth

Q: If I use this product, will it allow me to run my engine with no oil in it at all?

A: See the story on the next page about the *Consumer Reports* test for the answer to this one.

Do these questions sound familiar? They should. They are the result of the claims of the companies that manufacture these products, all based on personal testimonies. Where are the facts? Show me the scientific research. Show me where two identical cars were tested that had the same engines and the same equipment, one with the additive and one without. Show me where they ran them the same number of miles under the same conditions. Show me where each car had the same mechanical care and treatment over a defined and significant period of time. Finally, at the end of the test, did they disassemble both engines and examine them for comparable wear? To my knowledge, objective, controlled, scientific testing has not been done. Why do these product makers offer only personal testimonies and hype if they had scientific evidence to prove their claims? The answer is obvious.

COOLANT STOP-LEAK

How do stop-leak products work? When installed in a cooling system the stop-leak product rushes through the cooling system under pressure to the site of the leak. When it exits the point of the leak, it builds up on itself sealing up the leak. The problem? It only seals for a short time until either another leak springs or the existing leak gets larger. This is true for either an internal leak like a head gasket or an external leak in a radiator. With a head leak, either the gasket material is gone or the metal is cracked or warped, resulting in a leak. In the case of a radiator leak, more often than not another leak will spring somewhere in the core in short order because wear and degradation is relative to the age of the unit.

In the final analysis the engine has lost its sealing ability internally or externally. Mating and sealing surfaces or component integrity must be restored to stop the coolant leak. In extreme cases the overuse of radiator stop leak can clog up the heater core and stop the heater from working. It can also stop an entire bank of water jackets on one side of the engine, resulting in a constant state of overheating. To solve this problem, the expansion plugs have to be removed from the whole engine block and the block has to be power-flushed in order to clean out the stop leak product. This stuff harms more cars than it fixes. Period.

TRANSMISSION AND ENGINE OIL STOP-LEAK

This product is supposed to stop engine oil and transmission fluid leaks when installed in the engine or the transmission. It softens the hardened rubber seals that have shrunk away from the sealing surface. When softened, the rubber seals swell and fit tightly to the metal sealing surface, stopping the fluid leak. Once the chemical product wears out, the seals return to their hard state and the fluid starts leaking again. The only way to solve this problem is to restore gasket and seal-mating surfaces.

BEWARE ENGINE OIL ADDITIVES

The following is an actual account recorded by *Consumer Reports*. Read and learn.

Consumer Reports duplicated the test seen in the infomercial for the engine-oil additive Prolong to see if the product really does offer extra engine protection. The commercial said it added Prolong to the engine's oil supply, then drained the oil and ran the car with no oil plugs or filters. The product makers say they ran the car with no oil for four hours without damaging the engine. (The infomercial has a small-print disclaimer saying, "Never run your car without oil or water.")

Testers at *Consumer Reports* used two former taxicabs with rebuilt GM V-6 engines when they duplicated the infomercial test. After breaking in the engines and changing their oil, they added Prolong to only one car and drove them both more than 100 miles. Then they drained the oil and removed the filters, just like in the infomercial. Next, testers drove the cars around a test track to see what would happen. "We drove the cars around the test track at speeds between 20 and 30 miles per hour," *Consumer Reports* tester Marc McEntee said. "We were able to go for 13 minutes, 5 miles, until both cars died within about 100 yards of one another." Testers later took the engines apart. The damage to both cars, including the one with Prolong, was extensive.

Consumer Reports says save your money. Don't buy the oil additives and make sure to keep your eye on your oil gauge. My recommendation: Change your oil and filter every 3,000 miles or what's recommended in your owner's manual and drink from the Automotive Fountain of Youth!

PROJECT 15
Change PCV Valve

 Time Required: 15 minutes

 Tools Required: None (hands)

 Skill Level:

 Cost Estimate: $5–$15

 Tip: Remove the valve from the rubber grommet in the valve cover carefully to avoid damaging the grommet.

1

The PCV (positive crankcase ventilation) valve, if your engine is equipped with one, usually resides in the valve cover. Its job is to send combustion gases that escape into the valve cover up to the air intake, where they are drawn through the induction system and burned. Check your owner's manual for your PCV valve's service interval.

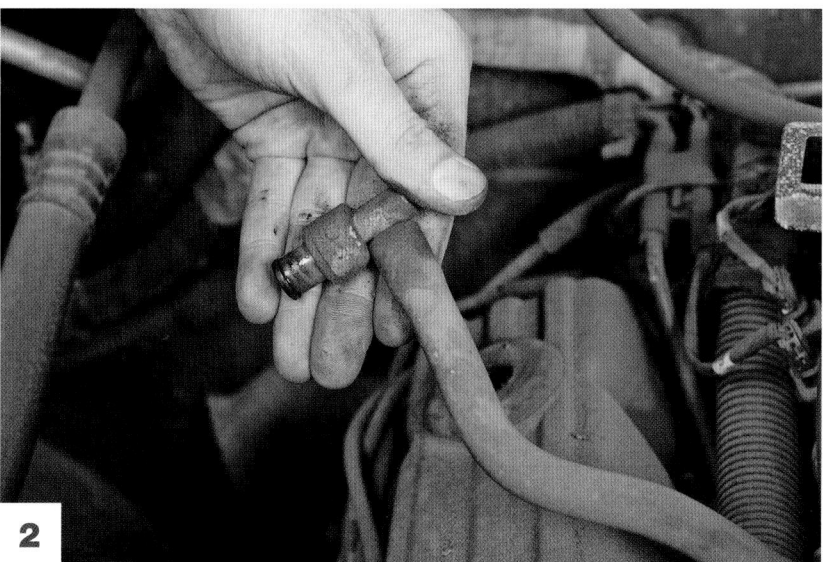

2

Once you have found the PCV valve, firmly grab hold of it and remove it from the grommet in the valve cover. Closely inspect the vacuum hose to see if it is brittle or soft. If either of these conditions is evident, replace the hose. You should also inspect the grommet and replace it if it is soft or brittle since this system must be sealed for it to operate correctly.

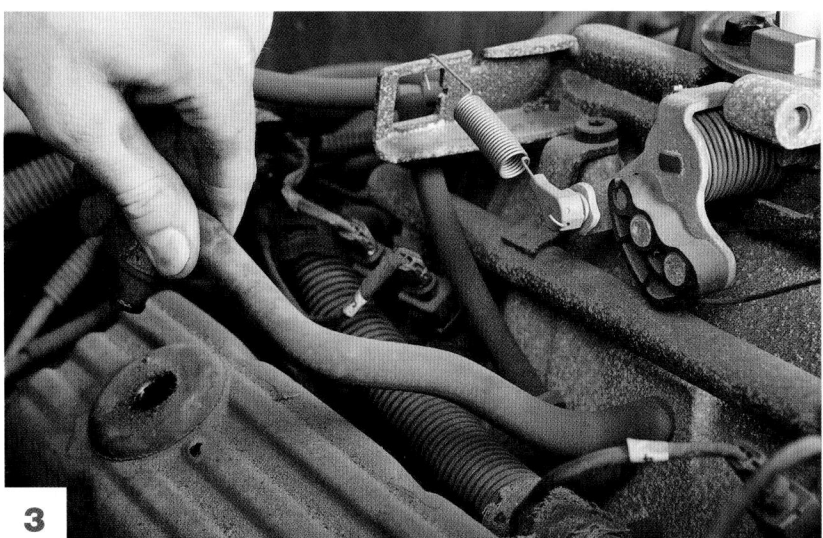

The valve may then be pulled from the hose running into the air cleaner.

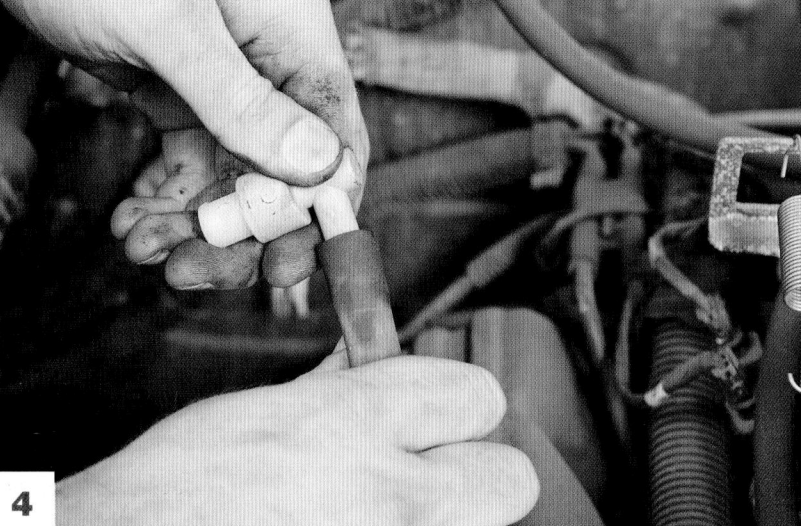

Push the new valve into the hose.

Press the other end of the valve into the rubber grommet in the valve cover. Make sure the valve is well sealed to the hose and valve cover.

Chapter 12
Maintenance-Free Cars (Is There Such a Thing?)

"One hundred thousand miles before the first scheduled tune-up!" "Coolant that lasts the life of the car!"

These seem to be the mantra of the marketing gurus of car manufacturers today. They promise cars that last forever, yet cars still break down consistently. Why this disparity? Why do our cars break down when they are supposed to last a long time without regular maintenance? This marketing ploy has created a lot of confusion. Allow me to bring some sense to it all.

100,000 MILES BEFORE THE FIRST "TUNE-UP!"

First, there's no such thing as a tune-up anymore. Years ago when cars operated on point ignition systems, yes the tune-up was necessary. Having a tune-up meant that the ignition system got new parts, filters, sparkplugs, wires, and so on. Today, with computerized ignition, most of the traditional ignition components are gone. Points, condensers, distributors, caps, and rotors are a thing of the past. All this stuff has been replaced with an intuitive computerized ignition that manages fuel and ignition automatically based on sensor input and environmental conditions.

What this marketing ploy refers to is sparkplug replacement. That's it. Most carmakers use platinum sparkplugs today because they last longer and have a hotter spark. And, yes, platinum spark plugs under perfect laboratory conditions probably would log 100,000 miles before giving up the ghost. But we're talking real world here. Enter the effects of bad fuel injectors, cold weather's effect on fuel mixture (richer mix) that fouls out the plugs, faulty sensors that cause incorrect engine adjustments (which fouls out plugs), mechanical malfunctions such as bad valve guides and seals that spill oil on the plugs (causing misfire), and worn pistons and rings that cause oil consumption (as well as poor performance and decreased fuel efficiency). Then, of course, we have air and fuel filters that get dirty and cause engine performance to go south as well. Oh, and what about the effects of bad gas?

Add the fact that most engines today are made of aluminum and the sparkplugs are made of an alloy metal, and when you ignore them for a long time, these dissimilar metals (of the cylinder heads and sparkplugs) "weld" themselves together, making them extremely difficult to remove and subject to cylinder head damage.

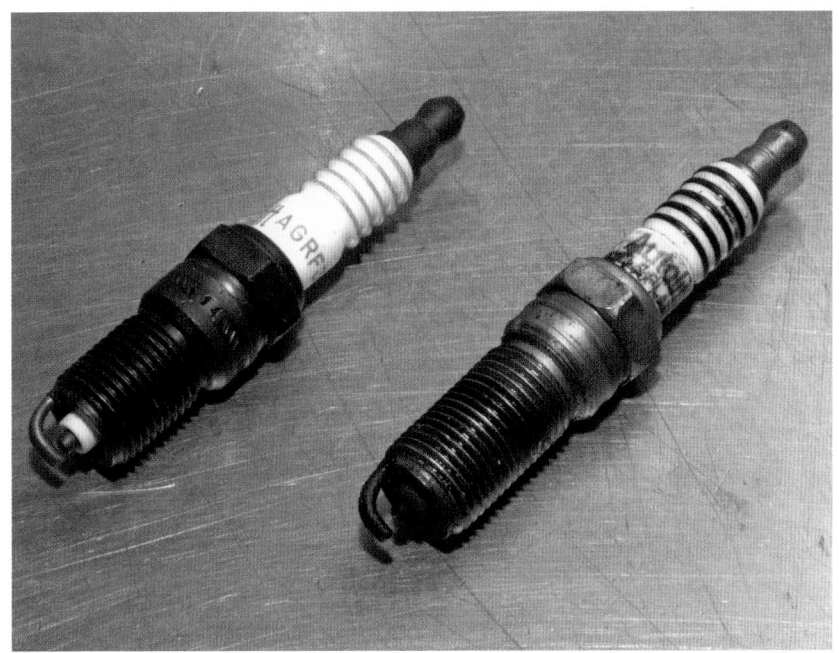

Here we have two sparkplugs. One is brand new, and the other has a heavy carbon deposit buildup. This is typical of sparkplugs in use for more than 20,000 miles. The reason for the carbon buildup is inefficient combustion from a weak spark. The spark gets weak from worn sparkplug wires, ignition components, and dousing of the spark with too rich and wet a fuel mixture. All these things figure into sparkplug life, hence the reason for removing, inspecting, and cleaning or replacing them every 25,000 miles. Leave them in too long and you have a recipe for drivability problems, poor fuel mileage, and increased tailpipe emissions.

In a perfect world with no dirt, grit, or grime to contaminate our cars' systems we might realize this kind of mileage between services, but this is simply not the case. Your car must have regular maintenance checks. Have the plugs pulled and inspected every 20,000 miles for misfire and wear. When reinstalling them, clean the threads, lubricate them with never-seize (a special lubricant designed to stop the welding of the threads), and re-gap them and reinstall (properly torquing them to factory specs). Head off problems before they cost you an arm and a leg.

COOLANT THAT LASTS MORE THAN 100,000 MILES

Twelve years ago GM introduced an engine coolant called Dexcool. It's supposed to last five years or 150,000 miles, but there have been problems with it. Cooling systems that use this coolant have experienced more acid buildup and rust in the system. The acid eats away at gaskets. Rust builds up in

Ethylene glycol antifreeze has been used for years without problems. The key is to inspect it every six months for protection and color and replace it every two years or 25,000 miles, whichever comes first. If the protection goes above −34° F, then I would replace it. Also, if the color gets dark, brown, or rusty, replace it and perform a cooling system flush to remove harmful rust and scale buildup in the system.

the system, inhibiting the flow of coolant flow, which causes overheating. Overall, numerous cooling system problems have been attributed to the use of this controversial product that GM sternly stands behind. There are class action suits against GM on this issue, but no settlement has been made to date.

Here's the bottom line when it comes to cooling system maintenance: Whether you are running Dexcool (the orange stuff) or ethylene glycol (the green stuff), inspect the coolant level and the condition and protection of the coolant at every oil change. In addition, completely flush and refill the system every 25,000 miles. These actions will avert the problems associated with Dexcool or any other coolant product.

Filters are one of the most neglected parts of our automobiles. Many people neglect proper filter maintenance because filters are simply "out of sight, out of mind." Add to this neglect the fact that computerized performance systems tend to compensate for problems caused by filters that need attention, and you have cars that seemingly run perfectly forever.

Clean filters are vital to the performance of your vehicle. In addition to grit and dirt that enter the engine and transmission from the air (and other environmental factors), your car also manufactures its own contaminants from condensation, chemical reactions, and wear. If it were not for these filters, some components in your car would self-destruct. Let's consider five important filters that need your attention: air, cabin air, fuel, transmission, and oil filters. What are their jobs? What are your maintenance responsibilities?

AIR FILTER

Air filters have always played an important role in automobiles. They keep harmful, abrasive dust and dirt out of the inside of the engine where it can do a lot of damage. However, they are even more important today with sophisticated computer-controlled fuel injection. A clean air filter is absolutely necessary to maintain the delicate balance of air-to-fuel ratio in a fuel injection system. A dirty air filter causes the fuel delivery system to go haywire trying to maintain balance.

Recommended replacement interval: Every 10,000 to 15,000 miles unless otherwise specified.

CABIN AIR FILTERS

With the increase of airborne contaminants, carmakers have designed more sophisticated air filtration systems in vehicles. They have installed cabin air filters in a lot of their models to filter out air impurities such as pollen, dirt, grime, and the likes. The cabin air filter is usually located under the hood inside the cowl area close to the air intake for the HVAC system (heating ventilation and air conditioning). The recommended replacement interval for the cabin air filter is around 15,000 to 20,000 miles, unless you live in a dirty, dusty environment. If that's the case, replace it a little more often based on visual inspection.

Air filters come in all shapes and sizes, as pictured here. Make sure you inspect the air filter every oil change, that way you catch a dirty air filter before it affects your gas mileage and performance. A clogged air filter causes diminished airflow into the engine, and thus the computer system tries to make adjustments to the extent of its parameters to make up for the decreased airflow it senses.

FUEL FILTER

Fuel filters are small yet critical members of the fuel delivery system. The injectors in the fuel injection system have small orifices through which fuel is forced under high pressure, creating a vapor of the air-fuel mixture (the best state for combustion and power). The smallest particle of dirt can clog an injector and thus disable an engine. To prevent this from happening, the fuel filter must filter out dirt and grime. In addition, fuel injection systems rely on electric fuel pumps to maintain the necessary pressure. They are usually located in the fuel tank behind the fuel filter. If the fuel filter is partially clogged, the fuel pump overworks trying to overcome the restriction ahead of it. If the fuel pump operates in this condition for a prolonged period of time, it will fail prematurely. To ensure proper performance and drivability, keep the fuel filter in your vehicle fresh.

Recommended replacement interval: Every 20,000 miles.

OIL FILTER

The oil filter is the storehouse for dirt in the crankcase. It traps dirt, metal filings, and sludge (all are by-products of the internal combustion engine). Without this filter, these contaminants flow through the engine causing friction, heat, and ultimately premature engine failure.

Recommended replacement interval: Every 3,000 miles.

Note: Always replace the oil filter with an OEM-quality filter that mimics the OEM design. This design has check valves to prevent "dry startup" (if so equipped) and fine-filtration filter media to filter out the tiniest speck of harmful dirt or grime.

Fuel filters vary in size and exterior design. On low-pressure systems the filter usually connects in the fuel line with hoses and clamps. On fuel-injected systems, which operate at higher pressures, the fuel filter connects into the lines with flare nut or compression fittings because of the higher pressure at which they operate. Fuel filters can be located under the body inside a frame rail, inside the fuel tank, on carbureted systems, inside the carburetor, and sometimes in the engine compartment.

Oil filters vary in size and oil capacity. Oil filters vary in quality as well. If cut open, a $2 filter will reveal many differences from a a $15 or $20 filter. Filter media will be very different in terms of filtration. Such features as check valves to prevent dry start up of the engine will probably be absent in the cheaper knockoff. Remember, you get what you pay for. Just because they look alike doesn't mean they are of the same quality and, more important, what your vehicle's engine needs.

Q Tom,
I own a 2008 Buick Enclave AWD. It has a 3.6-liter V-6 engine in it. The maintenance schedule says to replace the sparkplugs at 100,000 miles. Is this correct or a misprint? I have never let a set of sparkplugs go that long. Please advise.

John—Willingboro, New Jersey

A John,
I double-checked the maintenance schedule for your truck. The stated replacement interval in the schedule is correct. I too am uncomfortable with this recommendation. Especially when you consider the negative ramifications of leaving sparkplugs unattended for all that time. When left in the engine unattended for a long time, sparkplugs tend to get dirty from inefficient combustion of fuel. This results in carbon buildup. If the engine is given to oil consumption, sparkplugs get gummed up and heavily carboned up from oil spillage on the electrode. Finally, when left in a long time, the dissimilar metal of the plugs and cylinder head react to each other, resulting in the sparkplugs literally welding to the heads. This makes replacement hard and in a lot of cases, cylinder head replacement necessary because sparkplug threads are stripped out when removing old plugs that have wended themselves to the head.

I recommend removing the plugs every 20,000 to 25,000 miles, cleaning and re-gapping them, applying a never-seize thread compound to them, and reinstalling them and properly torquing them to factory specs. This will avert any sparkplug nightmares that might arise from leaving them in too long unattended.

Tom

Q Tom,
I have a 2007 Toyota 4Runner 2WD. The other day, I went to the service department at my dealership to have the transmission fluid and filter changed. The truck has 35,000 miles on it, and I thought it should be done at this mileage interval. The service manager told me not to worry about it, that the fluid did not need to be changed. Is this right? Doesn't the fluid need to be changed?

Rod—Warren, Pennsylvania

A Rod,
I checked the Toyota normal maintenance schedule for your truck. The manufacturer suggests checking the fluid only, no drain interval at all. I checked all the way up to 150,000 miles. Now based on this, Toyota says that hypothetically, the transmission fluid could last for the life of the vehicle. I simply do not agree with this. Transmission fluid is hydraulic oil, and oil loses its lubricating, cooling, and hydraulic properties over time. Call me excessive, but I would change that fluid every 35,000 to 45,000 miles. I have seen the inside of too many broken transmissions that have been left alone without regular fluid and filter changes to recommend anything else.

Tom

Q Tom,
I have a 2009 Chevy Silverado 1500 with 32,000 miles on it, and I drive it for work. My repair shop suggested I replace the engine coolant. I consulted my maintenance schedule and cannot find a recommended drain interval for the coolant. What's up with that? Is it supposed to last forever?

Charles—Detroit, Michigan

A Charles,
According to GM, Dexcool (which is what the coolant is in your vehicle) is supposed to last to 150,000 miles or more without needing to be changed. I checked the GM maintenance schedule for your truck and could not find a drain interval recommendation up to and over 150,000 miles. I simply do not subscribe to this service suggestion from GM. Too many problems have cropped up with Dexcool, but that is another subject dealt with in the cooling system chapter. Based on extensive experience, I recommend you flush and fill the cooling system every two years or 24,000 miles, whichever comes first. This way you head off problems in the form of rust, scale, and acid buildup at the pass.

Tom

Q Tom,
My 2003 Chrysler Sebring with a 2.7-liter V-6 engine has a check engine light on. The car runs fine, but the light still stays on. My brother told me to ignore that light and keep driving the car, that it would straighten itself out after a time. Is this right?

Wanda—Boca Raton, Florida

A Wanda,
The light is on because the computerized performance system of your car is telling you that there's a problem. Computerized automotive engine management systems are so good at masking problems through self-adjustment. The vehicle seems to run fine when in actuality there is a problem that, if left alone, will result in more system failure and thus, cost for repairs. Get it into a shop and have the system scanned for codes and repair the malady before it turns into a nightmare of expense to you. Oh, and tell your brother that if he's willing to pay for the eventual repair costs that will materialize as a result of his recommendation, that you will follow his advice wholeheartedly. That should shut him up.

Tom

Q Tom,
I am a driver of 50 years. The other day I bought a new Ford pickup. As with other vehicles I have bought over the years, I looked through the normal maintenance schedule to see when to do the recommended services, and it seemed to me that there was hardly any service to perform on this truck at all. Am I missing something or is this truck maintenance free?

Ron—Burlington, New Jersey

A Ron,
Excellent question. No, vehicles are not maintenance free. Carmakers just want us to think they are. Sparkplugs still wear out, ignition wires still degrade, filters still plug up, tires still need rotating, front ends need aligning, engines and transmissions still need oil and filter changes at regular intervals, and on it goes. Forget the normal service schedule and follow the severe service schedule for your truck. That should ensure that it continues to run trouble-free.

Tom

TRANSMISSION FILTER

The automatic transmission is a mechanical wonder in its design and function, making your car go forward and backward. The automatic transmission is nothing more than a giant hydraulic pump that lubricates itself. The fluid follows a pre-determined path under hydraulic pressure, creating what is called a "fluid coupling" or linkup between the engine and transmission, propelling the car forward. In order for all this to happen, the fluid must be clean and flow freely. The transmission filter plays a major role, keeping the fluid clean of debris such as dirt, sludge, and clutch material. A clogged filter inhibits the flow of fluid, causing the pressure to drop, the fluid breaks down, and friction and heat buildup, which affects the performance of the transmission (or worse, the transmission fails). It is extremely important to keep the filter and fluid in your transmission clean.

Recommended replacement interval: Every 25,000 to 35,000 miles.

Proper maintenance is essential if you want to make your car last and save a lot of money in the long haul. For maximum life, follow the severe service schedule of your owner's manual. When the service schedule suggests an extremely long service interval (in excess of 100,000 miles), get the advice of your service professional.

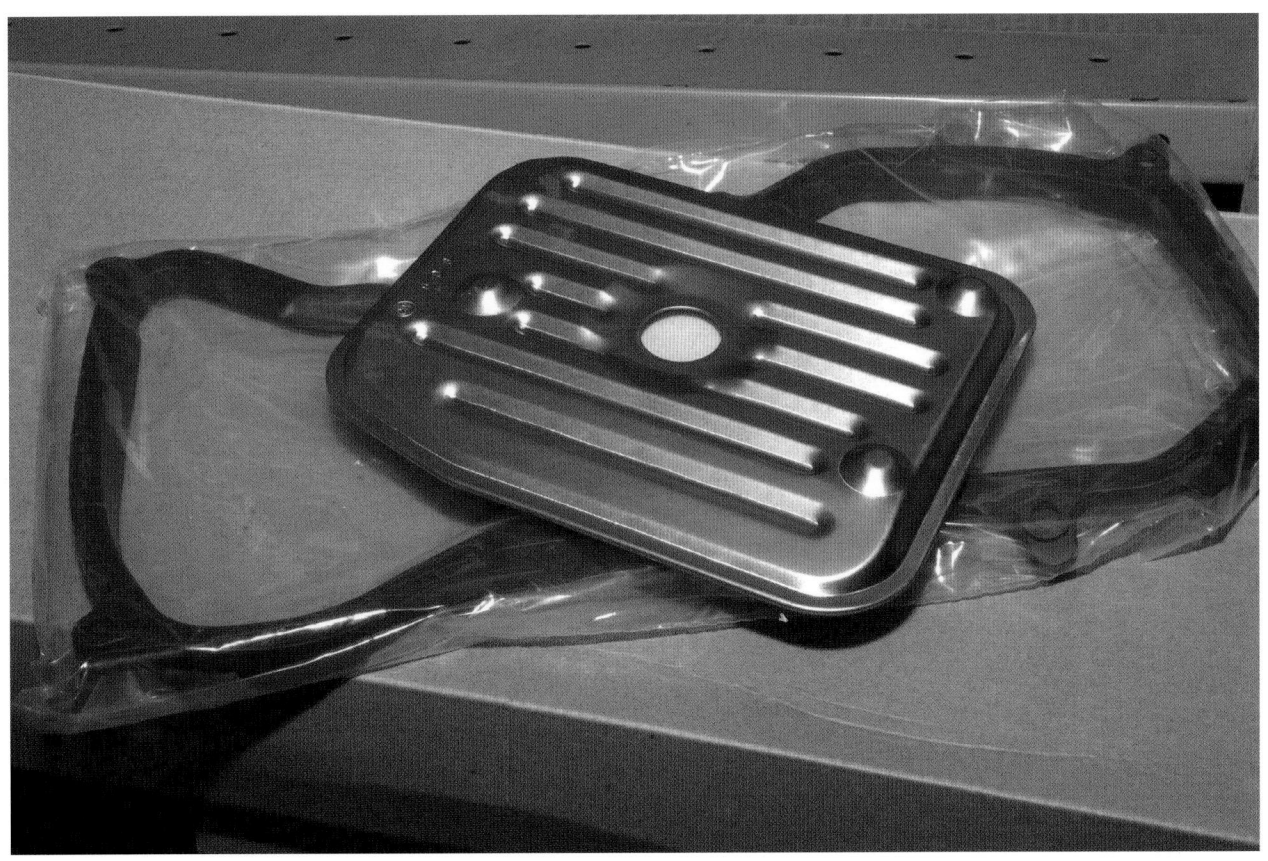

Transmission filters vary in shapes and sizes, depending on what model transmission they are designed to fit and filter. The filter is located in the transmission pan, where the transmission fluid is drawn into the filter to distribute throughout the unit after filtering it of impurities.

PROJECT 16
Replace Serpentine Belt

 Time Required: 15-45 minutes

 Tools Required: Socket, long drive handle

 Skill Level:

 Cost Estimate: $20–$50

 Tip: Observe the belt path carefully before you remove the old one and determine exactly how you want to thread the new one in to fit it properly

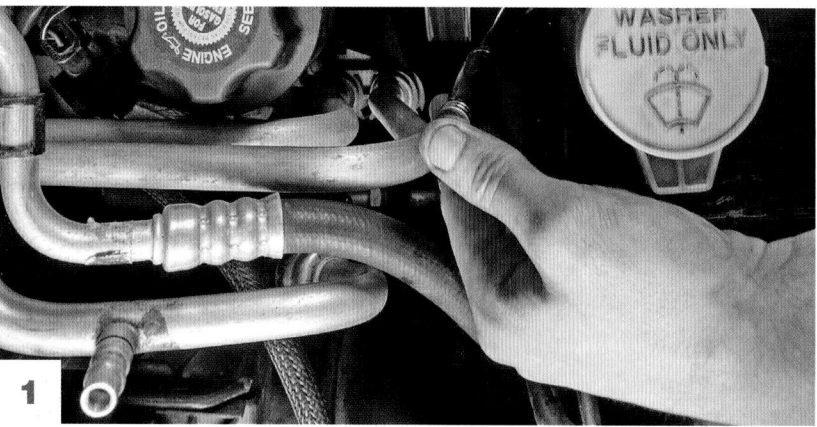

1

2

A placard or sticker in the engine bay will explain how your serpentine belt is routed over and around the pulleys at the front of your engine. To change the belt, you need to find and release the belt tensioner to loosen the belt and create enough slack to remove it. This Dodge uses a pulley on a spring-loaded arm. The pulley is identified in the sticker, which also shows which way to move it for release. Some vehicles utilize a long threaded bolt to tighten the belt that must be unscrewed to relieve tension on the belt.

Place a socket on a long-handled ratchet or breaker bar over the nut on the tensioner pulley and push or pull in the direction indicated (here, inward).

3

With the belt loose, you can lift it off one of the pulleys and then thread it out, using the sticker for guidance. Do this task in broad daylight or with a bright shop light. If the placard or diagram is missing, draw the belt routing on paper before loosening and removing the belt. Better safe than sorry. Tip: Remove the belt slowly and carefully. The easiest path for removing it is the easiest path for installing the new one. Installing the belt is a bit like a puzzle. Study the routing sticker carefully to determine which pulleys to put it over and under. Give yourself time to get it right. When you find the proper route, you will need to crank the tensioner in again to give the new belt enough clearance to sit properly. Once installed and tight, double check the routing and make sure the belt is fully seated and properly positioned on each pulley.

Chapter 13
Vehicle Exterior and Interior Maintenance

Your car's paint is exposed to a harsh environment, including contaminants such as bird droppings, tree sap, salt, and acid rain that eat into the finish of your vehicle. When this happens, the paint is exposed to harmful UV rays that fade the finish. It's important that you keep your car washed; however, there is a right way and a wrong way to wash it, and the wrong way can do damage to the finish.

If you wash the car yourself: When washing your car, don't work in direct sun because high surface temperatures cause chemical residues remaining on the finish to fade it. So park the car in the shade if you are outside. Before washing, rinse the car thoroughly with fresh water to remove harmful abrasives (dirt, grit, salt, or gravel). Make sure you use a soft cloth or washing mitt that is clean of dirt and a car wash solution that is pH neutral. Contrary to popular belief, dishwashing detergents are not safe to use on your car! These products are designed to cut grease. Consequently they will strip the protective wax coat, harm the clear-coat, and cause the car's finish to dry out and age prematurely. Remove bird droppings, bug stains, tree sap, and other such agents because this stuff discolors and stains the finish. Rinse thoroughly and dry with a chamois.

If you go to the car wash: Go to a car wash that is brush-less and uses fresh water (not recycled water). Harsh nylon brushes can scratch the paint, and recycled water may contain dissolved salt and other contaminants from previous vehicles that accelerate deterioration. Make sure that they remove bird droppings, bug stains, tree sap, and other such agents to prevent discoloration and staining of your car's finish. Good car washes dry your car before you leave, either with an automated strong air current or attendants who dry it by hand with a chamois.

Think hand-washing your car is too much of a hassle? Here's everything you need: A bucket, sponge, soap made for the job, plus a garden hose. Avoid the temptation of using dishwashing detergent, as this will strip the wax from the paint's surface.

Beware of acid rain: Beware of acid rain from industrial fallout. What is acid rain? Simply, it is the atmosphere's way of cleaning itself of pollutants. Chemical pollutants in the air combine with water vapor to form nitric and sulfuric acids. When it rains, this "acid rain" collects in droplets on your vehicle's surface. As the water evaporates, the acid concentration increases, and it eats into the paint surface (the rate accelerates with the heat from the sun). These harmful effects can be caused by dew or fog, as well as rain. Rinse and dry your vehicle often to prevent acid rain damage. Other things you can do? Park in a garage or carport, have a paint sealer or protector applied to the paint finish, and drive the car frequently so that water droplets blow off.

Wax your car: A sure shot way to protect your car's finish is to apply a good coat of wax twice a year and use a carnauba-based wax. This type of wax is tough and provides protection from harmful UV rays. For hand application apply the wax in a swirl pattern, let it dry, then buff clean with a soft dry cloth. If you use an electric buffer you must make sure you apply the wax on the slowest speed setting. If the buffer is moving too fast, it's easy to burn through the clear coat and paint. Bodywork experts repair a lot of paint jobs that were damaged from using a buffer at too high a speed or excessive downward pressure. When using a buffer, don't press down. The weight of the buffer is sufficient. Be careful.

Application of a high-quality wax is the best way to apply wax to preserve your paint. There are electric buffers available on the market that you can use. The problem with these tools is that use of an electric buffer can and does result in "burning the paint" if too much downward pressure along with too fast a buffer speed is used. I have told many DIY'ers who burned their paint because of improper use of the buffer that if you insist on using an electric buffer, get instruction from a pro before embarking. Otherwise, you could do some serious damage to your car's paint.

Touch up chips promptly: Chipped or scratched paint can cause blisters and surface rust. If you have to remove bumper stickers or decals, use a hair dryer to soften the adhesive, and then scrape the finish clean with an old credit card. Set the hair dryer on *low* to prevent damage to the paint.

In salt belt states: In areas that experience winter weather it's a good idea to wash the car every week and, more important, have the chassis (undercarriage) washed. Keeping the exterior clean of salt will cut down on corrosion and paint deterioration. If you keep the chassis clean, salt will not lay dormant. Dried salt on your car's undersurface will go back into solution the next time any water mixes with it, creating a concentrated solution that accelerates rust.

Cleaning wheels: Don't use Brillo-style pads on wheels or hubcaps. These are designed to remove baked-on food from pots and pans, not to clean the delicate finish on wheels and hubcaps. Some aluminum or magnesium custom wheels have a clear-coat finish. An abrasive cleaner will strip away the finish. Use a non-caustic cleaner with a soft brush or sponge.

Carpet and vinyl: Floor mats protect the carpet from dirt and wear. Just as important, they protect the carpet from harmful salt and other chemicals that break down the

Acid rain is a killer of automotive finishes. When allowed to sit on your car's finish, acid rain magnifies the sun's rays causing the toxic mix to etch into the clear coat layer of your paint. The clear coat is a protective clear finish applied at the factory that when exposed to acid rain is eaten away. The consequence is that the color coat becomes exposed to the acid rain as well as the sun's UV rays. This fades the paint and eventually eats through the primer coat, thus exposing the bare metal beneath to rust.

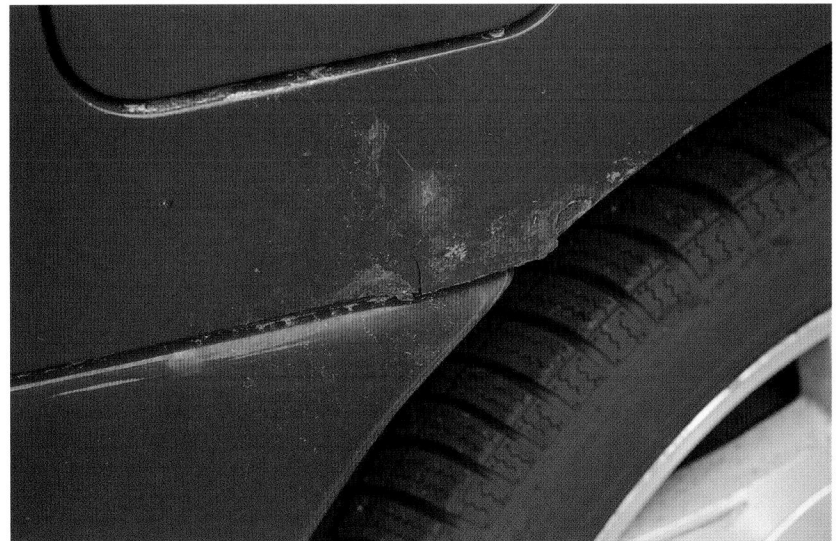

If let go, exterior paint chips can turn into major finish problems as well as body rust, and in extreme cases, compromise structural integrity of the part it's eating away at. When allowed to fester, exterior paint chips let moisture, salt, road dirt, and grime break in the paint. It then insidiously courses under the paint, setting up rust where you can't see it. Over time, a paint blister forms a few inches from the original paint chip. You will find after grinding away the paint to repair the rust that it has crept far and away from the paint chip. The best way to stop the progression of rust from a paint chip is to tend to it with some touchup paint as soon as you notice it.

Some car washes use recycled water. Stay away from these establishments. The salt from however many umpteen vehicles is in that water being pumped onto your car. Ask if the car wash uses fresh or recycled water. If recycled, find another car wash. Period. You pay enough for that vehicle; don't let the car wash help deteriorate it. *Shutterstock*

If your wheels have that black brake dust on them, don't try to scrub them clean. The dust is super-heated metal particles that have come off your semi-metallic brake pads when stopping. The heated material from the pads impregnates the wheels' surface. There are special cleaners designed for this. Be sure you use the correct type of cleaner for your car's wheels. Using the wrong type will seriously damage their finish!

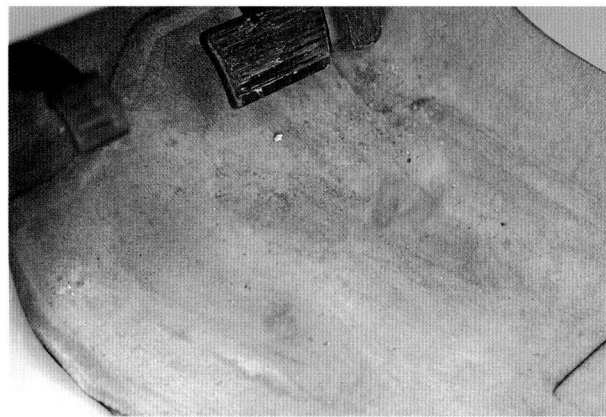

Carpets and interior vinyl take a beating. Salt and other road-clearing chemicals eat at carpet pile, causing it to come apart. Vinyl dries up from exposure to the sun. Make sure the carpets are protected with mats, and clean them twice a year. This will lift out the harmful chemicals that you bring into the car on the bottoms of your shoes. There are some great vinyl cleaning and dressing products on the market. If you're not sure what to buy, ask your local professional detailer.

carpet pile. Even if you don't live in a salt region, you still get chemicals on the bottoms of your shoes (for example, lawn fertilizers and bug sprays) that can permanently damage the carpet. Replace floor mats when needed; it's cheap compared to carpet replacement or lost value if you decide to sell or trade-in the car. Moisturize all vinyl. Interior and exterior vinyl should be treated once a year to prevent drying and cracking (especially if you live in a sun belt). Use a cleaner specifically recommended for vinyl. After cleaning, buff dry and apply a vinyl dressing.

Leather seats: Regarding the care of leather seats, check your owner's manual for recommended cleaning products and procedure. For any major cleaning it's a good idea to take the car for professional detail cleaning. A good quality detail shop uses up-to-date cleaning products and procedures. Careful about what you carry in your pockets and on your belt. Sharp objects like keys and such can do a number on your vehicle's leather (or any other kind of upholstery).

Keeping a clean car pays if you trade it in: Here's a statistic for you to consider regarding the value of keeping your vehicle clean. According to a national study done by the Car Care Council, auto auctions across the country reported that among typical four- to seven-year-old cars in all categories (which include sub-compact, compact, full-size, and luxury), an "extra clean" vehicle may be worth 50 percent more than an identical vehicle in "average" condition. Now that's significant.

PROTECT YOUR VEHICLE AGAINST THE ONSLAUGHT OF SALT

Salt attacks both the exterior and the interior of your vehicle and causes so much damage that we need to take a closer look at what you can do to fight back.

Several states use calcium and magnesium chloride, liquid sodium, and rock salt to keep roads clear of snow and ice in the winter to provide open roads and safe travel conditions. Although these chemicals do a great job of de-icing the roadways and keeping us safe, they take a big toll on your car. It is one of your car's worst enemies because its effects are devastating over time. So what can you do to slow the effects of oxidation (rust) of your vehicle caused by salt and other road clearing chemicals?

Wash your vehicle: Make sure you have your car thoroughly washed every week during the high salt-use season. Some of you choose the cheapest automated car wash cycle, which often doesn't include the undercarriage. Trying to save a buck will cost you a lot more in the long run. Include the undercarriage, because salt finds its way up into the cracks and crevasses of the car's underside, including the body seams, box areas of the frame, and the suspension components. If salt gets into the wiring via cracked insulation or a bad electrical plug, corrosion occurs. The rust inhibits electrical flow and causes malfunction of a component or circuit.

Remember, dried salt lies dormant underneath your car until mixed with water, which causes a chemical reaction causing oxidation (rust). Washing your car frequently during high-salt season flushes the salt from the hidden and exposed surfaces. Finally, wash the undercarriage weekly to prevent the negative effects of salt corrosion on the electrical wiring and connections of your vehicle.

Rust protection: If you intend to keep the car for a significant length of time (four years or more) have rust protection applied by a rust protection specialist. And I don't mean just undercoating or oil spraying. Let's take a closer look at these two methods:

- Undercoating seals up whatever rust has started and creates a waterproof underbelly where water and rust get trapped and continue to eat away at your car.

Leather interiors are expensive and idiosyncratic when it comes to care of them. Wipe all spills immediately as leather can stain easily. There are products on the market that can provide a protective coating to interior leather. Ask your car dealer or auto detailer about them. When cleaning leather seating, make sure you use products specifically designed to clean and nourish leather to stop cracking and fading.

DRIVERS ASK, TOM ANSWERS: EXTERIOR PROBLEMS SOLVED

Q Dear Tom,
I have stock rims on my 2005 Nissan Quest, and they look like something is eating away at the alloy. I live in Washington state; do you think it's the de-icer used by the road service during the winter? Is there anything I can do to curtail the corrosion and repair the damage?

Marty—Omak, Washington

A Marty,
What you described is quite common. Aluminum alloy wheels are affected by road salt, liquid sodium, and calcium chloride. The clear coat on the aluminum wheels breaks down, resulting in corrosion. The only thing you can do to stop it is to have the wheels buffed and clear-coated again. An expensive proposition to say the least. Get an estimate from a body shop and then decide if it's worth it to you. Should you decide to do it, ask the body shop about a special polyurethane coat which is tougher and stands up to the road-clearing chemicals.

Good luck.
Tom

Q Tom,
I own a '94 Chrysler minivan. The paint has begun peeling off the hood and roof; it looks like the wind is peeling the paint off. What could cause this?

Julian—San Francisco

A Julian,
This condition is called paint de-lamination. It is caused by the lack of chemical bonding of the paint to the primer coat and possibly the primer coat to the metal of the car's body if metal is exposed. Chrysler had this problem in the early to mid-1990s, so your minivan falls right into this category of vehicles affected by this defect. The only solution is to repaint the area affected.

Tom

Q Tom,
I own a '98 Sedan Deville with a water leakage problem. Every time it rains my carpets on the driver and passenger (front) get soaked. No one seems to know where it's coming from. I noticed there is no molding around my windshield. Could that be the problem?

Debra—Philadelphia, Pennsylvania

A Debra,
Water leaks in the body of cars can be tricky to locate. Water always finds its way to the lowest point in the vehicle. That said, the point of entry might be way higher than where it's welling up. Since the molding that goes around the windshield is missing, I would start there with a water test. If the vehicle has a sunroof, the drain hoses for it could be leaking or plugged, resulting in water finding its way inside the vehicle.

The best way to track down a water leak is to remove some interior body panels and then run a garden hose all over the vehicle until you start to see water coming in. Find the point of entry and repair the leak.

Tom

Q Tom,
What is the proper use of an electric buffer? I got one for Christmas from my wife and want to use it on my 1969 Camaro.

Jason—Miami, Florida

A Jason,
First off, if it has two speed settings never, never use the high-speed setting. This could result in paint damage. Set the buffer to low speed, apply your wax to the buffing bonnet, and just lay the tool on the finish. Do not apply heavy downward pressure to the buffer, as this will surely burn through the paint. Just the weight of the tool is sufficient, all you have to do is guide it across the area you want to apply or buff the wax on. The same instruction goes for buffing the wax after it had dried on the paint: low-speed setting with no downward pressure on the tool. Just guide it over the finish.

Tom

Q Tom,
I have a 2008 Cadillac Escalade. It has leather seating. What is the best way to clean the leather upholstery?

Linda—Reno, Nevada

A Linda,
There are some great leather cleaners on the market that you can use. The best way to start is to prepare the leather for cleaning first. Wipe the upholstery down with warm water and a cotton cloth. Make sure the cloth is almost dry, not soaking wet. You just want to get the dust and light dirt off the surface. Don't try to scrub any stains, as this can damage the leather. Let the cleaning product do that for you. After the leather is dry, apply the cleaner following instructions. For any tough stains that don't come out, take it to a professional as they have other methods of removing stains from leather.

Tom

Q Tom,
My Chevy Colorado has a scratch in the windshield from the windshield wiper. Can I buff it out with wax?

Sammy—New Jersey

A Sammy,
There are products on the market designed to buff out scratches in glass, not a wax but a rubbing compound much like jeweler's rouge, a fine jewelry-buffing compound. I tend to shy away from them because if not properly used, you can do more damage than good. If you must try this, apply the rubbing compound by hand and see if you can buff it out. It all depends on how deep the scratch is into the glass. If you must use a power applicator because the hand application is not touching it, try using a small fine buffing bonnet with a variable speed electric drill. Use low speeds in working the compound.

Good luck!
Tom

• Oil spraying creates a potential fire hazard if the oil is ignited by hot exhaust; oil can also cause rubber component damage. Also, with the first good blast of winter weather most of the oil gets washed off (along with any rust protection the oil might have offered). It's quite ineffective, to say the least.

Magic electrical boxes: You can forget about the magic electrical boxes that supposedly set up an electrical field to prevent rust. These systems were found to be fraudulent by the U.S. government. Giant electrical systems set up to protect bridges powered by high-energy generators might offer rust protection for bridges, but a little box powered by a 12-volt electrical system exposed to the weather is a waste of your money.

Carwell system: Living in the salt belt (Buffalo, New York) for more than 20 years now, and being in the auto repair industry as I have for the last 37 years, you can't imagine the myriad of rust protection "systems" and methods I have seen. Little boxes that are connected to 12-volt sources to stop rust, oil spraying, rubberized as well as polyurethane under coatings, anticorrosive foams that are sprayed into vehicle's body panels, and on and on it goes, yet cars still rust out at an amazing rate in Salt Belt Land.

A few years back I was contacted by the CEO of a rust protection company called Carwell. He claimed that he had the best rust protection on the planet. I yawned and said, "Show me the facts to substantiate your claims." He invited me to his office. When I arrived, he dropped on the desk in front of me a 5-inch-thick dossier with the U.S. armed forces logos on it. As I thumbed through this couple of thousand–paged document I realized that it was in-depth testing of this Carwell rust-protection product. The findings were incredible. It was tested in the salt belt states during wintertime and on the beaches of Florida, Washington, California, and Hawaii.

The bottom line: Carwell protects against rust better than any other rust-protection product or system out there. The armed forces had named this product the exclusive rust-protection product for all four branches of the U.S. armed forces.

After using it myself for several years I can honestly tell you it does work, and so I am telling you about it here in the pages of my book. Carwell is a formula designed specifically for its intended use: rust protection on vehicles. During a typical Carwell application, the specialist applies Carwell rust protection to the inside of the body panels and hard-to-get-at frame areas. The whole operation is similar to what happens when insulation is blown into the walls of your home, only in this case it's blown into the inside panels of your vehicle.

This chemical formulation attacks existing rust, flakes it away from the bare metal beneath, and chemically bonds to the bare metal. It also absorbs any moisture present and bleeds it to the surface, sets up a moisture barrier, and finally, it creeps to fill every crack and crevice in the metal.

That's total protection! Another great benefit of Carwell is that it insulates electrical wiring harnesses and connections, allowing only $\frac{1}{100}$th of a volt drop across connections. This is a great electrical system protector, especially when you consider the impact of salt corrosion on electrical connections and contacts. Carwell is one of the best rust protection systems on the market. Use it as a measuring stick when buying rust protection products. Find out more online at: www.carwell.com.

It's important to note that even if your car is rust protected, if you live in a salt belt you should still wash your vehicle at least once every week during high salt-use periods. And remember, *what counts the most is washing the underside*, especially under fender wells and other enclosed areas such as doors. Paint doesn't rust, the metal behind it does.

Keep out of heated garages: A study done in 1992 at Cornell University shows that most rust action is the result of road salt, and it is 20 to 30 times greater in spring than in winter. The reason? Rising temperatures, which trigger oxidation.

Cornell researchers warn to keep your car out of heated garages during the winter because heat increases salt corrosion. The Cornell team found that recycled water used by some commercial car washes often contains significant amounts of road salt from previous car washings. So if you use a commercial car wash, ask if they use recycled water. If they do, find another car wash.

Keep on top of rust: If you live in a salt belt state and intend to keep your vehicle a long time, have the body inspected regularly for rust. When a rust spot crops up, have it tended to immediately. This may require bodywork (cutting the rusty metal out and welding new metal in place), rust proofing, priming, and painting.

If you leave the rust alone, it will set up, creep underneath the paint, and "eat" the structural integrity of the metal body. When adding a new body part to the vehicle make sure to rust proof that part before installing it.

SUMMARY

• Wash your car (undercarriage included) weekly during high-salt use.
• Wax semi-annually. Apply a carnauba-based wax. Apply by hand in a swirl pattern, let dry, then buff clean. If using an electric applicator, be careful. Too fast with too much downward pressure will burn through the paint.
• If you are going to keep your car for a few years and you live in a salt belt, have professional rust proofing done on the car.
• During the salt-use season, do not park your car in a heated garage because heat triggers salt corrosion.
• Inspect for rust annually and repair as necessary; don't leave bare metal to fester into a rust spot and grow.
• When adding new parts to your vehicle such as a fender or door, make sure they're rust proofed before installing.

PROJECT 17
Change Wiper Blades

 Time Required: 15 minutes

 Tools Required: None, or a nail or small screwdriver depending on style of blade

 Skill Level:

 Cost Estimate: $15–$30

 Tip: Set new blades next to old ones and determine mounting method and orientation before removing old blades

1

When your wipers are not clearing the windshield cleanly during a rainstorm or when you use the washer, it's time for a new set. Changing them is an easy home project. Wiper arms are hinged near the base.

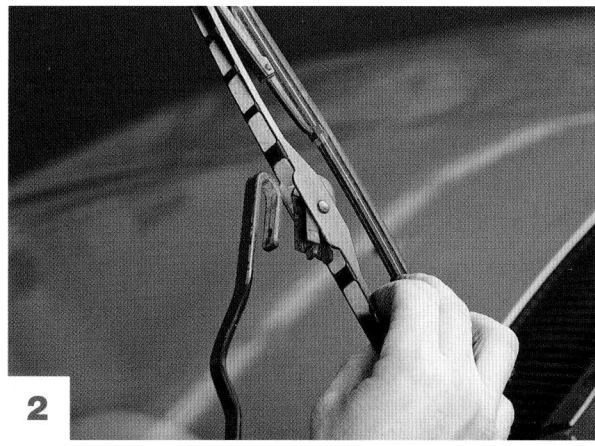

2

Most of these hinges allow you to lift the blade about perpendicular to the windshield, where it will stay. If not, you need to hold it up as you remove the blade.

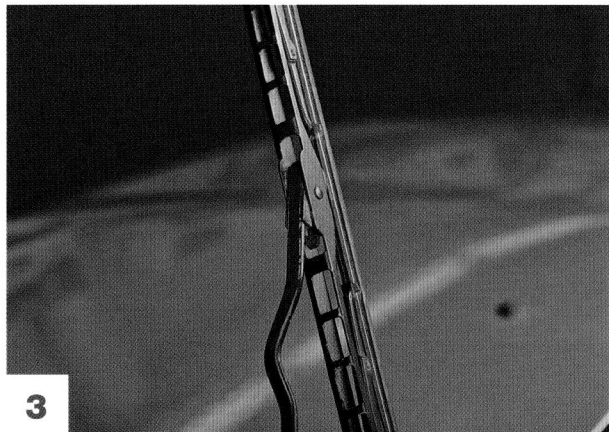

3

This common style uses a U-shaped clip that you compress to remove the blade. Find the little button inside the U and push it toward the other end of the clip. Another style attaches to a small, grooved shaft gripped by a spring clip. This style has a hole marked "push." You insert a thin object, like a nail, into the hole to release the clip and slide off the blade. The new blade clicks over the shaft.

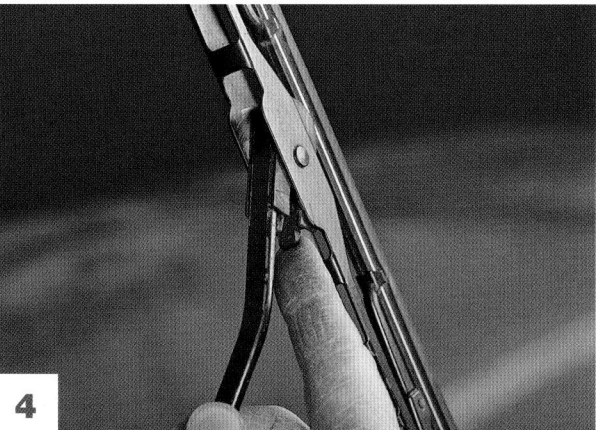

4

With the U-clip compressed as shown above, slide the wiper blade toward the base of the arm, which will cause the arm's U-shaped end to pull free of the clip. (Doing this will likely push the rubber blade out a bit.) Shift the arm end so that it clears the clip and passes out a hole above it, freeing the blade. To put the new one on, reverse the directions just given.

PROJECT 18
Replace Taillight Bulb

 Time Required: 15-30 minutes

 Tools Required: Socket wrench/screwdriver

 Skill Level: to

 Cost Estimate: $5–$10

 Tip: Check the bulb you remove to ensure that its filament is broken; a bad fuse, relay, or loose connection can also shut down your taillight.

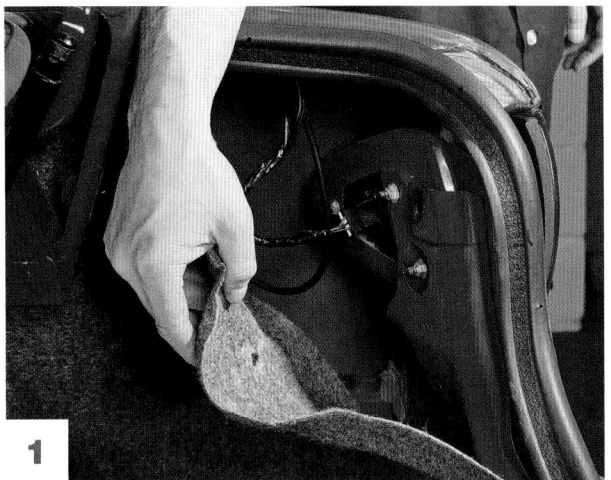

Find the wiring and harness. It may lie behind material lining the trunk.

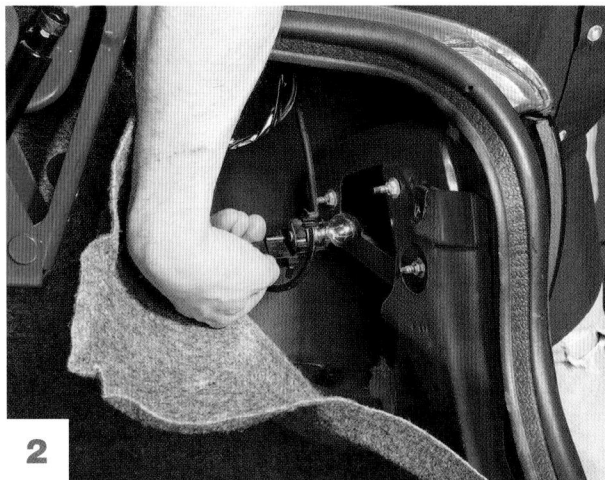

Most modern vehicles utilize a light socket that locks into place with a twist. To remove it, grip the plastic base the wiring runs into, and turn it counterclockwise. You can then slide the bulb out of the taillight lens assembly.

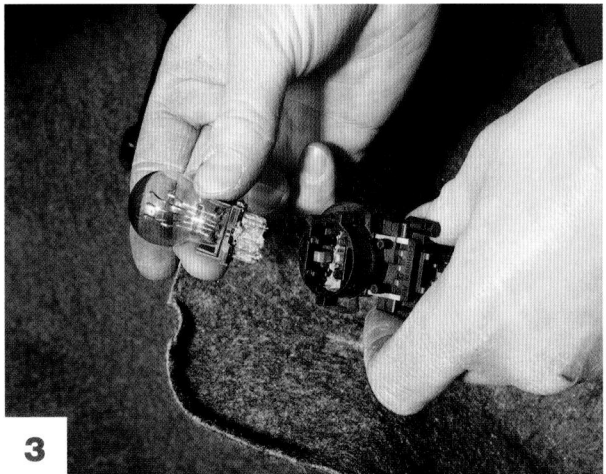

Grip the bulb at its plastic base and pull it out of the socket. The light brown grease in this picture is dielectric grease, which improves electrical connections and resists water. Do not use regular grease for this purpose.

Insert the new bulb, slip the socket back into the taillight lens assembly, and twist it into place. Any auto parts store or dealership has the bulb you need. Many of them are now standardized.

PROJECT 19
Replace Headlight Bulb

 Time Required: 15-30 minutes

 Tools Required: Socket wrench (possibly side cutters to remove body clip if present)

 Skill Level:

 Cost Estimate: $3 and up

 Tip: Be careful not to upset the headlight aiming screws

Some headlight bulbs are accessible from the engine bay and require removing nothing but the bulb fixture itself. With this Chevy Cavalier, we need to remove a plastic shield across the top of the front of the engine compartment.

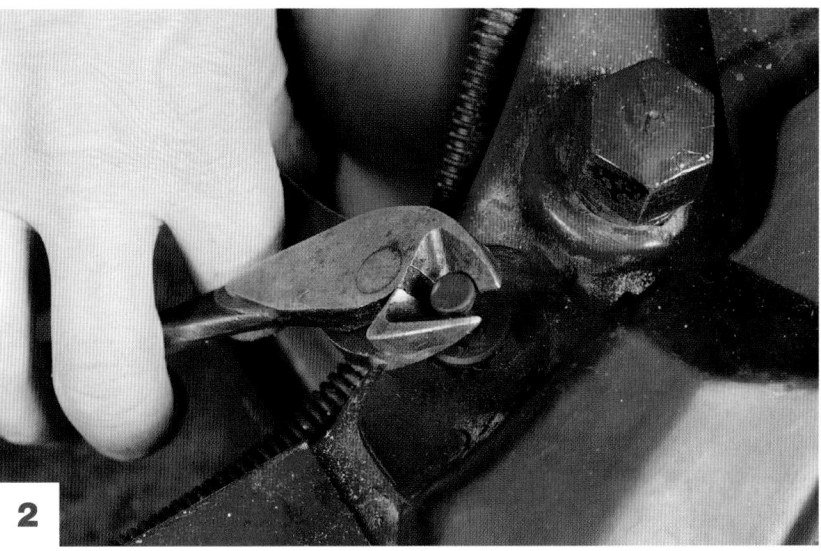

You can use a side cutter pliers to remove some body clips; use it as a wedge and lever, rather than squeezing the handles together to cut. This reveals the headlight housing mounting bolts.

Remove the bolts securing the headlight housing.

Now pull the housing forward to expose the electrical harness.

Rotate the locking ring or socket counterclockwise and pull the headlight bulb free of the headlight housing. Now unplug the bulb. Plug the new bulb in and reverse the removal procedure. Don't touch a halogen headlight bulb except at the plastic base. Oil from your fingers on the glass can cause the bulb to fail prematurely.

Chapter 14

Common Summer and Winter Woes (and How to Avoid Them)

Extreme weather changes affect vehicles. Extreme heat up and cool down causes expansion and contraction, overheating and freezing, and these environmental changes have an impact on vehicular operation. So let's explore common vehicular failures in summer and winter and how to avoid them.

SUMMER
Excessive Engine Heat

Today, car manufacturers must build cars under strict controls defined by the EPA standards, which require better fuel efficiency and lower exhaust emissions. One significant way they have complied is to manufacture engines with more aluminum, which is much lighter than the material of old, cast iron. The use of aluminum lowers the vehicle's overall weight, thus decreasing fuel consumption. That's the good news. The bad news is that aluminum has a lower melting point than cast iron, so it is not as forgiving when exposed to excessive heat. The catch is that in order to achieve low exhaust emissions, the engine must run at high temperatures. Factor into the equation the high temperatures of summer with the possibility of a coolant leak and you have *engine meltdown*. That's why it is critical that you maintain the cooling system.

Nothing kills an engine faster than overheating it. Most engines today are made of aluminum in one way or another, meaning that either the whole engine is made of it or a major portion is made of it, such as the cylinder head. Aluminum is unforgiving when it comes to overheating it. One excessive overheating and the aluminum cracks and warps, gaskets blow, gasket sealing surfaces are lost, and the engine fails. *Shutterstock*

If your car's cooling system is not up to snuff (clean and circulating the coolant to all parts of the engine), heat damage occurs. This damage shows up in the form of blown head gaskets, cracked cylinder heads, burnt or cracked valve seats and cylinder, as well as warped cylinder heads. Because they are submerged in coolant all the time, cooling systems build up sludge and rust or scale. This rust, sludge, and scale inhibit the flow of coolant through the engine, which causes elevated temperatures. In addition, the antifreeze wears out. Its chemical properties break down over time, rendering it ineffective. It's recommended that you have the cooling system cleaned and filled with new coolant every two years or 24,000 miles. This procedure is called a "Flush and Fill." In between, have a cooling system analysis done every six months. A proper analysis includes the following:

Cooling system pressure test, including the radiator cap. Repair any leaks.

Antifreeze protection test: Replace the antifreeze solution if it's worn out.

Check the condition of the hoses and belts. Replace any soft or brittle hoses and cracked belts. Tighten all loose hose connections.

Flow test to make sure that the coolant is flowing properly and that the engine is operating within acceptable temperature ranges. If not, replace the thermostat.

Summary: Equation no. 1
Aluminum + high temperatures + coolant leak =
ENGINE MELTDOWN

EXCESSIVE TRANSMISSION HEAT

Your car's transmission operates under tremendous heat. Many of the internal parts are referred to as "soft parts." These soft parts inside the transmission are made up of the rubber seals and clutches that are made of a soft friction material. The transmission oil is cooled by a transmission oil cooler located either in, or affixed to, the car's radiator. Overheat the transmission and ugly things start to happen.

The fluid (which is nothing more than a specific type of oil) reaches a boil, cooking the transmission in its own juices, so to speak. As a result, seals harden and there's loss of internal hydraulic pressure. The glue on the back of the internal clutches crystallizes, causing the clutches to weaken. Along with the loss of internal cooling capacity, there is a loss of internal lubrication. An increase in friction produces more heat, and the transmission fails in short order.

If you are going to tow a trailer this summer, make sure the transmission oil is adequately cooled while towing. Normally, transmission fluid is cooled within the transmission oil cooler located in one of the radiator tanks. During towing

Transmission fluid lubricates, hydraulically actuates, and cools the inside of the transmission. It is imperative that the fluid is cooled for the unit to operate trouble free. A small transmission oil cooler is located within one of the radiator tanks. Oil flows through this cooler where heat is transferred away from the oil. When you overheat the transmission from extreme use, the factory-installed oil cooler is not enough. I suggest installing an auxiliary transmission oil cooler to provide enough protection.

the fluid gets hotter and the standard oil cooler may not release the heat fast enough. This creates a "pressure cooker" effect within the transmission that hardens up seals, grinds up metal parts, and toasts the clutches. So if you're going to tow a trailer, have an auxiliary transmission oil cooler installed on your vehicle.

Keep your car's transmission in good health and running cool this summer by following this advice:

- Perform the manufacturer's suggested scheduled maintenance consisting of fluid and filter changes. Rule of thumb: every 25,000 to 30,000 miles. This helps fluid to flow freely and keep cool.

- Don't overwork the transmission by overloading the vehicle with a ridiculous load. Know your vehicle's GVW (gross vehicle weight) and respect it.
- If you are going to haul a trailer or carry weight, have an auxiliary transmission oil cooler installed to increase fluid-cooling capacity.

Summary: Equation no. 2
Poor transmission maintenance + poor transmission cooling + excessive towing load =
FRIED TRANSMISSION

EFFECT OF HEAT ON BELTS, HOSES, BRAKES, LUBRICANTS, AND FLUIDS

Belts: Drive belts are made of rubber and consequently dry up, crack, and break. When you add summer heat to the equation, as well as the increased stress from using the air conditioner, the "breakage factor" is multiplied significantly. Have the belts and tensioner checked regularly.

Hoses: The radiator and heater hoses carry the engine coolant. The coolant is forced through the hoses under high pressure at high temperatures. This harsh environment causes deterioration of the hose material, weakening them. Have the hoses checked regularly throughout the summer and replace any soft or brittle hoses.

Brakes: Brakes are always operating under high temperatures because of their very nature. Brake shoes and pads are designed to create friction in order to stop the motion of the wheels, which are attached to the brakes. This friction produces intense heat. Add the higher temperatures of summer and (if under extra load) the increased braking required when towing a trailer and it's like having a blast furnace attached to your wheels,

Have the brakes checked in the hot summer months (every tire rotation or 6,000 miles).

Lubricants: Summer heat causes lubricants and greases to break down and lose their lubricating properties. Lubricants and greases are used to lubricate the mating surfaces of metal

It's difficult to see here, but this belt is weathered and cracked. The reason for this is that over time, the rubber dries out, leaving it brittle and hard. Friction and expansion and contraction from the engine heating up and cooling down have created the cracks you see here. A belt in this condition is ready to break and leave you stranded on the side of the roadway. Replace a belt that looks like this.

Despite being subjected to excessive heat and cold, radiator hoses tend to last a long time without needing replacement. Regardless of a typical long life, it's a good idea to inspect them for condition every time you have an oil change. It's a simple inspection. Just squeeze the hose with your hand. It should be firm and resilient and rebound firmly. If the hose is soft or conversely brittle, replace it.

parts in suspension, steering, and drivetrain components. Parts such as CV joints, tie rods, ball joints, and control arms can fail without adequate lubrication. So make sure that these parts are lubricated as per manufacturer's specifications.

Fluids: Finally, your car won't perform well if the fluids don't do their jobs. During the summer, high temperatures break down the fluids more quickly. So check them regularly and replace as necessary. Remember, each type of fluid in your car has a vital function, whether it's lubricating, cooling, or creating hydraulic pressure for braking or power steering. It is vital that you have these fluids inspected (and changed, if needed) according to the manufacturer's specifications, especially during the summer months.

MODIFICATIONS FOR HAULING LOADS IN HOT WEATHER

Many of us haul trailers during the summer months. If you do, make sure your vehicle has been modified for hauling.

Vehicles that have trailer packages built into them usually have a beefed-up suspension, larger radiator, and auxiliary transmission oil cooler.

The need for a beefed-up suspension is obvious. A trailer taxes the vehicle's suspension because of the extra weight from the tongue, not to mention the weight that is dragging on the rear of the vehicle stressing the springs and suspension parts. Excessive towing by a vehicle that is not built for it causes premature suspension failure and excessive tire wear.

Hauling excessive weight also requires a larger radiator. Why? Because the engine produces more heat as it works harder. The coolant heats up faster and to higher temperatures. If the radiator is not big enough, the coolant passes through it too quickly, and the coolant doesn't have enough time to release its heat. Consequently, heat builds up in the coolant and the engine overheats.

To avoid transmission damage when hauling a load, you may need an auxiliary transmission oil cooler. When hauling a trailer load, the transmission produces more heat because it's working harder. Like the engine, the transmission must be constantly cooled. This is accomplished by circulating the transmission oil through an oil cooler located in one of the radiator tanks. If the cooler is too small, then the oil isn't cooled fast enough, and the transmission overheats and cooks the internal rubber transmission seals to a brittle crisp.

Another effect of overheating is the actual burning of the transmission oil. When it's burnt, the oil loses its lubricating and cooling properties as well as its ability to create hydraulic pressure within the unit. At that point, you might as well pour water into the transmission because the oil isn't doing anything anyway.

Having adequate brakes is essential to any vehicle, and even more so for one that is hauling a load on a trailer. When brakes get overheated because of intense use, they crystallize, which causes "brake fade." The friction material gets so hard from overheating that it doesn't stop the vehicle. No matter how hard you press the brake pedal, the vehicle keeps moving. Picture that happening while cruising down one of the mountainous highways in West Virginia. Makes you want to check out your brakes, doesn't it?

"Toy" Trailers: If you've put many miles on the roadways in the summer, you've seen refugees from junkyards masquerading as toy trailers careening down the highway behind some big SUV. Hauling a deathtrap behind you and compromising the safety of other motorists as well as yourselves is simply irresponsible. During the summer season, these trailers often carry boats and are submerged in water regularly. What do you think happens to the wheel bearing lubricant? How about the wiring and lighting, not to mention the effects of rust on the frame, suspension, and brakes of these trailers? At the end of the season, what do most people do? They put the trailer away until the next season. No maintenance, no upkeep, and no repairs. The

Proper brake operation is critical to you and your family's safety, and brake replacement is something that should not be done at the cheapest bidder's price. What I mean here is not to spend indiscriminately but to be a good steward when spending money on brake repairs. Get the best quality parts you can at the best price. Ask questions such as, what quality are the parts? What is the warranty? How do these parts measure up to OEM? Remember, just because they look alike doesn't mean that the brake parts that are cheaper are of like quality. Quality is in the unseen aspects of manufacture such as steel and friction material.

following season, they haul it out, plop their toy on it, and careen down the road in front of some family taking a Sunday drive. A message to boaters and personal watercraft owners: Take care of your trailers, please. Get your trailer inspected before hauling it down the highway.

A typical trailer inspection includes the following:
- Check the wiring for cracked or chafed insulation, poor electrical connections, or corroded light sockets.
- Check over the frame for compromised integrity from rust.
- Check tires and wheels for safety.
- Check the brakes.
- Make sure all the lights work: turn signals, brakes, and running lights.

- Inspect the wheel bearings and axles for wear or lack of lubrication. Make sure the wheel bearings have good seals and are adjusted properly.
- If the trailer has a wooden floor, make sure all floorboards are in good shape. Rotted or broken floorboards can cause your payload to shift in transit and fall off the trailer. An ugly scene indeed, especially for the guy following in the car behind you.

As you can see, hot outside temperatures can do serious damage to your car and cost you a lot in terms of money, time, aggravation, and compromised safety. The good news? Now you know how to avoid these problems and get the most mileage out of your car, with peace of mind and without having to take on a second job.

Q Dear Tom,
Does the electric corrosion control system, which is advertised to prevent a vehicle from rusting from road salt, really work? Or are these products just a gimmick?

Ed—Delaware

A Ed,
These "systems" have been found to be fraudulent by the Federal Trade Commission (FTC). They do not work. Cathodic corrosion protection works well on bridges because they are based in water and thus complete a circuit. Also, they use much higher voltage than the mere 12 volts used by the car devices. Add into the equation the rubber car tires that insulate the vehicle from ground (thus eliminating a closed-loop circuit) and you have a small 12-volt light in a box. It might look impressive, but it does nothing for rust protection. Don't waste your money.

Tom

Q Hi Tom,
I am the proud owner of a 1996 Nissan Maxima, which I bought new 13 years ago. This winter, even on days when it is 35 degrees, I have noticed that the heater does not blow warm air while the car idles. However, it does blow warm air when I step on the gas. Could the problem be the thermostat? The plastic reservoir of antifreeze appears to be below the "low" mark when the car is cold. Could this be the problem?

Guy—Walla Walla, Washington

A Guy,
Check the coolant level, fill it to proper level, and see if this solves the problem. It's possible that, due to low coolant, there is an air bubble traveling through the cooling system. This condition would cause a void of water in the heater core (and thus warm air) during times of idle. If the level is low, then have the system checked for a leak and have it repaired.

Tom

Q Tom,
I own a 2002 Buick LeSabre with 53,000 miles. I purchased it new and maintained it well. Recently, the car suddenly blew a brake line; there had been no leakage beforehand. My technician said the line just "rotted out." Fortunately it didn't cause an accident. I reported this failure to GM headquarters asking if it was a pattern with these cars and, if so, would they consider a recall. I never even received the courtesy of a reply to this serious safety inquiry. Can I have your thoughts on this?

Ed—Massachusetts

A Ed,
Don't expect to get a positive response from GM on this condition. They will claim that they have no control over where you choose to live and drive your vehicle. In your case, you chose to drive your car in the "Salt Belt" region of the United States where rock salt, brine, liquid sodium, and magnesium and calcium chloride are used to clear roads of snow and ice during wintertime, resulting in severe undercarriage rust. GM can do nothing to remedy such a condition. You'll have to bite the bullet and pay to have the brake line replaced. Understandably, no recalls here. Sorry about that.

Tom

Q Tom,
I own a '98 Chevy Blazer. When I turn on the heat only cool air blows. What should I do? It's cold here in Brooklyn during the winter!

Lisa—Brooklyn, New York

A Lisa,
I know all too well the cold of New York City, having grown up in Brooklyn myself. The basics of heater diagnosis begin with checking the coolant level. Make sure it's full. If the coolant is full, then check the thermostat and make sure it's opening at the proper temperature (usually about 212 degrees Fahrenheit) and that there is proper coolant flow. If the thermostat is good, check to see if the heater core is plugged. You can do this by checking the heater hose temperature. If one is hot and the other cold, the core is plugged and you need to replace it. If not, then the problem probably lies in the HVAC duct system, and the dash needs to be disassembled to find the problem. It's orobably a stuck air-blend door.

Tom

WINTER

The extreme cold of winter brings its own unique set of vehicular challenges. What are they? And what can you do to address them?

Engine Management

When winterizing your vehicle, make sure the engine-management system is up to snuff. This involves checking the spark plugs, wires, fuel filter, air filter, and a basic once-over of the performance system with a computer scan tool (to make sure there are no trouble codes logged in the system's memory). Codes indicate a problem the computer "sees" within the system. Sensors such as coolant temperature, air temperature, and oxygen can go bad resulting in poor performance and fuel mileage. With today's fuel prices, who wants to spend money on unnecessary fuel? Maintain your car's engine management system and reap the rewards: dependable cold starts, great performance, and good fuel mileage.

Protective Rubber Bellows and Boots

Have the vehicle checked from stem to stern for torn protective rubber boots and bellows on critical drivetrain/steering/suspension parts. Any parts that are exposed to the cold weather elements and dirt, road grime, and salt will succumb to premature failure.

Windshield Wipers

Make sure the windshield wipers on your vehicle are fresh, and clean the windshield properly before traveling. Wipers that skip, smear, or just move the water around are dangerous.

If your wipers are skipping, check the wiper blades to see if they are dried out. If they are, replace them. If the wipers smear the water, they are probably soaked with oil (oil gets kicked up from the road onto the windshield). Try cleaning the windshield with a water and cleanser solution. Dissolve the cleanser completely in warm water before applying it to the glass, and change the wiper blades. If the wipers just

Q Tom,
My car is very hot during the summer months. When I get in it I burn my legs. What can I do to cool it off?
  Sandra—Biloxi, Mississippi

A Sandra,
It just so happens I have written about this very subject for *AOL Autos*, so here's the rundown on keeping your car cool this summer from the Sultan of Cool:

- The most obvious thing we can do to keep the car cool is park in the shade. If there is no shade, try to park so that the sun comes in the back window. At least that way the front dash, steering wheel, and seats don't get as hot. A friend of mine keeps a white towel in her car and throws it over the dash and steering wheel. The white reflects the light and helps reduce the heat somewhat. Another technique I've used is to crack the windows about a half-inch to allow some airflow. And finally, use side vent shades on the backseat windows; they keep the sun off the backseat, keeping occupants cool.
- Turn on the air conditioner and open your windows a couple of inches as soon as you get into the car. Some people think they have to run the car for a while to warm up the engine before turning on the air conditioning. No truth to this. Start the car, open the windows, and turn the air conditioning on high. This will efficiently lower the interior temperatures because the cool air produced will displace the hot air, pushing it out the windows. As soon as it's cooled off, close the windows.
- Shield the windshield: A car sitting in a parking lot all day can reach temperatures well over 100° F. There are several companies that make windshield covers that block out the sun's rays. Not only do they lower interior temperatures, but they also stop the UV rays from damaging dashboards and fading fabrics.

If you want to spend the bucks and really lower interior temperatures, last year PPG released its Sungate EP automotive glass windshield, which the company claims significantly reduces the transmission of solar energy, keeping the interior cool and improving fuel economy. The new technology employs a glazing process built into the glass of the Sungate windshields, which reduces front seat temperatures 27° F and air-breath temperatures 16° F.

- Window tinting: Window tinting is very effective in lowering interior temperatures; however, there are different rules regulating window tinting for every state. Some states prohibit tinting of the front windows so police officers can see into a vehicle during a traffic stop. Other states allow tinting, but the degree of tinting is defined, which varies from state to state. So before having your vehicle's windows tinted, check with your state DMV to make sure you don't break any laws.

For those of you in the market for a car:
Choose cloth interiors, rather than leather. Leather tends to absorb heat, and it gets much hotter in the summertime. (It's also gets colder in winter.)

Opt for air-conditioned seats, if you're buying a luxury car. Small refrigeration units are built into the seats. When activated, they circulate cooled air up through the seat keeping your underside quite cool, dehumidified, and downright comfortable.

Rubber boots and bellows protect tight tolerance metal joints from weather elements, dirt, and road grime. If they tear or break from a projectile or just plain old age, the aforementioned elements are allowed to attack the joints and metal parts and wear them out in short order. Replace any compromised protective rubber boots immediately to avoid expensive part replacement.

move the water from one place to another on the windshield, check the wiper arm tension. The arms springs could be worn out and unable to apply enough downward pressure on the blades to clean the windshield.

Snow and ice often settle at the base of the windshield, binding the wiper blades. Many people think they can clear the windshield of snow and ice by turning on the windshield wipers. Nothing could be further from the truth! The wiper system was designed to clear the weather elements from your windshield while you're driving. Wipers aren't snowplows; they can't remove the glacier formed at the base of your windshield.

What are the consequences of overtaxing the wiper system by using the wipers to move packed ice and snow at the base of your windshield?

Windshield wipers come in many designs. Wiper makers come up with design innovations all the time. Designs include multiple blades, shorter and longer blades, multiple blades on one arm, shrouded wiper linkages, and whatever else you can think of. I have found the conventional one blade design to be most dependable. Winter blades incorporating the use of all-season rubber and shrouding of blade linkage is best for winter driving.

- Burning up the wiper motor
- Stripping out the wiper arms
- Damaging the wiper transmission (linkage system)
- Overheating the wiper motor wiring harness causing an electrical short or fire

Avoid this sort of trouble by clearing the wipers of all ice and snow before turning them on. Remember, they are called "windshield wipers" not "windshield plows."

Frozen Gas Lines

Ice forms inside the gas lines from condensation buildup. To avoid this problem, keep your gas tank at least half full at all times. In addition, use gas line antifreeze with isopropyl at least twice a week during extremely cold weather. It's compatible with electronic sensors and fuel injection systems.

Frozen Door Locks, Linkages, Windows, and Frames

The rubber gasket at the base of the window in your car door stops water from going down into the door. Unfortunately, on most cars this gasket is either rotted away or maladjusted, allowing water to get down into the door and freeze the lock linkage and window regulators. The only fix here is to either replace or adjust the gasket. If you have no intention of doing this, then here's a tip: Leave the car unlocked during the cold weather. With any luck you will be able to get into the car and warm it up enough to defrost the doors.

If you force frozen windows and locks to open, parts will break and you'll face major repairs. And don't think lock de-icer is the answer. It's designed to defrost the keyhole, not the inside of the door. Ever go to open the car door and the latch works, but you just can't get the door open? Chances are the doorframe gasket is frozen to the car, and it's either worn out or maladjusted. This gasket is designed to keep water from coming into the car. When it's not working, water enters, forming ice between the door gasket and the car's structure.

My advice? If the gasket is not torn, go to a shop and have the door adjusted to fit more tightly into the doorframe, sealing out water. Once this is done, lubricate the gasket with a rubber lubricant such as silicone. The lubricant will keep the gasket soft and pliable and, most important, set up a moisture barrier that will inhibit ice buildup. If the gasket is worn, have it replaced.

Damage to Exterior of Car

Keep the exterior and undercarriage of your car washed clean of road salt weekly during high salting times. Remember, salt plus water plus metal equals rust (the eating away of your dollars). If you haven't already done it, get a fresh coat of wax on the car to protect the paint.

Here we have a typical automotive doorjamb. Note the black rubber gaskets that outline the door cavity. These gaskets are what seals the door opening when you close the door. Over time, they can wear out and become brittle or soft, or they can tear, and when water is allowed to seep in between the door and the gasket, they can allow the door to freeze shut. Then, when you force the door open, the gasket tears even more, allowing more water to get inside the door cavity. Lubricating these gaskets with a silicone lubricant semi-annually will keep them supple and flexible and will help them continue sealing water and air out of the vehicle. Also, over time, the striker often goes out of adjustment, causing the door not to close securely. When a loose-fitting door is evident, have the striker adjusted so that the door pulls tighter into the door cavity.

Rust Protection

In salt belt states, highway departments use liquid sodium, rock salt, calcium chloride, and brine to clear roadways during winter. This plays havoc on the vehicle's undercarriage and body. Apply an effective rust protector to curtail the effects of rust and oxidation. Waxes, coatings, and paraffin that are sprayed onto the vehicle's undercarriage simply set up a place for rust to fester away at the metal. They actually can add to the problem. In a previous chapter, I outlined a rust-protection product called Carwell. It attacks existing rust and penetrates it so that the rust actually flakes away from the metal beneath it, then chemically bonds to the good metal, sets up a moisture barrier, and bleeds any existing moisture to the surface, where it evaporates.

Once this product bonds to the good metal, it creeps five inches or more in all directions, protecting every crack and crevice in the metal. In my opinion this is the definition

of an effective rust-protection product. Use this description as a guide to find an effective rust-protection product for your vehicle.

Diesel Engines and Cold Starting

For diesel-powered vehicles, make sure the battery is fully charged and has full cold-cranking amperage capacity. One of the keys to effectively starting diesels in the wintertime is a fast enough cold cranking speed. Diesel engines rely on a high-compression ratio to compress the fuel tight enough to induce combustion. If the engine doesn't crank fast enough on a cold morning, it won't start. In addition, use an anti-gel solution in diesel fuel, which keeps the fuel liquefied and flowing. If diesel fuel gets cold enough it can gel up, affecting the flow of fuel through the fuel delivery system. No fuel, no start. It's that simple.

Keep a diesel engine warm when not in use. Most diesel engines come with a block heater that plugs into a standard 110-volt outlet. A block heater is a heating element that keeps the engine coolant warm which, in turn, keeps the oil in the crankcase warm. When warm, the engine cranks over easily and attains the proper cold-start cranking speed for effective cold weather startup. If your diesel engine does not have a winter heater, get one. Diesel engine heaters come in two forms: engine block to keep coolant warm or an oil dipstick heater to keep the oil in the crankcase warm. Finally, another solution to the problem of a cold diesel engine startup is to install a battery blanket on the batteries. This will keep the batteries from freezing up, resulting in low cranking power.

Fresh, Clean Fluids

Make sure all engine fluids are fresh and clean. Fresh engine oil allows the engine to crank easily in cold weather. Clean power steering fluid makes for smooth easy steering. Brakes work more effectively with fresh clean brake fluid, and fresh clean engine coolant at a 50-50 mix prevents the engine block from freezing when temperatures drop.

A note about oil: One of the great properties of good synthetic oil is that it flows easily in cold weather. AMSOIL and Mobil 1 are the two best synthetic oils in winter flow tests. An engine with synthetic oil in the crankcase cranks easily when it's cold, resulting in a crisp startup.

Tires

Good traction is essential if you want to get around in winter conditions. Make sure there's at least 70 percent tread on your tires. All-weather tires will get you around on most snow-laden highways adequately. Ideally, experts have found that (on front-wheel-drive vehicles) four snow tires are the ticket to sure-footed winter travel. A vehicle with four snow tires will track much better around corners. With two snow tires on the traction wheels and non-snows on the trailing wheels,

There are many fine winter tires on the market today. Design innovation has excelled in this area. Winter tires are made of a rubber compound that does not freeze below 32 ° Fahrenheit, and the tread design is self-cleaning of weather elements. Tread lugs are semi-segmented to allow for better winter traction, and some tire tread designs have built into them ice cleats allowing for better ice traction. Ask your tire dealer about these design elements when buying tires. *Photo courtesy of the Goodyear Tire and Rubber Company. Used with permission.*

the end of the vehicle without snow tires has a tendency to spin out.

Engine and Transmission Oil Filters

Engine and transmission oils get heavy when outside temperatures drop, causing them to flow more slowly. Add to the equation a dirty clogged filter and you've got substantial loss of oil flow. A decrease in oil flow causes an increase in friction, which produces more heat. Over time, the ultimate result is the premature failure of transmissions and engines. So make sure engine and transmission maintenance work is current before winter starts. Pay close attention to the transmission and oil filters. Have them changed at the manufacturer's suggested intervals.

Belts and Hoses

Bad belts and hoses break down under the stress of cold temperatures. Make sure that all belts and hoses are in good condition. Soft or brittle hoses and belts that display cracks, glazing, or missing ribs (on serpentine belts) need to be replaced.

Cooling System

In addition to cooling the engine, the cooling system also protects it from freezing up. The coolant should be a 50-50 mix of coolant and water. This ratio gives a cold weather protection of –30 to –35° F. Have the coolant protection checked every year just before the start of winter. If the coolant tests out above the protection level, have the system flushed and refilled with a fresh 50-50 mix.

Don't Rock the Boat

Trying to "rock" the car out of deep snow is not good medicine. Let's say your car is stuck in deep snow. In an effort to get it out, you start rocking the car back and forth, accelerating first in drive then in reverse, in order to gain momentum. Do you have any idea what you are doing to the drivetrain of your car? The transmission and drivetrain are being stressed to the nth degree. Internal parts break under this pressure. CV joints, universal joints, and splined parts such as axles are also put under extreme stress and could break. Save yourself some money: dig out or get towed.

Steering and Suspension Damage

Another problem that occurs frequently during the winter season is suspension breakage caused when a driver overshoots a corner and slams into the curb. Ball joints, control arms, tie rods, and strut assemblies fall victim to curb damage. In addition, it's important to remember that, with front-wheel drive cars, you also have drivetrain components that get damaged (half shafts, CV joints, front hub assemblies, transmission tail shafts, and front differentials). Slow down when negotiating those turns during winter months.

SUMMARY

The minor investment of time and money preparing your vehicle for winter driving pays off in multiple dividends in the form of safety for you and your family, travel reliability, and prevention of weather damage to your vehicle. It saves you money in the big picture, so don't be a Scrooge and cut on car maintenance when working out the family budget.

PROJECT 20
Change Tire

Time Required: 15-45 minutes

Tools Required: Vehicle jack, tire iron,and spare

Skill Level:

Cost Estimate: $0

Tip: Check your spare tire and keep it inflated along with your mounted tires, so it can serve you when you need it.

1 Everyone who drives a vehicle should know how to change a tire. It starts with knowing where the jack, lug wrench, and spare tire are stowed in the vehicle. This minivan's tools lie beneath a cover at the rear. Instructions are on the inside of the cover. The vehicle must be on level ground to change a tire. Never jack up a vehicle on an incline because the vehicle can roll or shift when you lift the wheel(s) off the ground. Wear gloves to protect your hands.

2 With the tire on the ground, "break" the lug nuts free so they will turn easily once you raise the vehicle. If you jack up the vehicle first, the wheel will spin when you push on the tire wrench.

3 The jack is designed to fit in a particular place. On modern vehicles the jacking point is often where sheet metal comes together to form a ridge, called a pinch weld. Check the jacking instructions or owner's manual. This scissor jack rises when you turn a nut on one end. The wrench that turns the nut is the same one used to loosen the wheel's lug nuts. Do not work under a vehicle supported by a tire jack. It does not provide adequate lift, stability, or safety for that purpose.

4 With the lug nuts loosened, jack up the vehicle until the tire clears the ground. Take the lug nuts off, pull the wheel off, and set it aside. Tip: If the lug nuts are too tight for you to turn, put the wrench securely on the nut with the handle pointing to the left, then press it down with your foot for better leverage.

COMMON SUMMER AND WINTER WOES
(AND HOW TO AVOID THEM)

5

The spare tire in this Dodge Caravan is suspended underneath the van's rear end. To lower it, remove a plastic cap in the floor, exposing a nut that can be turned with the jack's wrench. Place the wrench on the nut and turn counterclockwise.

6

This lever releases the spare tire. Check your owner's manual for spare tire release procedures on your car.

7

Lift the spare tire onto the wheel studs. If it's too heavy to lift by hand, sit on the ground in front of the wheel opening and use your feet to help lift the wheel into place. Thread all the lug nuts onto the studs and hand-tighten them with the lug wrench. Lower the jack until the tread makes contact with the ground, but don't set full vehicle weight on it. This way, the wheel won't spin when you fully tighten the lugs using a crisscross pattern. Double check that all the lugs are securely tightened, lower the vehicle, stow jack, throw the flat tire in the back. Tip: Fix your spare as soon as you can, even if it's not a "mini" spare. If you let it go, you may need a spare again and not have one.

PROJECT 21
Fill Washer Fluid

 Time Required: 5 minutes

 Tools Required: None

 Skill Level:

 Cost Estimate: $2

 Tip: Use care when opening and closing the cap in cold weather, as thin ones can become brittle and crack.

The fluid reservoir is in the engine bay. It should be clearly marked with either the words "washer fluid" or a symbol of a windshield and wipers or both.

Lift the cap, fill the bottle with washer fluid, and close. Washer fluid is not stored under pressure, so it does not have the exacting fill standards as other fluids. Typical fill level is just below the cap.

SECTION 3
STRAIGHT TALK

INTRODUCTION TO CHAPTERS 15–17

Too often when we want the truth about something and we ask someone "on the inside" for the skinny, we sadly get spin. Unfortunately, many people go with questions unanswered, or worse, false impressions. In the following three chapters I present the naked truth to you about a few controversial issues in the automotive arena, in an effort to make it easier for you to navigate through the stormy world of vehicle ownership.

Chapter 15
Car Warranties—What's Covered and What's Not

During the past 37 years in the automotive industry, it's been my experience that whenever the phrase "it's covered under warranty" is used in auto repair, it's music to the ears of the motorist. Conversely, the phrase "it's not covered under warranty" is received with much dissatisfaction. To clear this up, I believe all that's needed is a little education.

First, a car warranty is not an entitlement; it is an agreement between you and the car manufacturer. You are responsible to follow the specified maintenance requirements set forth by the manufacturer. By doing so, you have fulfilled your responsibility to the warranty agreement. Now the manufacturer is obligated to you to perform any repairs due to a defect from poor workmanship, or a failed part for the time or mileage set forth by the terms of the agreement.

So why all the misunderstanding? I believe it's because of a commonly held assumption that a car warranty is an entitlement, not an agreement. A small number of "professionals" in the industry reinforce this mindset by telling their customers what they want to hear. "Oh no problem!" they say. "It's covered under warranty," when it's not. Then, when they can't back up their statement because the repair is not covered, the customer gets upset with the manufacturer and the shop can sympathize with them. Furthermore, there are a few unscrupulous service personnel that abuse the system by "sliding things in under the wire," covering repairs under warranty that don't quality. How do they do this? By falsifying mileage and time, VIN numbers, and who knows what else.

Engines in whole and in part are covered under the powertrain warranty, as these are manufactured by the carmaker, which stands behind them. Powertrain warranties vary in length or time and mileage. Make sure you understand what the coverage is before leaving the dealership or purchasing a warranty. Covered parts are explained in detail in your warranty information. *Shutterstock*

Opposite page photo credit: Shutterstock

Wearable items such as the drive belts and brake friction material shown here are not covered parts. That's because they are wearable in nature and are expected to go bad with age and use. Such parts are considered regular maintenance and thus the responsibility of the owner. Other items that fall under the wearable category are cooling system hoses, tires, filters, sparkplugs, and anything else considered regular maintenance as outlined in your maintenance schedule or new car warranty.

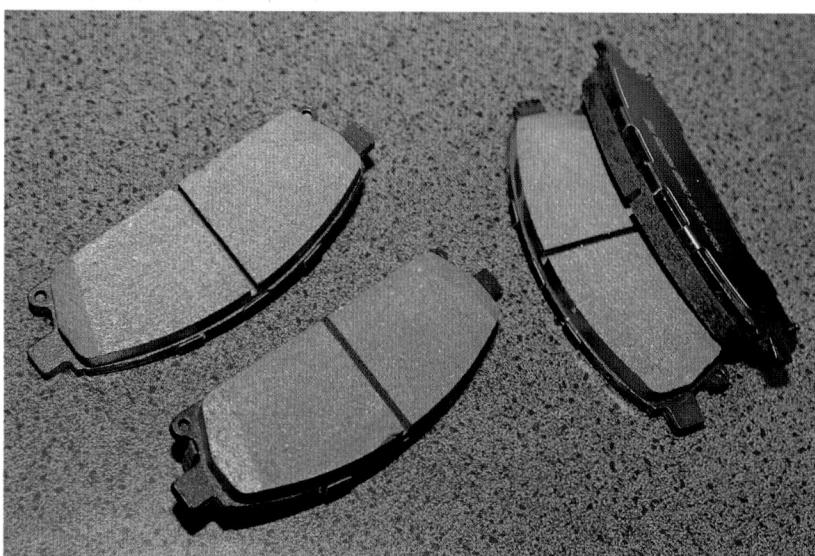

This kind of activity further reinforces the view that a warranty is an entitlement and not an agreement. Because of this underhanded practice, car manufacturers closely scrutinize every warranty claim that comes across their desks. Whenever anything questionable comes up, the magnifying glass comes out with laser-like intensity. The customer misreads this action, assuming that the manufacturer is trying to back out of the agreement. When, in fact, the repair in question doesn't qualify under the terms. A repair may not quality for a number of reasons, ranging from abuse, expiration of the warranty because of time or mileage, or a part that isn't covered.

What parts and services are covered under a warranty?
The car manufacturer is responsible for the parts it makes: the engine, transmission, suspension, steering, computers and emission control devices, instruments, chassis wiring, and a myriad of other parts that they manufacture. These components and systems may have different times and mileage coverage. Maintenance items such as filters are not covered. In addition, wearable items such as belts, hoses, brake friction material, and rotors, tires, and the likes are expected to wear out and are therefore not covered under the manufacturer's warranty.

There is one exception when wearable items might be covered in a warranty claim. If a part fails that is under warranty and this causes the failure of a wearable item, then the warranty will probably cover the replacement of the wearable item as well. For example, a brake caliper (covered under the warranty) seizes and will not release, causing both the brake pads and rotor to wear out. In this case, the pads and rotor will probably be replaced at no charge to the customer because the part with the warranty caused the damage.

There are many parts that are installed on your vehicle at the time of manufacture that are not made by the car manufacturer. Items that fall into this category include tires, aftermarket stereo systems, and conversion components. If you read the paperwork you receive at the time you purchase your car, you will find that these items are covered under their own manufacturer's warranty. So often I hear stories from consumers and service personnel alike about warranty nightmares where it was assumed that the part was covered and when a claim was filed reality struck. The key to avoiding this dilemma is to *educate yourself*.

COMMON WARRANTY-RELATED TERMS

Understanding a few warranty-related terms will go a long way in helping you through filing a warranty claim.

Bumper-to-bumper coverage is a comprehensive warranty that normally covers all items under the basic and drivetrain warranty for the period specified by the manufacturer. Time and mileage vary with each manufacturer so make sure you understand time and mileage terms before leaving the dealership.

Powertrain refers to engine components such as the engine block, cylinder heads, intake and exhaust manifolds, injection systems, flywheels, crankshaft, and pistons (basically anything related to the powerplant or engine).

Drivetrain refers to anything that drives the wheels, that is, the transmission, axles, wheel hub assemblies, transfer case, auxiliary gearbox, differential/s, driveshafts, clutch, pressure plate, throw-out bearing, and so on.

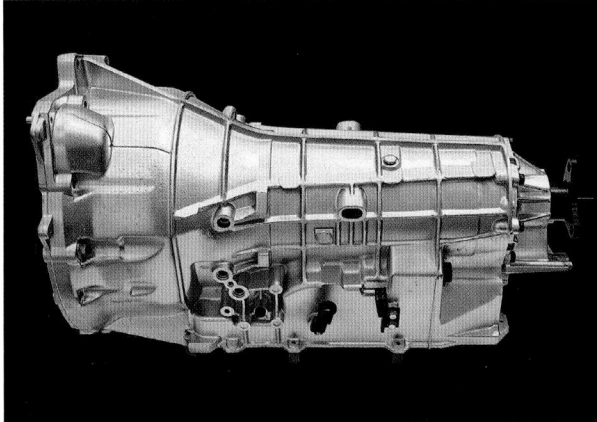

Transmission and related parts are covered under the drivetrain warranty. Such items as drive axles, CV joints, differentials, transfer cases, and overdrive units are included in drivetrain coverage. Once again, all covered parts are outlined in your drivetrain coverage. As with powertrain coverage, drivetrain is covered by the carmaker. Coverage mileage and time varies from carmaker to carmaker. *Shutterstock*

Corrosion warranty covers rust-through perforation from the inside out on sheet metal with actual holes. Surface corrosion from nicks, chips, and scratches are not covered because it is not the fault of the manufacturer but rather the driving environment. Corrosion coverage varies with each manufacturer, so read your warranty information or check with your dealer for specific details.

Campaigns and safety recalls, when announced by a manufacturer, are performed at no charge to any owner of an affected vehicle. Manufacturers may elect to perform campaigns regardless of time or mileage. Most dealers encourage owners to have them "run their VIN." The dealer plugs the owner's vehicle identification number into their computer. The computer searches the database (which is connected to the manufacturer's data) to see if the vehicle is covered under a campaign or any other actions the carmakers issued on that particular year, make, and model vehicle.

Customized conversions pertain to some vans or limousines that are covered under separate warranties for the add-ons not installed by the manufacturer. Be sure to obtain a written warranty disclosure when purchasing these types of vehicles. Also, make sure you (and your dealer) completely understand the ins and outs of conversion vehicle warranties. Don't wait until after you have taken possession of the vehicle. At that point it's too late.

Goodwill adjustments are when car manufacturers allow their dealers or field reps to make "goodwill adjustments" for a customer once the vehicle is out of warranty time or mileage. Decisions to do so are based on certain criteria such as owner's loyalty, time the vehicle has been in service, failure trends reported in the field, maintenance records, vehicle history, mileage, and whether any service contracts are in effect. Customers may be asked to share some of the cost of the repair with the carmaker in a goodwill adjustment. Never be afraid to ask for assistance from the manufacturer. You've got nothing to lose. I have been the benefactor of a goodwill adjustment myself. The paint on my Plymouth minivan had delaminated, and I asked for help. The van was out of warranty, but because of my impeccable service history and customer loyalty, the field rep opted to pay for most of the repair. A $400 job cost me $40.

Hidden warranty is not a goodwill adjustment. There is no such thing as a hidden warranty. Dealerships make money performing warranty campaigns. They get paid directly from the factory for any warranty work performed by their service department. So don't go beating up your local dealer because you think a certain operation should be performed under a hidden warranty. They would do the work if they could because it would be money in their pockets.

Emissions warranty is mandated by the federal government. Carmakers are required to provide extended warranty coverage on emission systems to ensure lower tailpipe emissions. Typical coverage is seven to eight years and 70,000 to 80,000 miles. If you have a drivability problem on a late-model vehicle, check with your dealer on emissions warranty coverage before paying for the repair. It could be covered under the emissions warranty.

Emissions warranties are longer than carmaker warranties by federal government mandate. Check your warranty for such coverage. Items covered are exhaust gas recirculation (EGR) valves, air pumps, evaporative emissions (EVAP) systems, catalytic converters, O_2 sensors, and anything else that is considered an emissions related part.

AFTERMARKET WARRANTIES

What happens if you install an aftermarket part and have to file a warranty claim for a problem with your car that crops up after the installation? Does this void your vehicle's warranty? In 1975 a law was passed to address this issue.

The Magnuson-Moss Warranty Act of 1975: How It Affects Your Vehicle's Warranty When You Install Aftermarket Parts

A summary of how the law reads:

Magnuson-Moss Warranty Act, Title 1, __101-112, 15 U.S.C. __2301 et seq. This act, effective July 4, 1975, is designed to "improve the adequacy of information available to consumers, prevent deception, and improve competition in the marketing of consumer products. . . ." The Magnuson-Moss Warranty Act applies only to consumer products, which are defined as "any tangible personal property which is distributed in commerce and which is normally used for personal, family, or household purposes (including any such property intended to be attached to or installed in any real property without regard to whether it is so attached or installed)." Under Section 103 of the Act, if a warrantor sells a consumer product costing more than $15 under written warranty, the writing must state the warranty in readily understandable language as determined by standards set forth by the Federal Trade Commission. There is, however, no requirement that a warranty be given nor that any product be warranted for any length of time. Thus the Act only requires that when there is a written warranty, the warrantor clearly disclose the nature of his warranty

obligation prior to the sale of the product. The consumer may then compare warranty protection, thus shopping for the "best buy." To further protect the consumer from deception, the Act requires that any written warranty must be labeled as either a "full" or a "limited" warranty. Only warranties that meet the standards of the Act may be labeled as "full." One of the most important provisions of the Act prohibits a warrantor from disclaiming or modifying any implied warranty whenever any written warranty is given or service contract entered into.

Translation (and How It Applies to You, the Motorist)

Under the provisions of the Magnuson-Moss Warranty Act of 1975, an automotive dealership or carmaker cannot void your warranty because your vehicle has been modified with aftermarket parts. The manufacturers have to prove that the failure was the direct result of the installed aftermarket part. Unfortunately, too many folks have gone to a dealer to have warranty service performed on their modified vehicle only to have the dealership refuse to cover the defective items. The dealer tells them that the warranty is void because aftermarket parts were installed. In such cases, they don't even attempt to find out whether or not the aftermarket part caused the problem. This is illegal. Period.

Below are illustrations of aftermarket installations that *would* void a vehicle's warranty.

Example 1

You install an aftermarket electronic cruise control. While you're driving down the road, the cruise unit develops an internal short; this causes the accelerator pedal to depress to the floor and over-rev the engine. After this episode the engine develops an engine knock under acceleration or under load. The car is still under warranty so you take it into your local dealer, and they determine that the short in the cruise unit over-revved the engine, causing the rod bearings to spin and thus damage the crankshaft and connecting rods. In this case, your warranty is void because the aftermarket cruise unit caused the engine problem. Not only are you responsible for the engine replacement, but the dealer is also within his rights to charge you for the diagnosis. Too bad, you lose.

Example 2
You install an aftermarket air dam system to channel more air to the cold air intake system that you installed. The air dam system causes the vehicle to overheat because it restricts airflow over the radiator. As a result of overheating, the engine blows a head gasket and a cylinder head is warped. The car is still under warranty. You take it to your dealer and they determine that the aftermarket air dam system caused the overheating and thus the cylinder head damage and gasket failure. The carmaker is not obligated to perform any repairs under the provisions of the warranty.

Example 3
You install a 6-foot "personal snowplow" on your SUV. The warranty expressly states that the installation of a snowplow voids all warranty if the vehicle comes in with frame, suspension, steering linkage, or any other damage that can be attributed to the plow installation and use. You install the plow anyway. While plowing you drive hard into a snow bank and the air bag deploys. You take it into your dealer and they determine that the airbag deployed because of the hard, sudden impact when the plow hit the snow bank. (But you took the plow off!) Yes, but the mounting brackets, winch, and hydraulics are still there, and there is indication of stress to the frame where the plow is mounted. Warranty voided! You are left holding the bag.

Example 4
You install a high-energy ignition system along with a special performance chip in your car's computer to increase performance, as well as aftermarket headers (of course, you had to disconnect the O_2 sensor). Maybe you're a street racer? The car is due for state inspection, and it fails the emissions part of the inspection. You take it into your dealer for warranty service to the emissions system. The dealer determines that the car failed because you modified the performance system as well as the exhaust system. Sure it runs like a racecar, but it will never pass the state emissions test with this set up. Oh, by the way, you just voided your warranty because the car was set up for racing and the OEM system was cannibalized.

In any one of these scenarios, if the dealer just lifts the hood, sees the modifications, and states that the warranty is void based on what they see without verifying that the failure is due to the aftermarket installation, the dealer would be in violation of the Magnuson-Moss Warranty Act of 1975. The cause of the failure must be searched out and proven in order for the carmaker to void a warranty.

If you want to "play it safe" when modifying your vehicle, consider the following: In today's competitive market, carmakers are heavily into manufacturing performance parts and accessory systems for their cars. So, before installing anything aftermarket on a vehicle that has a warranty in place, check with your dealer or carmaker to see if there are parts or systems available for your vehicle from the manufacturer that would accommodate your car's warranty. For instance, consider Scion. The accessory products that Scion and their parent company Toyota have come out with for this vehicle are numerous and impressive to say the least. Installation of this product line should not void your warranty or put it into question.

EXTENDED WARRANTIES
If you are keeping your vehicle beyond the average payment time period of 36 months, I highly recommend an extended warranty. Why? Consider the cost of electronics repair or transmission or engine replacement. The average transmission replacement is around $3,000. Engines cost in the neighborhood of $4,000. In-vehicle electronics can cost a small fortune to diagnose and repair or replace. Repairs of this nature can rifle most people's budgets and cause immediate hardship. This is precisely why I recommend an extended warranty on a vehicle if you are going to keep it beyond the factory or dealer warranty.

Pictured here we have a PCM (powertrain control module), a very expensive replacement should it go bad. Vehicles today can have as many as 28 individual computer modules like this one controlling different vehicular systems. While they are covered under the factory warranty, once the vehicle has gone beyond warranty coverage in mileage or time, such devices are not covered. Here's where an extended warranty is worth its weight in real cash. *Providing* the extended warranty covers these electronic devices. Note, I stressed the word *providing*; always, always make sure you understand exactly what's covered in your extended warranty before plunking down the cash. It's just smart vehicle ownership, period.

DRIVERS ASK, TOM ANSWERS: WARRANTY PROBLEMS SOLVED

Q Dear Tom,
I own a 2000 Audi and the engine light keeps coming on. I took it to my mechanic and he said I needed a new catalytic converter. I took it back to the Audi dealer, and they said I needed new sparkplugs. (They never mentioned the catalytic converter.) They put new sparkplugs in and the check engine light is still illuminated. They told me that the light would go off after driving the car for a few hours, which it did; however the light is back on again! I went for an inspection (California) and the car failed for emissions. The dealer wants to charge me again for a diagnostic and the car smells like rotten eggs! What is going on here?!
Samantha—Fresno, California

A Samantha,
Call Audi customer service and get with your local service zone rep. You should have documentation that the catalytic converter needed replacing before the warranty went out. This should be enough to get Audi to pay for the replacement of the catalytic converter, but make sure someone checked why the cat went bad. Usually they go bad due to the dumping of excess fuel into the engine, causing the cat to receive more gasoline than it can process. When this happens, a rock of carbon forms inside the cat, restricting exhaust flow. Catalytic converter replacement does not guarantee the problem is solved. Get to the root of the problem, the excessively rich fuel mixture, or this will happen again!
Tom

Q Tom,
My brother is interested in buying a 2007 Saab 9-3 convertible that was water damaged and has no factory warranty. It has a "flood title?" What do you think? Can a warranty be purchased for it? Is it worth the risk?
Sigmund—New York

A Sigmund,
This vehicle has a Flood Damaged Title issued from the insurance company. Such vehicles cannot be given warranties because of said title and extended warranty companies stay away from this type of preexisting condition. You see, with water-damaged vehicles the problems that crop up later are so massive due to the deep-seated corrosion resulting from water immersion that its not worth the risk to the warranty company, so they stay away from this type of situation completely. It's not worth the hassle for your brother either, even if he were to find an extended warranty company that would issue a policy on it. Tell your brother to walk away from it; there are other Saabs in the sea, Sig!
Tom

Q Tom,
I bought my 2006 Chevy Impala LS in September 2008, and the dealer sold me a warranty for the car, which cost $1,800. It doesn't cover anything on the car except the inside of the motor and the inside of the transmission. I know this because I had to replace the power steering hose ($140), the steering column shaft ($550), and the transmission lines ($175). All this stuff should have been covered by the four-month dealership warranty that I received from the dealership that closed down two weeks after I bought the car. I called GM, and all they could offer is a shoulder to cry on and no help with financing to fix these things. Do you have any suggestions?
Gil—Fort Worth, Texas

A Gil,
The warranty you bought is probably an extended warranty that a private company administrates. Based on what you described, it is a powertrain/drivetrain warranty. Powertrain/drivetrain warranties cover only the components that move the car: the engine, transmission, and sometimes differentials and gearboxes. Read the warranty information closely and contact the warranty company. They should be able to answer any questions you have. On a side note, you may be able to determine what you paid for by simply reading the warranty explanations within the paperwork you got from the dealer. Sometimes the answers to our questions are right in front of us. Success to you.
Tom

Q Tom,
I would like to know if you could tell me the difference between a powertrain warranty and a drivetrain warranty, please?
Shari—New York City

A Shari,
Powertrain includes all components that power the car: the engine, turbo or super charger (if equipped), and all related engine components. Drivetrain usually relates to the transmission, differential, axles, wheels, and anything that drives the car forward through gears and axles. I hope this helps clear things up a bit. Oh, one other thing: Read the warranty policy closely, it will explain exactly what is covered and what is not.
Tom

Q Dear Tom,
I own a new Lexus IS350 that requires premium gas. It seems like most foreign (European/Japanese) cars including this one require premium fuel. Why is that and will it void my warranty if I use regular gas?
Ann—Port Ritchie, Florida

The arena of extended warranties is one that has evolved light years in a short time. Just 15 years ago, extended vehicle warranties were either offered by the carmakers or by obscure companies selling a bill of goods. Having been a service manager, I can tell you horror stories of dealing with these huckster extended warranty companies that denied every claim that came into their "call centers" (probably a one-room shack in the middle of Area 51). Story after story riddled the highways of folks spending good money for perceived coverage, only to find out later that all they owned was a piece of paper.

The extended vehicle warranty market has evolved. Companies like AIG, Allstate, AAA, and NAPA have thrown their hats into the extended vehicle warranty ring, adding credibility and offering genuine coverage to motorists. The caveat here is to research the company before buying a warranty.

How does a good extended warranty company's profile look? One company that comes to mind that is exemplary is WarrantyDirect.Com, which has been in business for several years and has paid out more than half a billion dollars in claims. They deal with hundreds of car dealerships nationwide

AAnn,
Premium gasoline is required in all vehicles that have a high-performance engine. As a matter of fact, the engine in your new Lexus IS350 is a 3.5-liter V-6 is kicking out 306 horsepower. High-performance engines require high-octane gas because they run hotter combustion chamber temps than conventional engines. The lower the octane gas, the more volatile it is in the combustion chamber. The higher the octane fuel, the less volatile and more stable in the combustion chamber. When low-octane gas is used in a high-output engine like yours, it causes pre-ignition or "engine knock." The gas ignites too early, which results in hammering at the tops of the pistons, valve faces, and cylinder head faces. Over time this action damages the engine, and it will fail prematurely. Use high-octane gas where recommended. It will cost you less money in the long run, especially if you open a warranty claim for a failed engine from a melted piston due to prolonged use of low-octane fuel.

If you wanna play and drive high-performance cars, Annie, you gotta pay. Buy the high-octane fuel.

Tom

QTom,
I own a 2002 Ford Ranger. Recently the engine began pinging under acceleration. I took it to the dealership and was told by a mechanic that the pinging was inherent in this model and not to worry about it. Should I be worried? If it is a problem, how can it be corrected? Can I get it covered under warranty even though the truck is out of the time and mileage coverage, and Ford knows about the problem with the pinging?

Jim—Detroit, Michigan

AJim,
Ford issued a technical service bulletin for pinging on these trucks back in 2003. It involved reprogramming the computer with a software update. A bad mass airflow sensor can also cause this problem if the sensor is out of range. If your Ranger has a 4.0-liter engine, there have been problems with the primary timing chain too. The noise with the timing chain slapping against the timing cover is similar to that of an engine ping and will occur between 2,000 and 3,000 rpm. No, none of this is covered under warranty or recall since it's not safety related. Sorry.

Tom

and do business in 50 states. This is the kind of profile you want to see when selecting an extended warranty company.

Questions to ask before purchasing an extended warranty

Who is the warranty administrator? Do they have a good track record? How many car dealers do they work with? (If car dealers work with them, as well as sell their policies, chances are the company is easy to deal with when you have a claim.) Are they difficult to deal with when settling a claim?

To whom do you ask these questions? The best person is the service department manager or writer. These people deal with extended warranty companies all the time so they know who is reputable and who is not.

Make sure you know what's covered and what's not, as well as what your responsibilities are to the agreement. Some companies require the use of a particular chemical during scheduled maintenance. For example, the Wynn's product warranty brochure reads like this:

> Wynn's Product Warranty program offers a system of specially formulated automotive chemicals that are backed by the company's warranty on the product's performance. The program consists of a full supply of specially formulated chemicals that are designed to prevent the breakdown of internally lubricated components of a vehicle such as the engine, transmission, rear drive or transaxle, and power steering components. The Wynn's Product Warranty program is a perfect plan for the consumer who is purchasing an older, higher mileage vehicle. The standard "Powertrain" coverage is available from 3 Months/3,000 Miles up to 3 Years/36,000 Miles. The Wynner's Choice coverage includes powertrain, air conditioning, fuel and cooling system coverage and is available from 1 Year/15,000 Miles up to 3 Years/45,000 Miles.

The key here? Make sure you use the chemicals in covered components as prescribed by the chemical company and that you follow the time and mileage intervals. If you don't follow prescribed procedures, any warranty claim will be denied.

Some companies offer tiered coverage depending on vehicle mileage, year, service description (how it's used), and condition of the vehicle at the time of contract purchase. Most extended warranty companies require that you have an in-depth inspection of the vehicle performed by a company-approved inspection station before they will allow coverage. This is perfectly understandable when you consider pre-existing conditions like engine or transmission wear and damage.

Some companies offer plans with no deductibles or tiered deductibles. The method of payment of claims varies. Some plans allow immediate payment to the service provider via the use of a company credit card. These are the best, because the service provider gets paid immediately and therefore is more willing to deal with the extended warranty company. In addition, there's no out-of-pocket expense that has to be reimbursed. Other plans require that you first pay the bill, and then they will reimburse you later after you send supporting documentation for the claim to their fulfillment department.

The bottom line? Know who you are dealing with before purchasing an extended warranty (and read the fine print before buying).

PROJECT 22
Replace Turn-Signal Bulb

Time Required: 15-30 minutes

Tools Required: Combination or socket wrench

Skill Level: 🔧 to 🔧🔧

Cost Estimate: $5–$10

Tip: Check for a broken filament; if unbroken, check fuse, wiring, and relay for source of signal failure.

1 Turn-signal lamp replacement is much like replacing a taillight. For clearance, some vehicles, like this Ford Ranger, require that you remove the turn-signal housing from the body to access the bulb. The housing may combine nuts and bolts with fasteners that press into a clip.

2 The Ranger's turn-signal housing requires removing only one bolt.

3 Pull the housing free.

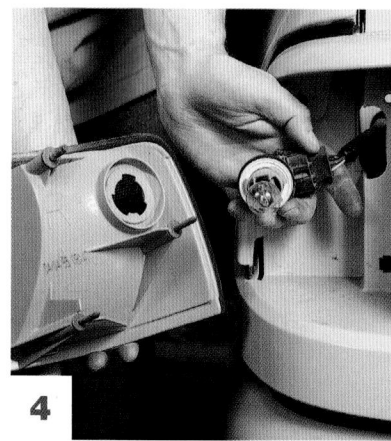

4 Turn the socket counterclockwise and pull it from the housing.

5 The bulb then pulls free from the fixture. Insert new bulb and reassemble in the reverse order. A small amount of dielectric grease (not regular grease) will aid the connection and repel moisture.

Chapter 16
Make Your Car Last Forever

This chapter is devoted to enlightening you on the following four topics:

- When faced with a major repair, when do you say enough is enough and replace the vehicle?
- When your vehicle needs repair, when should you use OEM (original equipment manufacturer) parts and when is it okay to use aftermarket parts?
- What are your options when making a decision on major repairs?
- What are the criteria for finding a good auto repair shop?

REPAIR OR REPLACE? THAT IS THE QUESTION

Many motorists find themselves in this situation. They have a car that's perhaps 8 to 10 years old with high mileage. Their technician gives them a repair estimate for what everyone tells them is more than the car is worth. They really don't want another car payment. Furthermore, they don't want to spend a lot of money on a used car that might have more problems than the car they have now. The last thing they want to do is "buy someone else's problems."

HOW TO DETERMINE WHETHER TO REPAIR OR REPLACE

Have a qualified technician do a complete assessment of the vehicle to determine whether or not it's worth repairing. It's important to have a good foundation from which to refurbish your vehicle. This type of inspection is the same as a pre-purchase inspection. The technician will closely scrutinize such things as the suspension, brakes, transmission, and engine, looking for any in-the-near-future failures. All potential problem areas should be identified, with estimated cost of repair using state inspection rules as a guideline (this way you are sure the vehicle will pass state inspection).

The technician should check over the condition of the frame and body, and I mean a thorough inspection. He or she should look at the undercarriage and frame closely for deterioration caused by rust. In addition, the technician should carefully inspect the inside of the car's sheet metal. The front and rear fenders, bottoms of doors, cowl (base of the windshield), and floorboards should be examined closely because water wells up in these areas and accelerates rust.

When faced with a major repair bill on a vehicle with high mileage, a new car looks alluring, to say the least. Dealers have car lots teaming with attractive new or used vehicles beckoning you to come in and sign on the dotted line. Well, before you sign, have a pre-purchase inspection done on your old buggy to determine if it's worth repairing. You might find that you have a perfect foundation from which to restore the integrity of your vehicle, thus avoiding a car payment! *Shutterstock*

You might have a car that functions well mechanically, but if the frame and body are disintegrating you may be better off shopping for another car.

Have a complete electrical and computer analysis done to detect any potential electrical failure such as wiring harnesses or alternators. In addition, a detailed electronic analysis will determine the health of the car's electronic performance system, as well as the engine's health.

Your ultimate goal is to determine if you have a good foundation to start with, before spending more money on the car. Look over your service history to see what has been done long-term. Repairs that fall under long-term maintenance can be defined as major engine repair, transmission replacement or overhaul, and total rebuilding of systems such as the suspension or brakes. Maybe the body had just been completely refurbished and repainted and the car has little or no rust. These are all good reasons to consider major work versus replacement.

An example of what the repair estimate might look like

Complete brake system overhaul	$ 650.00
New rack-and-pinion unit, including alignment	$ 595.00
4 new tires	$ 312.00
Shock and strut replacement	$ 450.00
New battery	$ 75.00
Minor body and paint work	$ 850.00
Subtotal:	$2,932.00
Tax:	$ 234.56
Total:	$3,166.56

The question to ask yourself at this point is this: Can I replace this car with another car of good integrity for the same amount of money?

In the above example let's say that you just had the engine replaced 20,000 miles ago and you had the transmission resealed last year. You know the transmission is in good condition internally because the fluid is clean and there was nothing more than normal wear material in the pan at the time of the reseal job. In this case, the car would be a good candidate for repairing versus replacing.

Now that you know what it will cost to refurbish the car ($3,166.56), take this figure and divide it by 36 (36 months is the average length of a car loan) and compare this monthly figure ($87.96) to the average car monthly payment, which is roughly $380 to $500.

Your choice to keep the car and fix it is obvious if you're motivated to act according to what's best for your budget; however, if you're just tired of the old chariot and would like a change in scenery, then you may decide to replace it even though it will cost you more. That's the beauty of living in America; it's your choice.

A final word about fixing up "old faithful." A wise salesman once told me, "Logic rides on the horse of emotion."

When faced with a major repair on your old vehicle, it's best to have an evaluation of the vehicle to see if you have a good foundation from which to work. A stem-to-stern inspection much like a pre-purchase inspection will tell you if the vehicle is worth repairing. A close scrutiny of the engine, transmission, brakes, steering, suspension, body, and frame by a professional will give you an idea of the overall condition of the vehicle. Then you can make an informed decision on whether to keep it or trade it in. *Shutterstock*

Get your logic in line and leave your feelings and emotions outside the door before making a decision on major repairs. There is a point-of-no-return when it's time to retire "old faithful." That point usually comes when repairs far exceed the value of the car. Remember these words the next time you're faced with this dilemma.

OEM, AFTERMARKET, REBUILT, OR USED PARTS: SO MANY CHOICES!

When repairing a car it's vital that you use good quality auto parts, parts that are durable and deliver peak performance. There are four options when considering part replacement: OEM, aftermarket, rebuilt (or remanufactured), and used. How do you decide what is best for your car and your pocketbook?

OEM VERSUS AFTERMARKET

Let's say that your repair shop calls you at home to inform you that your alternator needs to be replaced and the estimated cost is $120. This cost breaks down to $90 for the alternator and $30 for the labor. You say to yourself, "Wait a minute, where's yesterday's paper?" After rooting through the trash for 10 minutes you triumphantly return with the paper raised above your head looking like a victorious knight

OEM parts are made by the carmaker according to new car standards and specifications. Some repairs warrant OEM parts. Those include repairs for drivability problems for proper engine operation or in body repair of fairly new cars. OEM parts are the best and sometimes only option. Here's a true story to make my point: Years ago, the shop I worked at was approached with a new line of ignition parts by our parts distributor. They claimed that these parts were of OEM quality but at a much lower price. We could save our customers money, make money, and thus compete with the competition. We installed 12 sets of the new ignition parts over the next couple of weeks and 10 of the 12 cars stalled without starting again. The "OEM-quality" parts we installed all failed. We had to tow every car back into the shop and replace the faulty parts with OEM ignition parts to get the cars running again. We also recalled the other two cars that the parts had not failed in just in case. This is a perfect illustration of OEM parts outranking the aftermarket product. Use OEM in repairs where you want to be sure of dependability and performance.

Aftermarket parts are made by companies other than the carmakers. There are good aftermarket parts out there, and there are substandard aftermarket parts on the market as well. One has to be wise in choosing what aftermarket parts to buy. For example, I steer away from cheap ignition parts made by offshore companies because they tend to lack critical components essential for long-lasting and dependable service. Below you will find a guide to follow when buying aftermarket auto parts.

Rebuilt parts have been rebuilt to operating condition. Only that which was essential to replace to get it operating again was replaced. Rebuilt units are cheaper than new or remanufactured ones. Sometimes rebuilt parts are the only units available on the market to perform a specific auto repair. As the illustration above shows, its advertising says "Rebuilt CORVETTE Headlight Motors." New headlight motors for this particular year and model Corvette are probably unavailable, so the only option would be to go with a rebuilt unit. Rebuilt parts have their place in auto repair.

Remanufactured auto parts have been completely rebuilt to new standard and OEM specification using the best possible cores available. Jasper Engines and Transmissions is a good example of a premier remanufacturing company. All internal engine and transmission tolerances are restored to OEM specifications. New parts are used for bearings, valve springs, crankshafts, and camshafts, and virtually everything inside is replaced with the only used part being the engine block or transmission case.

In selecting a salvage yard from which to buy a used auto part, learn to spot a chop shop from an organized yard. Chop shops tend to leave their yard unorganized; engines, transmissions, and other major components might be left out in the weather to rust. Sensitive electrical components are also left in the cars that are outside and exposed to weather. This is not good for these components and can result in a prematurely failed part. Perfectly good body sheet metal is eft to rust and corrode rather than being removed and placed in a protected environment. Good salvage yards have computer cross-reference programs to show part fitment. They also usually belong to a hotline of salvage yards across a region or the whole country that allows them to access each other's inventories. In short, in selecting a salvage yard, look for organization, cleanliness, and safe inventory of parts.

---

who just returned from battle. You exclaim, "Here it is! I knew I saw a sale on alternators!" The ad pitches "the same" alternator on sale at the local discount auto parts store for $29.95. You call your garage back and tell them you're going to supply the parts (Why not? You'll save about $60). The garage says they will install the part, but there will be *no* warranty. You agree, no problem. The part is installed and goes bad in four months (just 30 days out of warranty!). Both the garage and the local discount auto parts store deny any warranty responsibilities. You have to purchase another alternator and pay to have it installed. Wasn't such a bargain after all, was it?

This scenario plays out in repair shops regularly. Why? Because most people don't realize that the $29.95 alternator is not of the same quality as the $90 alternator. The issue here is not the price of the part; it's an issue of the quality in construction of the part. Remember, you get what you pay for. Externally both alternators look alike. They have the same connections, markings, castings, and so on. However, most people are unaware of the difference in the quality of the internal construction. A good rule of thumb to follow when selecting parts is to look for consistency not only in price, but also in warranty, product specifications, manufacturer, and the country of origin.

CONSISTENCY IN PRICE

After some experience with shopping parts prices you will get a feel for what the average price should be for a particular part based on warranty, specs, and manufacturer. Be wary of drastic differences. A higher price tag doesn't necessarily mean it's better, and downright cheap usually means it's inferior. Also, don't count out factory-rebuilt units such as AC Delco for GM, Motorcraft for Ford, or MOPAR for Chrysler. In recent years car manufacturers have realized that there's a huge market for aftermarket parts, so they've jumped into the arena, offering factory rebuilt parts at competitive pricing with great warranties.

To illustrate this point I will tell you a story. A few years back I owned a Chevy Lumina. The rack and pinion steering gear went bad, so I got an estimate for an aftermarket one (including installation) from a local tire dealer in town. The dealer's price was more than $700. Just as a matter of diligence I priced the same job at the local Chevy dealer. Their price came in at $450 using factory-rebuilt parts with a lifetime warranty. That's quite a difference, to say the least.

WARRANTY

A warranty is only as good as the manufacturer that's backing it. Make sure it's a solid company and that the warranty is comparable to other respected manufacturers' warranties.

PRODUCT SPECIFICATIONS

Remember, just because two parts look the same doesn't mean they will perform the same. The product specifications will tell you what the product is capable of. If the specs don't meet the needs of your vehicle, then *stay away from it*, even if it's cheaper! (It's cheaper because of poorer quality.)

MANUFACTURER AND COUNTRY OF ORIGIN

The manufacturer and the country of origin are especially important with respect to quality. Offshore companies want to capture as much of the market as they can, so they often put out products that are inferior in both design and the raw materials used. These factors greatly reduce the durability of their parts. For instance, offshore brake rotors can cost about one-fourth of the price of domestic rotors. But they simply don't hold up under normal operating conditions because they are made of poor quality steel. For this reason they warp prematurely and wear out quickly. Ignition parts also fall into this category of "wonder-priced parts." They might look the same, but an internal inspection reveals their inferior design compared to the genuine product.

Aftermarket parts should at least match up to the expectations of the OEM parts. I illustrated the disparity between offshore and OEM ignition parts on television a few years back. I presented two brand new ignition modules designed to fit a GM vehicle. One module was an OEM GM part; the other was an offshore knockoff that cost about $60 less. I opened both modules to show the audience that the GM part was stuffed with electronic components, while the electronic components of the offshore product filled only 25 percent of its case. As the saying goes, "A picture is worth a thousand words."

Now this is not to say that all aftermarket companies offer substandard products compared to OEM. On the contrary, there are great aftermarket parts companies out there that reverse engineer OEM parts, find their weaknesses, correct the design, and come to market with a superior product. You just have to make sure you use these good quality parts from good companies. Talk to your parts supplier or repair shop and ask for such information. Your repair facility should be offering you good quality parts that meet manufacturers' specifications with fair warranties. In return, you should expect to pay for just that. Don't shortcut on auto repair. You and your family are driving and riding in that vehicle.

REBUILT, REMANUFACTURED, AND USED AUTO PARTS

You're faced with a major auto repair such as an engine, transmission, or differential replacement. Your service provider asks you, "Do you want rebuilt, remanufactured, or used parts?" The price differences are significant. To make an educated decision, you first need to know how these three solutions to the same problem compare. And only then can you decide which one is the best choice.

Rebuilt Parts

If you choose rebuilt parts, the rebuilder will use your vehicle's old part and replace just the worn components. If your vehicle's old part cannot be rebuilt because it is too worn, he will use a part from another vehicle (referred to as a "core"). If a core is used, then he will replace only what is needed in the core. For example, if an engine is rebuilt, maybe just the bearings and piston rings need to be replaced (the original crankshaft, pistons, and connecting rods would be used). This approach, in lieu of using new or remanufactured parts, usually saves the customer money.

There's just one glitch. Mechanical wear is relative. In other words, before rebuilding the unit, all of the components within the unit are equally worn. After rebuilding, some of the components are new, and some are used. Although the used components still function and do not need replacing, they are worn to some degree. Factors such as heat stress and cracks cause wear that is invisible to the human eye. Consequently, other problems could crop up later, resulting in premature failure of the repair.

Remanufactured Parts

What is a remanufactured part? The term *remanufactured* usually refers to a part that, for all practical purposes, has been completely remanufactured to the standard of a new part. Using a remanufactured engine as an example, mechanical tolerances have been restored either by re-machining, or by installing the necessary mechanical inserts to restore original mechanical tolerances. Either way, the engine meets the standard for OEM tolerances, durability, and quality. New pistons, connecting rods, rings, bearings, camshafts, lifters, and oil pump are installed.

All related bearing surfaces are restored, and the upper half of the engine, which includes the cylinder heads, is rebuilt. Usually the only component from the old engine that is used is the bare engine block, and this part is only used if it's in top-notch condition, to ensure longevity of service. These same rules apply to other remanufactured auto parts, whatever they may be. You will find that remanufactured auto parts usually carry a longer and stronger warranty, covering parts and labor for longer periods of time as compared to rebuilt parts.

Used Parts

What about used auto parts? Let me start with a well-known Latin expression, *caveat emptor*. Translation: "Let the buyer beware." Yes, used auto parts have their place in auto repair. And no, I am not discouraging the use of used parts. But be careful when buying them.

When selecting a salvage yard from which to purchase used auto parts, look the place over. Is it clean and well organized? Are the parts in order and sheltered from the environment? Too many times I have seen delicate electrical components laying out in the weather and then picked up off the ground and sold to an unsuspecting customer. What kind of cars does the salvage yard have in its inventory? Late model, import, or old clunkers? There's nothing wrong with a good mix of all of the above. If the yard is loaded with outdated rust buckets, however, move on.

There are many respected salvage yards that take pride in their businesses and in serving their valued customers. Be especially careful when buying certain used auto parts, specifically engines, transmissions, transfer cases, differentials, hydraulic units, and electrical parts. They are subject to the environment and can rust and wear away internally where you can't see it. Look for a salvage yard that has an organized dry storage building on the premises, with everything neatly stacked and categorized. In addition, I like to see an up-to-date computer system used to cross-reference parts. I also like to see the salvage yard connected to a network of salvage yards via computer across either the region or nation. This is especially helpful if you need a hard-to-find part for a particular year, make, and model.

When selecting used parts, ask about the warranty and the return policy. Also, watch the way in which the part(s) are removed from the vehicle. I've seen yard attendants use oxygen-acetylene torches to remove parts that should have been removed with wrenches and hand tools. I've also seen yard attendants use forklift trucks to carry parts across yards and then drop them in front of the facility, denting or damaging the part. Am I condemning salvage yards? No, just the "chop shops." Ask around. You'll find out who they are.

REBUILT PARTS, REMANUFACTURED PARTS, OR USED PARTS?

When selecting auto parts for an effective auto repair, first determine exactly what plan you have in mind for your vehicle. To keep it long term? Mid-term? Or to "get by" until next spring when you replace it? For most of us who do not work on our own vehicles, it is our service advisor's job to determine what we need based on our plan for the vehicle. Our responsibility lies in communicating this information effectively. Only then can he find the right parts for an effective repair based on our budget, needs, and goals.

When I was a service manager, I always asked my customers a lot of questions. Who drives the car? How often? Will the car be used to make long trips frequently or periodically? Is it your son's or daughter's car and is he or she going to college? All these factors come into play to help you make a wise repair decision. So make sure that you have a trusted advisor leading you through significant repair decisions.

ASK YOUR SERVICE ADVISER FOR REPAIR OPTIONS

Too often, during the auto repair process, service advisers do not give customers repair options. As a matter of fact, early in my career I failed to offer customers options when they were faced with major auto repairs. Luckily, I had an excellent

mentor who straightened me out. Allow me to give you two examples that illustrate this point.

Example 1

Suzie Customer comes into XYZ Auto Repair because her 1998 "Zorch" is making awful noises on acceleration (reminiscent of those sounds at the racetrack when a racer's engine blows up shortly after leaving the line, knock-knock-knock-rattle-rattle-rattle). Joe, the mechanic, diagnoses the sound: crankshaft bearings. He gives Suzie a repair quote that's more than the car is worth. She tells Joe she can't afford it, but she needs the car. Can he fix it cheaper? Joe tells Suzie he won't do it any cheaper, because he can't guarantee the job would last. He advises her to take the car elsewhere for repairs. Could this situation have been handled differently to help Suzie? Or is she a lost cause?

I used this example because, several years ago, I found myself in such a situation while working at a large shop as the assistant service manager. A single mother in dire financial straits came into the shop with a car that sounded like it had 12 angry trolls banging their hammers under the hood. I didn't know whether to get a gun before opening the hood, or to call a priest proficient in the rite of exorcism. It turns out her car's engine had major damage, and it would be a costly repair. I swung into action checking out her options. As I saw it, she had four repair options:

Option 1: Rebuild the old engine. After pricing it out, this option was simply too expensive. With the cost of parts, machine work, labor, and incidentals like wire, bolts, fluids, and so on, the price was way beyond her means.

In automotive repair, effective communication is key to getting the job done right the first time. If service advisors have done their jobs properly, they know exactly under what conditions the problem occurs. They know what the customer's concern is. During the repair process, they have kept the customer in the loop so there are no surprises when he or she comes to pick up the vehicle. If the job is a big one, they have discussed what the customer's intentions are for the vehicle and have come up with repair options that they have fully explained to the customer to help them make an informed decision. *Shutterstock*

Option 2: Partially rebuild the old engine. This option was a little cheaper; however, I had some legitimate concerns. For instance, if we rebuilt the lower half of the engine (crankshaft, piston rings, bearings, and so on), we would still have a problem with the top end. By restoring the compression to the bottom end and not doing anything to the top, we would still end up with loss of compression because the top end had sustained the same wear as the bottom. Taking into consideration that the customer wanted to keep the car for some time, this option was a no-go.

Option 3: Install a "new rebuilt" engine. Too costly. Period.

Option 4: Install a used engine. This option was the ticket for her.

Now my challenge as her service adviser was to find an engine that had middle to low mileage, was in good shape mechanically, didn't smoke, use oil, knock, tap, or have any other problem that could or would leave her stranded (and cost a lot of bucks down the road). And it had to fall within her budget!

I found such an engine and got the job done within her price range. The car ran for a long time after the repair and she was a happy customer. The solution to her problem was a result of communication. An assessment of her needs and what she could afford helped me determine the best fix for her car. The perfect solution mechanically is not always the best solution for the customer. Each situation is different. Various factors come in to play when deciding the direction to go for some car repairs.

DRIVERS ASK, TOM ANSWERS: SERVICE PROBLEMS SOLVED

Q Dear Tom,
I have a '92 Dodge Spirit (four-cylinder) that has 76,000 miles on it. The car has an oil leak, but is not so bad that I can't drive it (it's a slow drip leak). I had it checked out and the mechanic told me that since the car is 10 years old, it would not be worth fixing. Is this true?
Randy—Massachusetts

A Randy,
While I would agree that one should exercise caution in performing extensive repairs on an older vehicle, I would disagree that "it isn't worth fixing" without proper evaluation first. Have a professional technician determine the source of the leak and get an estimate for repairs. Then, have the vehicle evaluated to determine its overall condition. Only with this information in hand can you make an informed decision as to whether or not to repair it. For example, if the underside of the vehicle is rotted and it appears as though extensive repairs will be required to the fuel tank and fuel lines, brake lines, and floorboards (in addition to fixing the oil leak), then I would back away from repairing it.

If the overall condition of the vehicle were good, then I would strongly consider fixing the oil leak if the repair estimate is within reason and you're OK with driving the car. A good repair shop would be willing to help you make this decision. Good luck.
Tom

Q Tom,
I took my car to a local quick lube to get my oil changed. They didn't put enough oil in my car, and they didn't put the drain plug on tight enough. This caused the oil that they did put in to leak out. Now my car is making a loud noise (knocking sound) and my husband thinks the engine is bad. What do you think?
Tamesha—Pennsauken, New Jersey

A Tamesha,
It sounds like the car has a rod knock (engine damage). The quick lube's actions could have caused the damage. How long has it been since the oil change? If you can prove that the oil loss was due to their mis-installation of the drain plug and that the low oil levels caused the engine damage, then the quick lube could be held responsible for the damage and have to make it right for you legally. After verifying the engine damage, consider talking with an attorney to see if you can take legal action.
Tom

Q Tom,
I just moved to a new area and need to find a repair shop. What do I look for in selecting a shop for auto repair?
Lucille—Astoria, Pennsylvania

A Lucille,
You are smart to find a repair shop before you need it. This way you are not forced into a making a decision under pressure. Good decisions are never made when under pressure. Ask your local AAA for a good shop in your area. If there's no AAA in the area, visit a few shops in the area. Look for ASE certification and any other training programs that the technicians might have attended. Also ask about equipment: Is it up to date? Does the shop have computer programs to get the latest repair information? Ask to see letters from satisfied customers. This should be a good guide for you to follow. Good luck.
Tom

Q Tom,
I have an older car that needs some repair work. The shop I am going to won't put anything other than new parts in it. They claim they can't properly warranty the job without. It needs an engine, and I simply can't afford a new one. What should I do?
Nicole—Joliet, Illinois

A Nicole,
Ask the shop to find you a good used engine with mid-mileage on it. If they refuse, find another shop to do the work. Good salvage yards guarantee their used auto parts. Make sure the shop person selecting the engine sees and hears it run before buying it. If a right engine is selected for your year, make, and model vehicle, there should not be too much modification required. Also, if your car is equipped with computer controls, make sure you match up the computer controls with the replacement engine, as this can be a nightmare if not followed.
Tom

Example 2

Let's say that the brakes on your car are bad. You need both front and rear brakes, and the hydraulics have worn out as well (the rubber seals within the system). Your service adviser suggests that you replace the master cylinder with a new one because the old one is showing signs of seepage. Based on his experience, when hydraulic systems are refurbished without replacing the master, the original master usually goes bad shortly after the brake job. You have enough money to fix the brakes, but not enough to install a new master cylinder. He tells you that he cannot guarantee the job without replacing the master with a new one. Is there any option? The service adviser could consider replacing the master with a good quality rebuilt (less money), rather than insisting that a new master must be installed.

COMMUNICATION IS THE KEY

There are all kinds of repair options that an adviser can offer to a customer. As a customer, you should ask if there are any options. If you have financial concerns, communicate them. If you are a service adviser reading this, you need to listen to your customers, ask questions, and find out how best you can meet their needs. Look at the job as if you were in the customer's shoes. Is the car too worn out to warrant an expensive new part? How long do they intend to keep the car? Ask questions. A happy customer means repeat business and good word of mouth, and this is the best advertising you can do for your business. As the service adviser, a good relationship with your customer should be your main goal. You want customer loyalty, and it cuts both ways.

A caveat for repair professionals: When exercising repair options for your customers, always confirm the quality of either used or aftermarket parts. Also, make sure that you properly prep the part. For example, if it is a used rotor, measure it with a micrometer to make sure there's plenty of "meat" on it (if you have to machine it). In the case of a used engine, make sure you see and hear it run; make sure there are no knocks, taps, or smoke. If it's a used electronic part, make sure it was properly stored (not exposed to weather elements/moisture, which cause oxidation). In short, treat the repair as if it were *your* family's vehicle and *your* money that is being spent. With such a perspective, you will deliver a good quality job and you will make a customer for life.

At this point the question arises: How do you find that trustworthy auto repair facility? Read on.

CHOOSING A SHOP IN THE LABYRINTH OF AUTO REPAIR

A few years back, a woman called my radio show. Her husband of 32 years had passed away and she was left to take care of the family car. Her question? "How do I know if I'm going to a good auto repair shop?" A great question.

I have been in the automotive radio talk show business since the early 1990s, and every year the number of people who ask me this question grows. Why? In today's society, people are living (and thus driving) longer. People are moving to different cities and towns at a phenomenal rate. The auto repair business is changing. For example, dealerships' service departments are in serious competition with the independent repair facilities. Vehicles are evolving at a rapid pace and are more hi-tech, requiring repair facilities to continually upgrade their equipment and educate their technicians. Automotive advertising and marketing is drowning the marketplace with excessive mailings and Internet, television, and newspaper ads. Everyone is having a big sale! Is it any wonder that many of us find ourselves lost in this labyrinth of auto repair? Is it any wonder that more and more people are looking for a guide to take them through it?

That's my job. So let's start our journey and answer the question: How do you find a good quality auto repair facility?

First, you should start shopping for a repair facility before you need one. Why? Because making a sound decision is more difficult when you are faced with a broken down vehicle that you need to have fixed immediately because it transports your family and gets you to work. Intelligent decisions are made after evaluating the facts. Emergencies create an emotional environment that thwarts clear and decisive action.

Call local repair shops in your area and find out if they belong to professional automotive repair associations such as: Automotive Service Association (ASA), International Automotive Technicians Network (iATN), I-CAR, National Institute for Automotive Service Excellence (ASE), MAP, or American Automobile Association (AAA).

In the illustration above we see a labyrinth or maze. Imagine being dropped in the middle of this thing at night and being expected to find your way out of it safely. Along the way, there are dangers and encumbrances that could harm you or cause you loss. Does this sound daunting? Of course it does. Yet customers in auto repair facilities experience the same anxieties I just described every day. What do you look for when choosing an auto repair shop? In this section I will discuss what to look for and what questions to ask in an effort to relieve those anxieties. *Shutterstock*

ASSOCIATIONS

Membership in the associations listed here usually means that the shop cares about the quality of business it does. Such associations require the shop to subscribe to a code of ethics, meet a certain criteria for membership, or keep itself up to speed with technology and training. Shops of this caliber usually have access to online technical repair information, are abreast of the latest technical trends, and can track down a problem in laser-like fashion.

Here are the web addresses to each association:

Automotive Service Association, http://www.asashop.org

International Automotive Technicians' Network, http://www.iatn.net

Inter-Industry Conference on Auto Collision Repair,
  http://www.i-car.com/index_us.shtml

National Institute for Automotive Service Excellence, http://ase.com

Motorist Assurance Program, http://www.motorist.org

AAA Approved Auto Repair, http://www.aaa.com/AAA_Travel/
  AutoRepair/automobile_repair.htm

Membership in these associations usually means that the shop has met certain criteria to be a part of the association. For instance, to become a AAA Approved Auto Repair Facility, a shop must undergo a rigorous investigation. In addition to having state-of-the-art equipment, training, qualified technicians, and information systems in place, the shop must score high with its customers. AAA contacts about 100 of the shop's most recent customers and conducts a Consumer Satisfaction Index (CSI) study.

AAA asks customers questions like these:

- Was the estimate accurate compared to the actual bill?
- Was the job done on time?
- Did they fix it right the first time?
- What kind of warranty did they give you?
- Was the shop clean and presentable?
- Did they offer you a ride to work or somewhere you needed to go?
- Was there a comfortable, pleasant, and clean waiting area?

If the repair facility passes the test, it can hang the "AAA Approved" shingle. As you can see, membership in associations such as this is a significant qualifier when evaluating a facility.

Involvement in such organizations tells you that the owner of the repair facility cares about the quality of the workmanship and most likely operates by a code of ethics as required by the organization he or she belongs to. In addition, membership in these associations usually requires that the shop subject itself to an arbitration process that is binding, should the need for arbitration between customer and shop arise.

Visit the shops you're interested in and ask yourself about each shop: Is it clean and orderly? Or does it look like it ought to be condemned by the health department? Ask customers why they shop there. Answers like, "They are the cheapest," "They offer a lot of specials," or "The owner is a friend of my father's," don't offer much credibility. Look for responses such as, "They fix my car right the first time," "I can trust them to do the job at a fair price," "They welcome my questions and concerns and take the time to answer them," "I never get any surprises when I come to pick up my car," and "They explain in plain English what the problem is and what my options are—patiently." Good word-of-mouth like this is a great qualifier.

While at the facility, look for certifications displayed on the wall. If they have none, ask to see their qualifications. This will tell you a lot about the facility. What shingles and certifications should you look for?

Do the technicians have certifications from ASE, AC Delco, ASP, or manufacturers such as GM, Ford, Chrysler, Toyota, Nissan, and so on? Do they have aftermarket training from such leaders as NAPA/Echlin, Moog, Carquest, TRW, or Bendix? How about continued education from a technical training course or college?

These shingles are evidence that the technicians have taken the initiative to go beyond the call of duty and keep up with changes in their field. Not only are they trained in the latest technology, but they also show a serious interest and pride in their work. They know how to fix your car. Continued education and certifications also convey that the owner of the shop cares about the quality of the work, because it's usually the shop owner who foots the bill for extended training.

Another factor to consider when choosing a repair facility is the equipment. Does the shop have state-of-the-art equipment such as hand-held computer scanners and diagnosis software, digital volt-ohm meters, logic probes, lab scopes, and on-line computer systems like CAS, Alldata, or Mitchell-On-Demand? Don't be afraid to ask the shop if they have this equipment. These systems and tools are necessary to diagnose and repair your high-tech car accurately. Without them, fixing your automobile is a hit-and-miss proposition.

Sometimes it's best to take your car to a specialist. Specialists cost more money initially, but because they are specialists, they often know how to pinpoint and repair certain types of problems more efficiently and effectively. Why? Because they deal with these problems every day; thus they have the knowledge, equipment, and information systems necessary to go directly to the problem. While Joe down the street is busy replacing parts and floundering, the specialist usually diagnoses with laser-like accuracy, locates the problem, and replaces only what is necessary. Consequently, less guesswork and fewer parts are being replaced, as well as a lot less labor time, saving you money. Don't be "pennywise and pound-foolish." The cost of diagnosis is often far less than the cost of the trial-and-error method when repairing today's high-tech vehicles.

COMMON AUTOMOTIVE SPECIALTIES

Transmission and drivetrain
Computer, drivability, and electrical
Collision repair
Foreign car repair
HVAC (heating, ventilation, air conditioning)
Radiator repair and cooling system repair

SHOP SIZE

Some people think that because a shop is either smaller or larger, the price will vary greatly. That's not true these days. With the high cost of equipment, training, and information systems, the prices between dealers, large independent shops, and small independent shops are balancing out. As a matter of fact, in a lot of cases I've seen the larger entities (dealers and larger repair facilities) actually offer more competitive pricing compared to the little guys in an effort to capture a share of the auto repair market. If the criteria we have discussed are in place, and the quality of the parts and warranties are equal, probably the pricing will be close. At that point, it's just a matter of whom you feel most comfortable with.

PRICE OF REPAIR

The next issue that arises when selecting a repair shop is the price. Let's say that you *do* know that your car needs the shock absorbers and struts replaced. You call around to four places and (assuming you car is not an exotic) you get a price for the job over the phone. For the sake of argument, let's say that you get prices of $200.00, $215.00, $195.00, and $129.95. Wow! Why such a difference between the first three and the last one? Whenever you run across a drastic price difference, get the answer to these questions: How do the warranties compare? How does the workmanship and quality of the parts compare? Does the shop have the equipment and training to do the job? Does the shop employ qualified technicians?

Remember, you get what you pay for. That is a fundamental law of business, as rock solid as the law of gravity. Make sure you know why the differences exist; only then are you ready to make an informed decision on repairs.

IMPORTANCE OF BUILDING RELATIONSHIPS

Finally, I'd like to comment on the importance of building relationships. When customers and repair shops take the time to build relationships over a cup of coffee, watching each other's families grow up, or perhaps sharing the loss of a mutual acquaintance, trust and mutual respect grow. So when the customer calls with a problem, the shop responds

to the customer's needs based on the relationship established. Even though they may have a full workload for that day or week, they get the car into the shop.

Perhaps the customer has a car that needs major work. The shop then becomes an advisor to the customer, suggesting the best repair options based on the customer's need, budget, and the condition of the car. When it comes time to buy a car, the shop will check out the vehicle for the customer and evaluate its integrity.

Don't float around trying to find the best deal. The best deal is found in competent auto repair. Deal shopping is shortsighted and, in the long term, the most costly way to do car repair. I strongly urge you to find a high-quality repair shop where you are able to reap the rewards of a good working relationship. I like doing business that way. I'm sure you do too.

You can't fix the vehicles of the new millennium with 1968 auto repair technology. Today's vehicles have computer systems in them that analyze hundreds of electrical impulses per second and make adjustments on the fly to realize optimum engine performance and efficiency. The diagnostic equipment required to analyze these systems is expensive and complicated and requires a highly trained technician armed with the latest repair techniques to track down and solve such problems. Wheel technology is such that it requires high-tech balancers that can cite the most minute imperfection in a wheel. Up-to-date diagnostic and repair equipment is a must for effective auto repair.

Chapter 17
How to Kill a Car

What does it take to kill a car? Many of you can come up with ways of your own, but let's look at some of the most common forms of abuse that cause vehicle failure.

NEGLECTING SCHEDULED MAINTENANCE

More cars find their way to the junkyard by neglecting basic scheduled maintenance than any other cause. This list includes such things as neglecting oil changes and transmission services, driving too long on the same set of sparkplugs, ignoring check engine lights and charging system or temperature gauges that indicate trouble, turning a deaf ear to brake squeals, belt squeals, clanking, banging, and clunking.

Think about this: Airlines have aggressive maintenance checks on their planes based on how many hours they have been in the air. Ocean liners and submarines keep a full-time maintenance crew on hand at all times to attend to mechanical problems as they crop up. Race teams have a pit crew on hand during the race to ensure the vehicle continues to deliver peak performance safely throughout the event.

What makes those of us who drive a car every day think we are immune to mechanical breakdown? And what makes us think that we can drive our vehicles indefinitely without regular maintenance? Our cars need maintenance checks to ensure that they run safely and efficiently. There are an untold number of accidents that occur as a result of mechanical problems that were caused by neglect of basic maintenance issues. And there are many more cases of massive and unnecessary repair costs for the same reason.

A lot of people think that if the car runs, why spend money on it? If there's no obvious problem, wait until there is and then fix it. If you think like this, you are being pennywise and pound-foolish. In your lifetime you are spending far more money on cars than the guy who does what it takes to maintain a healthy car. Compare it to the physical health of your body. In the past, people used to go to a doctor only when they were sick. Today we know that preventative care has improved the quality of life as well as extended the length of life. And it costs less money! Insurance companies want to pay for yearly checkups because problems can be diagnosed early before they cost an arm and a leg to treat. Cars are no different. Follow the suggested maintenance schedule for your vehicle and you will get longevity, peak performance, and efficient operation out of your chariot.

OVERLOADING TOWING AND HAULING CAPACITY

Have you ever followed a car towing a small boat trailer that's loaded with a very large boat? Picture it. A large boat is hanging over a trailer on all sides and towering over the tow vehicle; the trailer's tires are flattened, and the vehicle's front end is pointing upward. It's a mess looking for a place to explode, and this is not an uncommon sight. Talk about a safety issue. Not only are the people in the tow vehicle at high risk, but so are the motorists who share the same roadway space.

Vehicles come from the factory with a specific towing capacity. Some vehicles come made with a towing package that is designed for safe towing. Check your owner's manual or call your manufacturer's customer service department to find out the towing capacity of your particular vehicle.

What happens when you pull a trailer that's too heavy for your vehicle? Engine damage from overheating, undue stress to the frame, damage to the suspension and braking systems, and transmission damage from overheating.

Overheating

Vehicles designed for heavy towing that have a towing package from the factory come with a high coolant capacity radiator and sometimes a heavier water pump. When hauling a heavy load on a trailer with a vehicle that is not designed to haul such a load, the engine heats up far beyond the ability of the radiator to cool it down. The result is overheating, blown head gaskets, and cracked or warped cylinder heads. This is not to say that you should never tow a trailer with your vehicle, just find out what the towing capacity is and do not exceed it. On vehicles that tow heavy loads regularly, it's a good idea to add an auxiliary engine oil cooler to ensure the engine oil in the crankcase is thoroughly cooled, because intense heat causes the oil to breakdown and lose viscosity.

Undue Stress to the Frame

Vehicles with high towing capacities generally have strong frames that allow for hanging the additional weight of a trailer in them. When hauling a trailer that is too heavy with a vehicle not designed to haul such weight, the frame buckles and damage to the structural integrity of the vehicle is incurred.

Suspension Damage

The suspension is designed to handle the weight of the vehicle plus the specified maximum trailer-towing weight. That's it. Overload the vehicle and suspension problems occur. Leaf and coil springs or torsion bars are overtaxed and either break or wear out prematurely. U-bolts and shackles that hold leaf-spring-packs together break, coil springs crack or snap in two, and torsion bars break free from their securing brackets in the vehicle's frame.

Brake Damage

Brakes are overtaxed when a vehicle that is loaded beyond capacity has to stop. Most small trailers do not have brakes of their own so the brake system of the towing vehicle bears the burden of the entire load. The additional stress on the brakes causes the friction material to overheat and harden or crystallize, rendering it ineffective and unable to stop the vehicle. This condition causes "brake fade." When you press down on the brake pedal, no friction material wear occurs because the crystallized friction material is too hard to wear away when it comes in contact with the rotors or drums. The brake shoes or pads just ineffectively slide against the rotor or drum surface like locomotive brakes (steel on steel) and make lots of noise, but there's no stopping power. Overheating the braking system also increases the temperature of the brake fluid to the point where it cooks the rubber seals and the entire system is compromised.

Transmission Overheating and Damage

An excessive load causes the transmission to overheat, which causes the transmission fluid to reach temperatures that compromise the soft internal parts such as rubber seals and clutches. The heat hardens the rubber seals, causing loss of internal hydraulic pressure. In addition, the glue that secures the clutch friction material to the steel backings hardens and clutch strength is compromised. If you're going to haul a trailer, install an auxiliary transmission oil cooler.

THE NEUTRAL DROP

A Neutral Drop is when you rev the engine high in neutral and, at the peak of revving, you drop the transmission into low gear. In the case of a car equipped with a manual transmission, you dump the clutch in first gear after revving the engine high. This action causes the tires to squeal as you speed off the line. The problem with this practice is that it puts excessive stress on the drivetrain components. Driveshafts break or bend, universal or CV joints snap, differentials are damaged, axles twist and break or strip out, transmissions break internally,

Neutral dropping a vehicle is not a good thing to do. I have been inside transmissions that have been vaporized as a result of this practice. Transmissions have heat-treated steel parts inside of them that last long under normal operating conditions, but when severely shocked from this type of practice snap and break. This causes damage to the other parts inside the unit.

and clutches burn out. In short, it's a high price to pay just to experience a little tire squealing. Not good.

INSTALLING A PLOW ON A VEHICLE THAT CAN'T HANDLE ONE

This kind of vehicle abuse often occurs in parts of the country that get a lot of snow. In recent years plow makers have come out with what they call "personal plows" for regular-duty vehicles such as small or mid-sized SUVs. Usually these plows are made of lightweight materials such as Plexiglas, aluminum, or a synthetic material that the maker claims will not overtax the vehicle. So what's the problem? Although these types of plows are not too heavy for the vehicle, they are intended for light use. The problem is that people tend to overwork them.

Often a driver will plow so hard into a snow bank that the air bag deploys. In addition, although the driver is not aware of it, the vehicle also sustains frame, suspension, steering linkage, and some body damage that can be attributed directly to the plow installation.

In this scenario, let's say this guy gets away with using the personal plow for a couple of years. During year three he notices a high-pitched whine coming from the transmission; then it quits altogether. He takes it to the shop. The diagnosis? The transmission is burned up due to excessive plow use. What happened? The transmission in his light-duty truck was not intended to push several hundred pounds of snow and ice around. It gave up the ghost after just three years of plow work. The damage was a result of the hard impacts of the plow into snow banks, ice, and other obstructions hiding under the snow. Had he installed the plow in a vehicle capable of handling it, there would have been no damage.

ROCKING THE VEHICLE OUT OF SNOW OR MUD

Ever get stuck in snow or mud? Rather than calling a tow truck, what's the first thing we do? We rock the vehicle back and forth, switching from forward to reverse while gunning the engine. This action often causes the vehicle to gain enough momentum to get the vehicle out of the rut. It often works, but at what expense? The stress on the transmission and drivetrain can cause internal hard parts (case hardened gears and sprockets) to break under the pressure. CV joints, universal joints, and splined parts such as axles can twist and break apart. Save yourself some money; dig out or get towed.

DRIVING WITH THE TEMPERATURE GAUGE ON HOT OR THE LIGHT ILLUMINATED

You're driving on a country road out in the middle of nowhere when you notice that your temperature gauge is buried in the "hot" zone. Rather than stop and call a tow truck, you keep driving, hoping you can make it to a repair shop. The engine overheats, coolant spews out of the overflow tank, and the engine gets so hot it stalls. You have to call a tow truck anyway. The shop tells you your engine's got a blown head gasket and cracked cylinder head. The cause? A $12 thermostat. The repair would have cost you $12 plus the cost of installation and coolant and the cost of a tow job (unless you have AAA or the equivalent). Instead you end up with an $800 repair bill because you were too stubborn to call a tow truck. Many a good vehicle has been undone because of this mistake.

DRIVING WITH LOW OR NO OIL IN THE ENGINE

While driving at highway speed the oil light comes on. You either don't see it or choose to ignore it. Sometimes an engine noise (usually a "knock") can be heard when the light comes on. You hear the knock but choose to turn up the radio (don't laugh; people actually do this). All of a sudden the engine starts to lose power and it eventually stalls, leaving you stranded on

Just a small suggestion here: *Don't ignore a hot temperature gauge. It will cost you a lot of money.* Most engines today are made of aluminum and are easily damaged when overheated. The best course of action when you notice a hot temperature gauge is to pull over, stop the vehicle, and call a tow truck to stop any or further damage to the engine. That's all I have to say about that.

This is another practice that will result in major engine damage. Here's what happens when you run the engine with low or no oil; first friction and heat build up from lack of lubrication. Metal mating surfaces that need lubrication heat up and start to grind away at each other. The ensuing heat causes the engine to overheat, expansion of the metal takes place, aluminum parts warp or crack, and the engine dies. Sometimes the bearings get so hot that the crank seizes to the rods and main bearings. In short order, the engine becomes nothing more than a boat anchor, essentially useless. When you see a low oil light turn on, pull over and stop the engine to prevent damage.

the roadside. You call a tow truck and the vehicle is towed to a repair shop. The diagnosis: The engine has seized because there was no oil in the system and you have to replace it.

How can this scenario be avoided? Stop at the first sign of low oil, whether it's the low oil pressure gauge, a lit oil light, or a knocking sound. Often major damage can be averted if the engine is shut off in time. Sadly most people choose to ignore the warning signs.

IGNORING AUTOMATIC TRANSMISSION WARNING SIGNS

The warning signs that something is wrong with your automatic transmission are quite distinct. Whining, dropping out of gear, and banging into gear all fall under this category. If you observe any of these symptoms, stop driving and check the fluid levels. Driving an automatic transmission on low fluid results in greater friction and more heat. The longer the transmission is driven in this condition, the more likely irreversible damage will occur. Remember, heat hardens the rubber seals and crystallizes the clutch glue, compromising the system. When you first notice any of these symptoms, check the fluid and proceed with diagnostics before driving any farther to avoid costly repairs and down time.

OVERSHOOTING A TURN AND HITTING A CURB IN THE SNOW

When you drive too fast on snow-covered roads, your vehicle slides rather than tracks through the snow. This action can cause frame, suspension, and steering damage if it occurs while trying to make a turn. For example, let's say you are approaching an intersection and realize at the last minute that you have to make a left-hand turn. Because your vehicle is going too fast, it slides as it turns and slams into the curb on the right side of the cross street. Overshooting a curb in the snow is a common occurrence, costing anywhere from hundreds to even thousands of dollars in repairs.

As you can see, there's a lot of vehicle abuse that can be avoided. Use common sense, know your car, observe changes in sounds, vibrations, warning lights, and other detectable variations, and don't ignore possible problems or put off getting them diagnosed. Your car is a major item on your family's budget. You can't control the price of cars, or the cost of car insurance, or the cost of gas, but you can control how much you spend to maintain your car, and how long it lasts, and how safe your family is when they ride in it. Take charge in these areas where you have control and you'll always have a reliable and safe vehicle that performs well and lasts long enough to make you feel like you got your money's worth.

ADDITIONAL DRIVING TECHNIQUES TO AVOID TO MAKE YOUR CAR LAST FOREVER
Feathering the Clutch

Have you ever seen someone in the car next to you on a hill, revving the engine and causing the car to lunge forward then hit the brakes, only to watch the car creep backward and the whole process starts again? I guarantee you that this driver is "feathering the clutch." What they're doing is equalizing the clutch halfway engaged and gunning the engine in an effort to make the car stay put on a hill. This practice results in a failed clutch in short order every time. By partially applying the clutch and racing the engine, you burn clutch disc material off the disc, rendering it useless and costing you hundreds or over a thousand dollars in repairs, depending on the damage done. It's best to learn how to start a stopped car on a hill with a clutch rather than this idiotic move.

Power Braking

When power braking, one foot is held on the brake while the other foot floors the gas pedal. When the light turns green, the driver releases the brake and the car races off at a high rate of acceleration. The problem with this practice is that engine and transmission mounts are taxed and over time break. If there already is a broken engine mount, the engine could lift up and chock the throttle linkage open resulting in uncontrolled acceleration. In addition, internal automatic transmission parts can fracture and break, brakes wear out when the tires break loose against the applied brakes, transmission and oil cooler lines become stressed and break causing a massive fluid leak and potentially do internal engine or transmission damage. And this is just a few problems that could crop up.

Drafting

Some people think they're NASCAR's Tony Stewart on the roadways, drafting semis and other vehicles while driving on the highways. Not only is this dangerous if the vehicle in front of you has to make a quick stop, it's also expensive in terms of paint work. Think about it: All the stones and projectiles on the roadway rolled over by the leading vehicle gets kicked up onto your vehicle's body, paint, and windshield. Think about the paint and body damage, not to mention glass damage you are setting yourself up to experience. Slow down, Tony. It's safer and cheaper….

Pulling a Fishtail

The other day I was waiting at a stoplight and heard the most annoying noise you can imagine. This guy was driving a small pickup truck, and he gunned it as he turned the corner. It was on a wet road surface so the rear wheels spun and the rear end of the truck fishtailed with him smiling behind the wheel as he lumbered down the highway (sped off would not be an accurate statement because the truck had a small four-cylinder engine in it). What happened if the truck spun out in that crowded intersection? What kind of damage would he have done to his truck and the other cars? If there was snow on the ground and he had hit a curb that was hiding under that snow, he would have pulverized the suspension and drivetrain (not to mention the wheel and axle damage he could have sustained). I have seen vehicular undercarriages literally destroyed from this type of abuse. Bad practice; stay away from it.

Well, that does it from me. 'Til next time, keep rollin'!

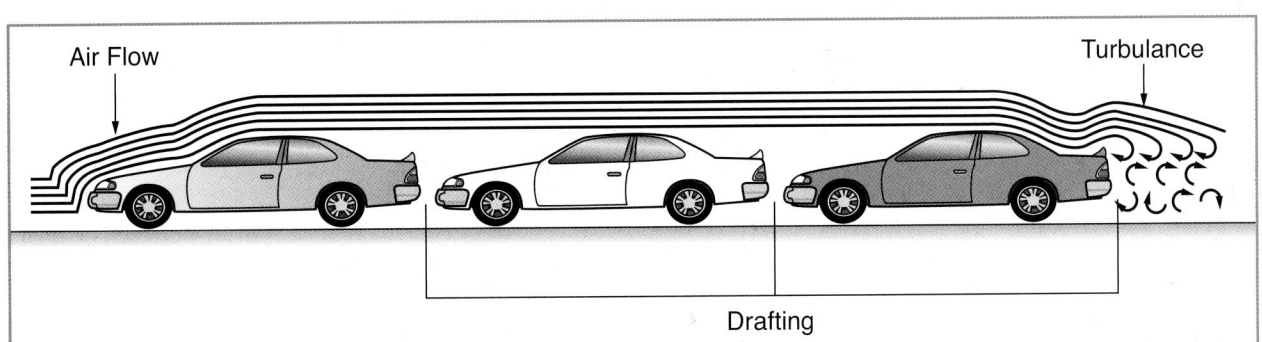

Drafting on the racetrack is acceptable and benefits racers, but it's just plain stupid on the highway. Period. What happens if the lead vehicle suddenly needs to stop? What if you're in dense traffic? Now other people are at risk all because you want to imitate Dale Earnhardt Jr. I have seen cars literally destroyed because they slammed into the rear of a semi they were "drafting" behind. While the truck sustained little damage, the unfortunate people in the car lost their lives. Drafting is dangerous and of no benefit to regular drivers. Leave this dangerous practice to racecar drivers, where it belongs.

Q Tom,
How long can I go between oil changes without doing harm to the engine? I have a 2000 Ford with a 2.0-liter engine in it.

Sally—Baton Rouge, Louisiana

A Sally,
What do you expect to accomplish by performing this feat other than destroying your engine? When you leave the oil in the engine for too long, it loses its ability to lubricate, cool, and keep dirt in suspension to be filtered out by the oil filter. Not to mention the fact that the oil filter gets clogged with dirt and inhibits oil flow through the engine. This practice is simply no good for your engine and will result in major engine damage over time.

Tom

Q Tom,
My sister and I have a difference of opinion regarding the practice of rocking the car out of a snow bank when stuck. She says it doesn't hurt the car at all and is a cheaper option than calling a tow truck. I say if you can't dig it out, call a tow truck because you do damage to the transmission and engine. Who is right?

Michelle—Buffalo, New York

A Michelle,
In short, you are right, period. Rocking the car out of a snow bank can result in all kinds of transmission and drivetrain havoc. And yes, the engine can get damaged if it gets overheated or over-revved. I have seen twisted axles and driveshafts, vaporized transmissions and transfer cases, damaged viscous couplers, damaged undercarriages, broken suspension components, bent wheels, blown differentials, torn gas and brake lines, broken motor mounts, bent frames, and other mechanical carnage as a result of this abusive practice. Not a good practice. Tell sis to cease and desist or suffer the eventual consequences.

Tom

Q Tom,
The other day I street raced my Honda Accord. When I launched off the line from neutral, I heard what sounded like nuts and bolts in a blender. Now it doesn't move at all. The car is an automatic. What did I do to my car?

Carlos—Los Angeles, California

A Carlos,
You probably destroyed the transmission when you "launched" off the line. What happens is when you do a neutral drop into gear while revving the engine at high speed, the transmission gets shocked beyond belief. Hard parts inside the transmission get fractured or break. In your case, it sounds like you broke some hard parts like a drum, planetary gear set, ring and pinion, carrier, or something along those lines. Get it into a shop to drop the pan and see what kind of metal is in the pan. You will probably end up replacing the transmission because of extensive internal damage. Sorry.

Tom

Q Tom,
I own a Toyota Rav4 with a 2.4-liter four-cylinder engine. I put a hitch on it to tow my 22-foot boat last year, and the truck just kept overheating. What can I do to stop this? Will it damage my SUV? It seems to me that it should be able to tow a silly boat, don't you think?

Sal—New Mexico

A Sal,
Your truck could tow a trailer that weighs about 1,500 pounds. Anything over 3,000 pounds requires its own braking system and a heavy-duty vehicle set up for towing. You did not give me the particulars of the boat, so I had to do a little homework. On average, a 21- to 24-foot Searay sports boat weighs anywhere from 3,000 to 5,000 pounds, depending on how its equipped. The cabin cruisers are even heavier.

Sal, at this towing weight, you are 1,500 to 3,500 or more pounds overweight. This is a recipe for disaster. You will damage the frame, destroy the brakes, and overheat the engine and transmission to the point of meltdown, not to mention the safety risk you pose to yourself and others while towing said boat. Sal, get another truck or sell the boat. Don't tow it anymore with this vehicle. It's dangerous and will destroy the vehicle.

Tom

Q Tom,
I just bought a small SUV; it's a KIA Sorento. I have a small house with a small driveway that needs to be plowed during the winter months. I have been shopping for one of those personal snowplows for my SUV. This would work perfectly on my driveway. What make personal snowplow do you recommend I buy?

Tammy—Burlington, Vermont

A Tammy,
I recommend you not buy a snowplow Tammy. This vehicle is not equipped for snowplow use. You will find that out the first time you plow hard into an ice and snow bank. The air bags will probably blow, and if they don't, over time you will do damage to the frame, suspension, drivetrain, and body. Not to mention the possibility of voiding your new car warranty. Forget the plow and call a plowing service Tammy. You'll be glad you did.

Tom

Q Hello Tom,
My father suggested I write you because he listens to your national radio show on XM radio. I own a 1982 Ford F-150 pickup truck with four-wheel drive. I put 311050R17 tires on the rear and 21570R15 tires on the front. This made it look jacked up. It drove fine until I put it in four-wheel drive. The truck acted like the brakes were on, and it came to a stop. Now when I put it in four-wheel drive I just hear grinding and it doesn't move. What happened?

Josh—Pineville, North Carolina

A Josh,
You destroyed the transfer case. This vehicle is equipped with part-time 4WD. This means that when the vehicle is shifted into four-wheel drive, all four wheels are locked together and turning at the same rate of speed. The transfer case has no way of differentiating between the two tire sizes and the different rpm they turn at. When you put the truck in four-wheel drive with the tires turning at different speeds, the transfer case gears bound up against each other and eventually failed internally. It's no wonder the truck acted like the brakes were on. The transfer case was twisted and binding up internally. Sorry to be the bringer of bad news, but you probably have to replace the transfer case. Next time, make sure all four tires installed on the truck are the same size.

Tom

About the Author

With 40 years in the automotive industry and close to 20 years in automotive talk radio, Tom Torbjornsen makes learning about cars easy with his personal approach, his expert advice, and his high-energy style. Tom's varied experiences have given him a firsthand look at the automotive industry from many perspectives. Tom is a writer for AOL Autos, Edmunds, CNN, and many other websites. He's also the creator and host of the widely acclaimed radio call-in talk program, America's Car Show with Tom Torbjornsen, which airs on the XM-Sirius Satellite Radio Channel and the SSI Radio Network. Find Tom online at www.americascarshow.com. Tom welcomes your questions at tom@americascarshow.com.

Index

   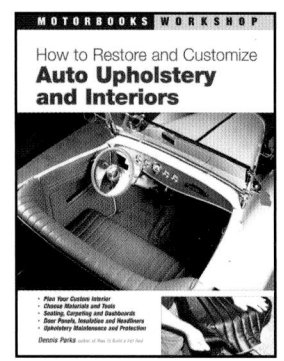